In a Class by Herself:

The Yawl Bolero and the Passion for Craftsmanship

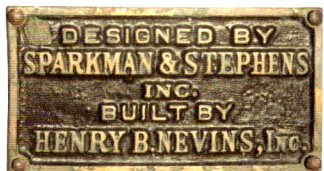

In a Class by Herself:

The Yawl *Bolero* and the Passion for Craftsmanship

JOHN ROUSMANIERE

Title page photos © Dan Nerney

Mystic Seaport
75 Greenmanville Ave., P.O. Box 6000
Mystic, CT 06355-0990
www.mysticseaport.org

© 2006 by John Rousmaniere
All rights reserved. First edition 2006
Printed in Singapore

Designed by Darcy Magratten
Prepress work by Meridian Printing, East Greenwich, Rhode Island
Printed by CS Graphics, Singapore

ISBN (cloth): 0-939511-13-4

Cataloging-in-Publication Data

Rousmaniere, John
   In a class by herself : the yawl Bolero and the passion for craftsmanship / John Rousmaniere.—1st ed.— Mystic, CT : Mystic Seaport, c2006.
   p. : ill., ports. ; cm.
   "Sources": p.
   Includes index.

   1. Bolero (Yawl). 2. Brown, John Nicholas, 1900-1979. 3. Stephens, Olin. 4. Stephens, Roderick, 1909-1995. 5. Nevins, Henry B., 1878-1959. 6. Yacht building—New York (State)—New York. 7. Yacht racing—History. I. Title.

GV822.B65 R6 2006

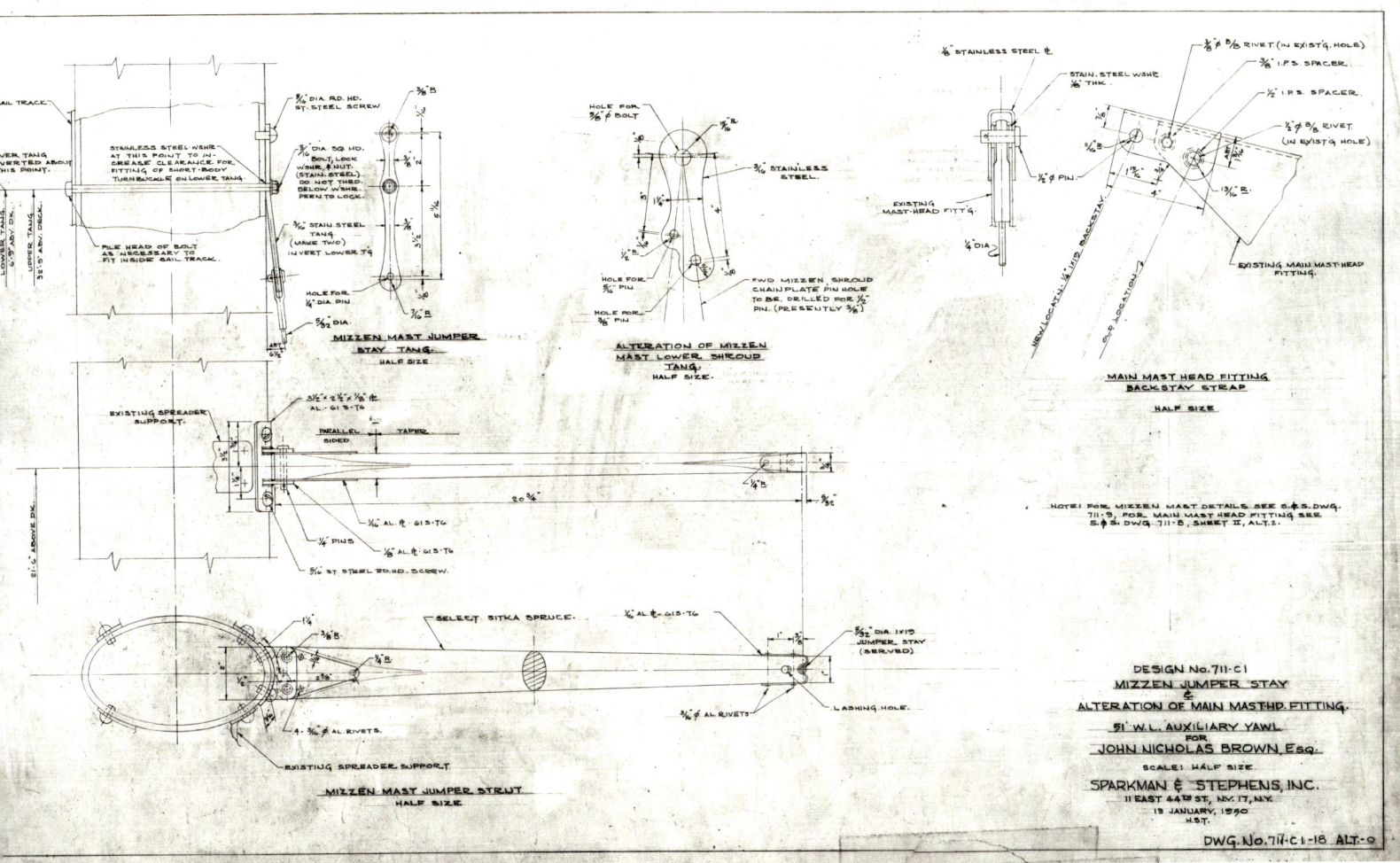

(DESIGN AND DRAWING BY SPARKMAN & STEPHENS, © 2005 BY SPARKMAN & STEPHENS, INC.)

Contents

Foreword, Edward Kane		iv
Preface, John Rousmaniere		vi-vii
1	The First Break for Freedom	11
2	A Comfortable Cruising Boat	21
3	The Two Adventurers	29
4	Olin Stephens and the Matter of Balance	45
5	The Nevins Way	60
6	Shown Through Heaven: Building *Bolero* with Rod Stephens	80
7	Grand and Glorious Sensations	98
8	The Queen, Four Owners, and Ted Turner	116
9	Doing the Right Thing for the Boat	129
10	*Bolero*'s Kanes	143
Notes		157
Sources		161
Index		163

Preface

During the *Bolero* restoration, I was asked to speak about the project at a Cruising Club of America dinner at the American Yacht Club in Rye, New York. After my talk, Dooie Isdale, a former commodore of the New York Yacht Club who had been involved in campaigning our restored Herreshoff New York 40 *Marilee*, stood up and asked, "What drives you to undertake these restorations?" I did not have a good answer then, and I'm not sure I do now, but I have certainly thought a lot about the question in the last three years. Perhaps I can attempt to answer it here.

Classic yachts have appeal in three different ways. First of all, they are works of art, and their beauty is often compared to that of famous paintings, works of sculpture, or architecture. People describe the works of Olin Stephens, Nathanael Herreshoff, and Philip Rhodes with the same words used to evaluate the creations of Picasso, Michelangelo, and Frank Lloyd Wright.

Second, they are a functional means of transportation and housing and can be used for recreational purposes, such as racing or cruising. Thus, someone who appreciates beauty can actually sail away in this piece of art.

Third, they are historic. The history of the design, construction, launching, racing, problems (sinking, collision, dismasting, etc.), and past owners and crew is fascinating. Every one of these boats has its own unique story, and discovering that history provides us with the gratification often achieved by archeologists.

Is my answer then simply that restoring classic yachts involves the confluence of art, function, and history? No, there is something else. I became interested in doing restorations not when I saw classic yachts or even when I sailed on them. Rather, it was when I read about them. The wonderful books that have been written by authors like John Rousmaniere and others provided a strong stimulus for me to learn more about the process. And in learning about the process, I began to meet the people and, as I met the people, I realized that I wanted to become a part of this community. Herein lies the answer to Dooie's question.

The yacht designers, brokers, yard owners, shipwrights, workers, captains, mates, crew, and others involved with classic yachts are some of the finest people I know. I sometimes marvel at the wealthy, powerful, and influential classic owner observing with awe the sawdust-caked, flannel-shirted laborer spiling a plank, each wishing he could change places in life with the other.

When these boats are moored in Antigua, St. Tropez, or Newport, owners and crew are instantly invited aboard each other's vessels. Conversations take place in multiple languages and spontaneous friendships develop. I have had the good fortune to be able to travel the world and have a broad variety of experiences; nowhere have I witnessed the camaraderie that readily exists in this community. I restored *Bolero* because while the boats are magnificent, the people are even better!

Edward Kane

 Fully restored, *Bolero* sails the Caribbean in 2004. (© DANIEL FORSTER)

Introduction

"We built a nice sailing yawl for the assistant secretary of the navy. I forgot his name – the name of the boat was Bolero *and that's a fancy boat."* — Nils Halvorsen

This book will not please people who believe that the story of a boat is a plodding account of construction details and race results. There is at least one sailboat that must be regarded in a very different light. Not only is *Bolero* "the best of her class" (as someone said of her), but she was created and restored by a diverse company of people who were the best of their classes. *Bolero* is one of those cultural heirlooms that is constantly being rediscovered in ways that would astonish even her creators, and her story is of a vast and varied world of laughter and tears, triumph and failure. The same boat that was featured in *Time* magazine and broke a Bermuda Race record was nearly wrecked on Cape Hatteras and, only 15 years ago, was rotting away in a Florida canal.

Very early in this project, I made three discoveries that shaped this book. The first was that this glamorous racing boat was in fact conceived as a family cruiser. After placing the order for "a comfortable cruising boat with a turn of speed," John Nicholas and Anne Kinsolving Brown — her wealthy, artistic owners, and patrons of magnificent buildings — devoted the better part of two months not to honing the boat's beauty but to making their boat practical. Almost their sole concern lay with the three sleeping areas for themselves and their children. This came full circle when I later spoke and sailed with Ed Kane and Marty Wallace, who made it clear that when they restored *Bolero* in 2003, they also made her a part of their tight family.

The second discovery was that *Bolero* was the last creation of one of the historic collaborations not just in yachting history but in maritime history. This was the relationship between the boatbuilder Henry B. Nevins and the naval architecture firm of Sparkman & Stephens. Contractors and architects usually are notoriously distrustful of each other; yet Nevins and his people, and the two Stephens brothers, Olin and Rod, were conspirators in a mutually agreeable, ongoing project, which was to build fine boats. Understanding these three remarkable men is as important to understanding Bolero as is appreciating John and Anne Brown. This is only partly a story of technology; it is a story of values. Henry Nevins would interrupt his instructional writings and lectures about boatbuilding with deeply felt manifestos on virtuous living, which he summarized in the word "craftsmanship" — an idea that, expressed one way or another, permeates *Bolero*, her people, and her story. When Olin Stephens spoke of the value of a boat with balanced ends, he seemed also to be talking of the value of the balanced life that he discovered during a personal crisis when he was at the peak of his career.

Third, I rediscovered that the power of what John Nicholas Brown called "the visual," a mystical appreciation of beauty, has absorbed many of *Bolero*'s people. They include Nevins, Olin Stephens, the boat's romantic racing skipper, Cornelius Shields, and on through Nils Halvorsen — the half-blind, stubborn old Norwegian who lofted Stephens's lines — to the people who restored *Bolero* in 2003, Ed Kane and Marty Wallace.

As a youthful sailor in the 1950s, I sensed that this boat was a superstar of the sailing world, an icon, a nautical Marilyn Monroe in beauty and alluring name. The Browns learned that early. Within weeks of the boat's launching in June 1949, they discovered that despite their own considerable personal accomplishments, they were prisoners of an icon: they were "the *Bolero* Browns." One of the boat's builders would forget their names, but not the name of their boat. In 2004, at the Sparkman & Stephens 75th anniversary celebration at Mystic Seaport, people stood gazing at *Bolero* as though she were a shrine.

Her inherent sleekness — her aptitude for unruffled, confident power — was sensed as easily as it was seen. "The greatest of all sensations," declared John Nicholas Brown, is "the *Bolero* feeling under sail." On the racecourse, she compiled a remarkable record that began with a famous rivalry with her near sister ship *Baruna*, extended through hundreds of races in Europe and San Francisco and Florida, and was still growing in 2004 when *Bolero* won almost half her races on the classic yacht circuit in the West Indies and New England.

If this boat seems larger than life, it is because so much life has gone into building, sailing, and restoring her, as I hope this book proves.

There are many to acknowledge in the creation of this book. My first thanks go to Ed Kane and Marty Wallace for their support, their hospitality, and their willingness to be subjected to questioning by their self-appointed "yachting therapist." Nick Brown, Angela Brown Fischer, Dick Goennel, and Olin Stephens generously offered memories of their many years around or on Bolero, and Dick and Olin provided their personal copies of the beautiful albums of onboard photos taken by Norry Hoyt and created by his students at St. George's School

Three archives have been exceptionally valuable: the City Island Nautical Museum, City Island, New York (Tom Nye, director); the G.W. Blunt White Library, Mystic Seaport, Mystic, Connecticut (Paul O'Pecko, director); and the John Nicholas Brown Center for the Study of American Civilization, Providence, Rhode Island (Joyce Botelho, director, and Holly Snyder and Ron Potvin, curators). I also conducted research in the Avery and Butler Libraries of Columbia University; the Ferguson Library of Stamford, Connecticut; the New York Public Library's Humanities and Social Sciences Library; and the library of the New York Yacht Club.

For providing speaking or writing forums where I tried out ideas, I thank Michael Tower of the Pratt Institute School of Architecture, Brooklyn, New York; Paul O'Pecko and the Fellows of the G.W. Blunt White Library, Mystic Seaport; and Herb McCormick of Cruising World magazine, where portions of chapter 10 first appeared.

Andy German, director of publications at Mystic Seaport, understood the aims and means of the project, and was remarkably patient about deadlines that seemed always to be set back.

In a year of joy, sadness, and change, Leah Ruth Robinson Rousmaniere encouraged me to attempt to understand one of the oldest of all mysteries, which is how in this flawed world so much beauty can spring out of the joint efforts of people who come together, it seems miraculously, in pursuit of a common purpose.

John Rousmaniere
April 15, 2005

Bolero's combination of grace, large size, and high polish are obvious as she knifes through the water during an early trial. Her afterguard inspects the mainsail as a professional sailor near a coffee grinder winch awaits commands to trim the jib. (© MYSTIC SEAPORT, ROSENFELD COLLECTION)

Arriving home from work one evening, a man was told that an impressive big boat was anchored in a nearby harbor.

"The name's *Bolero*, something like that," his wife told him.

"THE *Bolero*?" he replied.

"Big and black."

The fellow ran out the door and raced through the twilight to catch a glimpse of the most famous yawl in America.

The First Break for Freedom

On a warm morning on City Island, New York, in early June 1949, a lanky man in a blue blazer and a state of controlled fussiness was inspecting the incoming tide. John Nicholas Brown's passion for perfection would not brook delay. Over the previous eight months, dozens of craftsmen, guided by almost that many drawings and plans, had transformed piles of wood, tons of metal, and many gallons of paint and varnish into the gleaming black-hulled yacht that sat in the sun upon a sturdy wooden cradle on the iron rails lapped by the rising salt water.

By 11 a.m. the 83 guests had picked their way through the crowded Henry B. Nevins Yacht Yard to their seats. Many signed the guest book with their names and addresses, though there was one guest, Henry Taylor, who gave his address only as *Baruna*. This was a hint of a challenge. It was the name of his boat, widely expected to be the arch rival on the race course to John Nicholas Brown's new black yawl.

The Brown family took their appointed places. The boat's two sponsors, Anne Brown and her 12-year-old daughter, Angela, positioned themselves on a platform under the bow with a bottle of Champagne to crack across the stem. Standing above them on the boat's foredeck were the 49-year-old owner, grinning broadly alongside the boat's 41-year-old architect, Olin Stephens, his shy demeanor belying his authority as the world's most successful yacht designer.

The boat's builder was unable to join them. After 40 years of constructing some of the best-known, most successful boats of his era, Henry Nevins at 71 was frail and almost sightless. Waiting quietly on shore, he confided to a friend that

Here is the invitation to *Bolero*'s launching, almost three years after she was conceived. (COURTESY JOHN NICHOLAS BROWN CENTER, BROWN UNIVERSITY)

A beaming John Nicholas Brown poses with the boat's cosponsors, his wife Anne and daughter Angela, before the launching at the Nevins Yacht Yard in 1949. He wrote of another of his great building projects, "Through what seems endless detail there runs joy in creation which is [the] sine qua non of great art." (© MYSTIC SEAPORT, ROSENFELD COLLECTION)

Flanked by John Nicholas Brown and a launching guest, an ailing and almost blind Henry Nevins stands by for what he correctly predicted would be the last launching he would attend at the yard he founded in 1907. (© MYSTIC SEAPORT, ROSENFELD COLLECTION)

this was the last launching he expected ever to attend. So blind that he probably could make out only the big black hull, Nevins was alert to the familiar noises of a launching – the owner's hearty welcome to his guests, the foreman's slightly anxious instructions to workers manning the machinery, the spectators' excited comments on first seeing the massive boat looming above them. After more than 800 launchings in his yard, these sounds were almost as familiar to him as the usual noises of a busy boatyard – the whoosh of a plane putting a bevel into a mahogany plank, the thump of an adze shaping an oak keel, the whine of a file smoothing the edges of a bronze cleat fresh from the machine shop.

Such sounds were evidence of the authenticity of the boatbuilder's trade – or, as Henry Nevins preferred to call it, the boatbuilder's *craft*. To him, building a yacht was a far more ethical enterprise than a mere business or technical exercise. When he spoke of building wooden boats, he used words like "integrity" and "pride" and "character." Henry Nevins, in short, was a believer.

He heard the familiar smash of a bottle across the boat's metal bow fittings, and the cheers of the crowd, and the squeal of wheels as the cradle slid down the ways, and then the splash as the bottom of the new boat, now called *Bolero*, was kissed by salt water. Then came the groan of the wire cable as it was snubbed and stretched, and the silence as the crew clambered below to inspect the bilge for leaks. And finally the gratifying cry "All clear!" before the newly afloat *Bolero* broke free of the cradle and slowly slid into her natural element.

What Henry Nevins did not know was that there had been a slightly comical hitch in the proceedings involving the younger of the two sponsors. "I vividly recall the launching," Angela Brown Fischer looked back with mixed feelings, "and also my mortification at swinging the champagne bottle all tightly wrapped in red, white, and blue interlaced ribbon, only to have the thing swing back at me unbroken – three times! Someone from the yard finally stepped up and rescued me with a forceful bash which finally broke the bottle." Chagrined, she found relief in the usual way of the Browns, in an act of creation. On the first page of the guest book she jotted down a couple of bars of musical notation for a lilting tune, and under it wrote a personal note: "I know I'll have fun, even though I'm in the Dog-House." It was typical Brown playfulness. *Bolero*'s "dog house" was not a gloomy prison in the bilge reserved for miscreants but a handsome small cabin (also called the deckhouse) half-projecting above the deck and delegated as Angela's sleeping cabin when the boat was cruising. Completing her half-serious complaint, the girl ran off to join the celebration at one of old City Island's famous fish restaurants.

Olin Stephens, her designer, and John Nicholas Brown wait near the deckhouse for the inspectors below to report that there are no leaks. Soon *Bolero* will be floating free and her masts will be stepped. (© MYSTIC SEAPORT, ROSENFELD COLLECTION)

"Well Done, Young Lady"

After she went in the water, *Bolero* remained the property of the Nevins yard until she had been checked out. Over the next 11 days, when workers were not installing fittings the designers, builders, and the Browns were testing the electronics, engine, and sails. The sailing trials were the charge of Rod Stephens, the rigging and construction expert at Sparkman & Stephens who, though still in his thirties, had a knowledge of boats so authoritative that admirers were known to refer to him behind his back as "Rod-God." So that the stretchy cotton sails would be broken in without strain, he delayed the sailing trials until the first dry day with a light breeze so they could be slowly stretched into shape. When a jib ripped to shreds despite all his cautions, all were put on notice that as pretty as *Bolero* looked, she was one powerful and potentially dangerous vessel.

When everybody was finally happy, *Bolero* sailed over to Glen Cove, Long Island, where the Nevins yard's acting president, Arthur Gauss, presented the boat's title to John Nicholas Brown. The professional captain, Fred Lawton, recorded the moment in the log with due formality: "Commodore John Nicholas Brown accepted delivery of *Bolero* from Mr. Arthur Gauss and placed ship in commission in the presence of Mrs. Brown, Mr. Rod Stephens, Mr. Gauss." That legal requirement dispatched with, the boat was promptly taken out into Long Island Sound so Stephens could take a look at her racing sails.

More work continued until June 22, when the Browns finally extracted *Bolero* from the workmen and headed east. "*Bolero* slipped her mooring off Nevins' Yard at City Island and made her first break for *Freedom*—and the world," Anne wrote in her journal. There was a crew of seven: John and Anne Brown, their sons Carter and Nicholas, and the three professionals—Captain Lawton, the cook, and a paid hand. Their destination, 120 miles down Long Island Sound, was Fishers Island, New York, and their summer home, Windshield.

Anne felt like a new mother as *Bolero* ran under spinnaker before a gentle northwest breeze. "We lounged about, watching the stars, the racing sea, debating, identifying the lights ashore, and every so often, giving *Bolero* a surreptitious pat of endearment, trying to express the pride and pleasure we all felt in this,

As *Bolero*'s sails are stretched during her sailing trial, John steers and Anne looks aloft, while Olin Stephens tends the winch for the running backstay. Two observers perch comfortably on what Anne called *Bolero*'s "complicated, aristocratic fanny."
(© MYSTIC SEAPORT, ROSENFELD COLLECTION)

our first collective project in parenthood." Just after midnight, they sailed past a pair of round-top islands at the mouth of Fishers Island Sound. "Off the familiar Dumplings, made less familiar always by the depth of a moonless night, we heaved to & took in sail, then groped our way to the anchorage under power," Anne reported. "When we dropped the hook just under Windshield & tucked *Bolero* in for the night, each one of us breathed a sign of content & bowed in murmuring, 'Well done, young lady, you've got what it takes!'"

"The Young Lady Could Go"

Ten days later, on Massachusetts Bay, *Bolero* was sailing her first race and handily leading the fleet when a turning mark went missing so badly that Rod Stephens, who was navigating, could not find it. Though the boats were sent home, there was a happy ending to the fractured maiden race. She had proved fast, and John Nicholas Brown had made an impression by sportingly attempting to persuade the race committee to award a trophy to a competitor who had been winning when the race was abandoned. "*Bolero* lost no friends by this race," Anne Brown noted in her journal, "and most important of all, we discovered that the young lady could go."

Proving her abilities daily, the new boat completed her first races on the annual cruise of the Eastern Yacht Club, based in Marblehead and one of New England's oldest and most prestigious yacht clubs. In such an old institution, the annual "cruise" is not the lazy, aimless passage that word suggests but, rather, a series of races run between ports along an interesting coast – on this occasion, Maine's deeply indented and tideswept shoreline of granite ledges, pine trees, and fishermen's bait shacks peeking out of the fog. Whether sponsored by the Eastern Yacht Club or their home New York Yacht Club, an organized event like this was a favorite of the Browns, who had a knack for balancing privacy with gregariousness. During the days, their crew of children and friends raced, almost always successfully (here *Bolero* took two firsts and two seconds in the four races). At night, they went ashore to parties.

On one of those nights they were anchored at the little Down East harbor of Blue Hill. "When we stepped aboard the launch to return to *Bolero*," Anne wrote, "the moon was shining tall on the superb harbor with its high, pine-crested hills rising steeply from the shore, the fleet, gaily lighted, riding at anchor below, and the peak of Blue Hill in the distance. In spite of a long day, such beauty was too disturbing for sleep, and we sat on deck a long while, listening to the revels of the young and admiring the night."

The idyll was interrupted by the boat's first breakdown. The three-foot bronze centerboard stuck part-way down in its slot deep in the keel. Deciding to fix the problem immediately, Brown took *Bolero* into Boothbay Harbor to century-old Sample's Shipyard. With the marine railway set up for husky fishing schooners and lobster boats, not slim yachts, there was a certain amount of experimentation before a suitable cradle was made and *Bolero* could be pulled up the ways by a huffing engine. Anne wryly made much of the contrast between the polished yawl and the rough-hewn working waterfront:

Bolero was regularly hauled at Nevins and other yards for one of the many rigorous bouts of what Captain Fred Lawton called with some understatement "general ship's maintenance." (COURTESY NORRIS HOYT)

With a typical crew of many ages, *Bolero* slips rapidly along a rocky New England shore under all the downwind canvas she can set—mizzen, mizzen staysail, mainsail, parachute spinnaker, and an experimental spinnaker staysail called, inevitably, a "half-bra." The navigator looks ahead for a turning mark. The genoa jib (hoisted in loops of light line called "stops") is ready to broken out for the next leg. (© MYSTIC SEAPORT, ROSENFELD COLLECTION)

"Finally *Bolero* appeared, very stately and insouciant, at the foot of the railway, looking in her finery like a society queen gone slumming," she wrote. "She started up the railway with great dignity, disdainfully ignoring the excitement of the Sample family, who raced about giving orders, and of a large section of the population of Boothbay who had gathered on the roadside to see the show…. One, twice, three times *Bolero* sallied forth up the railway, only to retreat before the Sample judgment that the throne that was to bear her from her proper domain to the [illegible] land was not sufficiently secure – in other words was not yet tailored to fit her complicated, aristocratic fanny."

The Nevins yard dispatched a man to drive up overnight to fix the problem, and on the next high tide *Bolero* was slid back in the water.

Cruise over, she set out on the long route down the New England coast, all the way to City Island for a week of intensive fine tuning guided by the lengthy punch lists that Captain Lawton, Rod Stephens, and the Browns had been compiling in the weeks since *Bolero* had left her birthplace. Sticking doors and bureau drawers, baggy sails, balky running rigging, inconvenient storage areas, and countless other minor problems of the sort that surface when a new boat is tried out—all were attended to. When the checklists were crossed off (though new ones would continue to be made), Captain Lawton and his crew threw themselves into to the first of many long exercises in delicate touching up and vigorous scrubbing down that a perfectionist like Lawton and John Nicholas Brown considered normal procedure aboard any decent vessel, and which Lawton euphemistically called "general ship's maintenance."

In her state of high polish *Bolero* headed east once again, this time to New London, Connecticut, for the start of the New York Yacht Club Cruise – and her first, much anticipated race against her near-sistership *Baruna* in a duel that, off and on over the next 13 years, would become legendary.

The Bolero Browns

Already *Bolero* was a celebrity. Only three weeks after she was launched, a Boston boating writer in a preview of the Eastern Yacht Club Cruise wrote, "The presence of John Nicholas Brown's super-ocean racer *Bolero* insures national interest." Carter Brown believed that to some extent this interest was an outburst of pent-up demand in the wake of war for glamorous new sensations.

But there was something more. *Bolero*'s designer, Olin Stephens, had made her drop-dead gorgeous. "Olin's lines," Carter wrote, "reach right into your heart." As though she were Marilyn Monroe, another postwar sensation, eyes and cameras latched onto the boat intimately and obsessively. Her photograph appeared in newspapers and magazines from Boston to Des Moines to Los Angeles. Whatever harbor she entered, she was greeted, Carter Brown would say, by "flotillas of small boats coming to ogle." The sight of *Bolero* under sail was permanently recorded not only in film but in memory. After Bill Robinson of *Yachting* magazine looked down on Bolero from a Newport-Bermuda Race patrol plane, he wrote, "She made a brave sight…, romping along at a great clip, a broad vee of white almost like a steamer's wake streaming out astern of her." More than half a century after the 1954 Bermuda Race, two Bermudians who had been in the finish-line spotter boat, Helen and Kirk Cooper, became emotional when they described how a great black yawl had erupted out of a squally night – a white bone in her bow's teeth, her sails and winches glistening with rain.

Such was the world's image of John Nicholas and Anne Kinsolving Brown's *Bolero*. Though it pleased them, the celebrity at first was a little daunting. A few weeks after the launching, a friend of theirs passed on a remark made by his son. Hearing that the Browns were coming to dinner, the boy had blurted out, "Not the *Bolero* Browns!" Anne was shocked. "It was," she would write, "as if one's pet pony had turned out to be Man O'War." What had started as a family cruising boat had become an icon.

With a bone in her teeth even in a moderate breeze, *Bolero* pulls away from the fleet after the start of a New York Yacht Club race in 1954. The jib is made of Dacron, a new shiny, low-stretch synthetic polyester fabric.
(© MYSTIC SEAPORT, ROSENFELD COLLECTION)

18 | FIRST BREAK FOR FREEDOM

"Sailors frequently are individualists, as a yacht designer should know."
—Olin Stephens

A Comfortable Cruising Boat

Although *Bolero* is famous as a racing boat, the Browns' first concern was for her cruising accommodations. From a vantage point near the small owner's stateroom and the Brown boys' cabin, the camera looks up the main companionway into the deckhouse, where Angela Brown stands at the chart table near her bunk. (COURTESY JOHN NICHOLAS BROWN CENTER, BROWN UNIVERSITY)

Almost three years before *Bolero* was launched, on a hot August day in 1946, John Nicholas and Anne Brown came down to New York City to talk with Olin Stephens about a family dream that John called "a comfortable cruising boat with a turn of speed." The boat would have to be the largest size for racing and suitably impressive to serve as the flagship of the New York Yacht Club. But, most important, she had to be a family boat. Out of these hopes came design number 711, and, three years later, a boat.

The Browns' dream of building a boat to suit their needs was born soon after their marriage in 1930, grew slowly as they learned from boats they purchased second-hand, and took hold for good during the 1946 sailing season, the first since 1939 when Americans were able to sail freely without being confined to bays and harbors by anti-submarine nets and other security measures. As the Browns and their three young children cruised and raced along the New England coast in their 64-foot sloop, *Courante*, they imagined a new boat. She would have to be bigger than *Courante*, a prewar Sparkman & Stephens design that was originally named *Orient* because she had been built in Hong Kong, but that they, in Brown style, had renamed for a dance, in this case one involving quick running.

Anne Kinsolving Brown had introduced her husband and later their three children to the sport. John Nicholas Brown may not have been a natural sailor, but he was a romantic and fascinated one who was exceptionally proud that his family's fortune was founded on merchant shipping. He also was by nature a creator. A professionally trained art historian, an amateur architect, and a fulltime visionary, he was intrigued by the challenge of building big, beautiful, intricate, and at the same time practical objects. Already, he had meticulously supervised the creation of two spectacular buildings, one a Gothic chapel at his old prep school and the other the modernistic summer home, Windshield, at Fishers Island. Now, with John's successful wartime duty as the U.S. Army's chief advisor on handling plundered European art behind him, and with their teenage

 When they posed for this photograph with Drake Sparkman and the plans for the New York 32 Class sloop in 1936, Olin Stephens (center) and his brother, Rod, a construction and rigging expert, were still in their 20s, yet Sparkman & Stephens was the country's most successful yacht design firm.
(© MYSTIC SEAPORT, ROSENFELD COLLECTION)

sons, Carter and Nicholas, eager to do some racing, John and Anne throw themselves into a third big family building project – a great new yacht.

For advice, Brown went to Drake Sparkman, the president and chief salesman at the yacht design and brokerage firm of Sparkman & Stephens. Sparkman, who had sold him *Courante*, understood the Browns' tastes and needs, and in early August he introduced them to his partner, the world's most prolific and successful yacht designer, Olin J. Stephens II.

"Drake was more influential than I was in landing the job, and he brought the Browns in one day for a talk," Stephens recalled many years later when, at the age of 95, he was enjoying an exceptionally active retirement, writing books and traveling around the world to sail in boats of his design that had been restored to their original beauty. Out of his discussions with the Browns came two preliminary sketches and a set of parameters for a boat that was identified as Sparkman & Stephens design number 711. The Browns at first surprised Stephens by making very few demands. "Some people who want a cruising boat are quite particular," he looked back, "but all the Browns said was that they wanted a good combination of cruising and racing ability in a boat that was 72 feet on deck, which was almost the maximum under the rule for the Bermuda Race."

In other words, she would be a "maxi" like *Baruna*, the prewar 72-footer that Stephens had designed for Henry Taylor. Designed and built along the same parameters that the Browns were setting, she was a very fast, very big, and very striking family cruising and racing yawl at the very top limit of boats allowed to enter the world's oldest regularly scheduled ocean race, from Newport, Rhode Island, to Bermuda. Taylor and his sons had won the Bermuda Race in 1938, the last one before World War II; they would win it again in 1948.

22 | A COMFORTABLE CRUISING BOAT

An Evolving Design

According to a memorandum that Stephens sent to his staff, he and the Browns agreed on a few alterations to the *Baruna* template. One concerned looks: the stern would be stretched out a little farther than *Baruna*'s. Another feature that the Browns requested at this early meeting was that their boat be a cutter. Over the centuries, the word has meant so many things that the authoritative *International Maritime Dictionary* requires 57 words to define it. Over the centuries, cutter has meant a ship's small boat; a deep, narrow, singlemasted racing boat (as against a shallow-hulled, beamy sloop); or—in the mid-twentieth century—a single-masted boat with at least two jibs. The last definition applies to *Bolero*'s first sail plan, with its towering mast. Since *Courante* had this rig, the Browns obviously were guided by familiarity. The projected boat, however, was so much larger than their old one that they wisely allowed themselves to be persuaded to replace the single stick with a two-masted yawl rig like *Baruna*'s, with the large sail plan divided into smaller, more manageable sections while providing an additional big sail, the mizzen staysail, to be set off the mizzen when sailing downwind in races.

Bolero's cabin arrangement and the design of the deckhouse were inspired by the Browns' experience with their previous boat, the 64-foot Sparkman & Stephens-designed *Courante* (the former and future *Orient*). In their initial discussions with Olin Stephens, they said they also wanted *Bolero* to be a cutter like *Courante*, but she was so much larger that the yawl rig made more sense.
(© MYSTIC SEAPORT, ROSENFELD COLLECTION)

A COMFORTABLE CRUISING BOAT | 23

The Benchmark: *Baruna*

At first, in 1946, Sparkman & Stephens design number 711 had the same dimensions as design number 222, *Baruna,* built in 1938. *Baruna*'s principal dimensions were these:

72' Length Overall (LOA)
50' Load Waterline Length (LWL)
14'10" Beam (Bm.)
9'6" Draft (Dr.)
88,130 pounds Displacement (Disp.)
2,342 square feet sail area (SA)

Bolero's final dimensions

In the fall of 1948, design number 711 was enlarged to these dimensions:
73'6" LOA
51' LWL
15'1" Bm.
9'6" Dr.
93,800 pounds Disp.
2,480 square feet SA

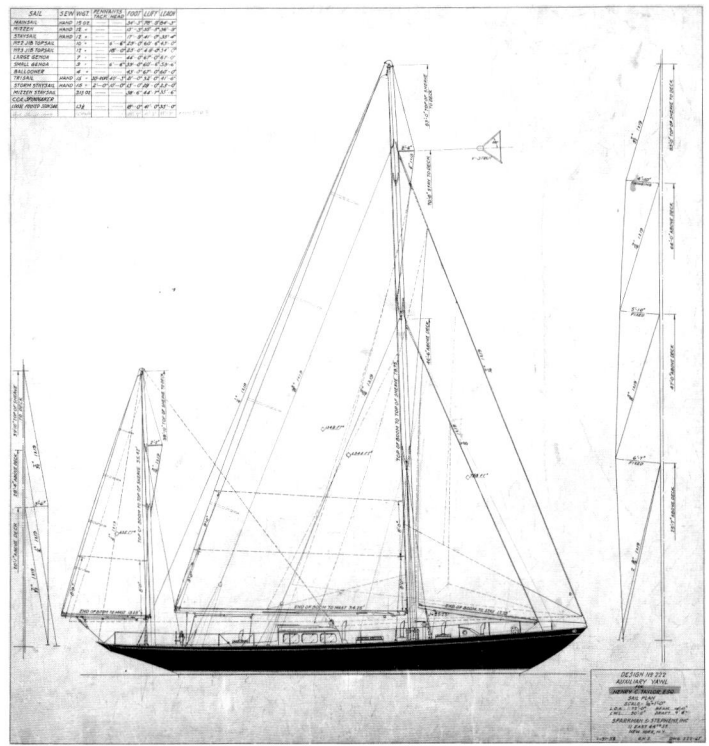

These profile plans by Sparkman & Stephens – *Baruna* (design number 222) on the left, *Bolero* (design number 711) on the right – bring out the varying ideas about accommodations as represented by the deckhouse placement. *Baruna*'s wooden masts required jumper struts while *Bolero*'s aluminum masts did not. For years on both the East and West Coasts the two big yawls engaged in one of the longest, closest, and at the same time friendliest duels in yachting history. (DESIGNS AND DRAWINGS BY SPARKMAN & STEPHENS, © 2005 BY SPARKMAN & STEPHENS, INC.)

Bolero was based on Henry Taylor's *Baruna*, a 1938 Sparkman & Stephens yawl that won the 1938 and 1948 Bermuda Race. The most obvious difference between the two is the deckhouse placement and shape, which reflect varying approaches to living arrangements. (© MYSTIC SEAPORT, ROSENFELD COLLECTION)

If the Browns had asked the cost of such a big boat, they would have learned that, depending on details and the rapid pace of post-war inflation, construction at the Henry B. Nevins Yacht Yard on City Island – one of the most respected builders of first-class wooden boats – would probably run over $100,000, with annual maintenance running at least $20,000. In the end, *Bolero* had enough special features to bring her price, without sails and electronic instruments, up to about $150,000. This was a fair price for an icon in the 1940s. It was, for example, what Judy Garland charged for making an MGM movie musical like *Easter Parade*, but half again as much as Joe DiMaggio's $100,000 annual salary. Today it is the equivalent of almost $1,500,000, which is nowhere near sufficient to pay a movie or baseball star – or, for that matter, to replace a boat like *Bolero* in a time when labor costs are many times higher than what Henry Nevins's workers were paid in 1949. (Fully equipped, the new boat cost about $175,000.)

Had Brown harbored any doubts about the cost, he might have consulted *Baruna*'s owner, Henry Taylor. Taylor undoubtedly would have offered Brown the same assurance that he gave the man who bought *Baruna* from him in 1953, James Michael of San Francisco. When Michael wondered out loud whether he could afford to own the boat, Taylor told him that the same worry had bothered him, but that considering everything that *Baruna* had given his family, she was the best investment he had ever made.

A COMFORTABLE CRUISING BOAT | 25

While this rationale would have made perfect sense to John Brown, the price would not have stopped him because, first, he could afford it, and, second, he had a profound appreciation for fine objects, from furniture to paintings to automobiles to architecture of radically different styles.

"Something to Think About"

If monetary considerations lay in the background, not so with considerations of family. When the Browns began to assert themselves about the details of their new boat, the main issue was not beauty or speed or structure, but living accommodations. "A ship is a matter of infinite compromises," Brown would say after *Bolero* was launched. "If you want speed, you have to sacrifice something else. If you want comfort, you have to sacrifice speed, and so on. In *Bolero*, we aimed at flexibility. We tried to have a maximum of comfort as a family sailing ship, and yet to have as much speed as possible." Speed he left to Olin Stephens. Comfort was his responsibility, which was why the rig and the shape of the stern were relatively minor considerations for the Browns compared with their concern for the living arrangements for themselves and their children.

The accommodations received two mentions in Olin Stephens's initial memorandum to his staff. One was that there had to be sufficient headroom to keep the six-foot, five-inch owner from banging his head when he was below decks. The other point was that the deckhouse – the cabin half-projecting above the deck that Angela Brown would call the "Dog House" – must be like *Courante*'s, which was located far aft and not toward the middle of the boat like *Baruna*'s. The first request was relatively easy to meet in such a big boat. The second request, however, involved some complications that took some thought.

The reason for the aft deckhouse was that it made room for the sleeping arrangements that the Browns wanted. In most boats over 70 feet, a 'midships deckhouse like *Baruna*'s gave the owner a very spacious, very private aft stateroom. But the Browns did not wish to be isolated; what they wanted was a family suite in which their own stateroom, with a double bed, would be near their children's sleeping quarters.

Just how this would be arranged was the subject of an intense effort in August and September, 1946, when six sets of plans flew between the Sparkman & Stephens design office and Fishers Island, Newport, or wherever the Browns were staying. All five Browns threw themselves into the problem of fitting in a private cabin for a tall woman and an extra-tall man who wanted to sleep in the same bed every night, and still have their children nearby. "These two studies will give you and the rest of the Brown family something to think about," Drake Sparkman wrote.

There was plenty to think about. A sailboat hull that is 72 feet long on deck,

 Continuing the family policy of naming boats for dances, the Browns called their new one *Bolero*. Under the ownership of Ed Kane and Marty Wallace more than half a century later, the boat gained an apt symbol in this graceful Bolero dancer designed by Chip Barber.

26 | A COMFORTABLE CRUISING BOAT

"A ship is a matter of infinite compromises."

15 feet in maximum width, and 50 feet along the waterline may be a big boat, but it is a very small house. The two sides sometimes worked at cross purposes as they tried to make everything fit around the Browns' wishes for the cabins. When Anne Brown complained that the wash rooms seemed cramped and proposed lengthening them by half a foot, Stephens replied that his assistants had already snatched six inches to enlarge the galley. Eventually, Stephens advised the Browns that the only way to gain more space was to add at least a foot to the waterline length. "Personally I would rather do this than make the main cabin the least bit cramped."

The boat was not lengthened (at least then), and after a great deal of pushing and squeezing, the Browns got their family suite. At the bottom of the steps leading down from the deckhouse there were (and remain) two smallish cabins side by side for the parents and their sons, while Angela slept in the deckhouse itself. To relieve any sense of crowding, and to open the interior up when the boat was raced, the designers and owners came up with the ingenious solution of building the two cabins with side panels that could be easily removed.

In October 1946, plans were drawn up and some specifications were drafted to give to the Henry Nevins yard, with which Sparkman & Stephens had a long relationship so intimate it could be called conspiratorial. As big as the boat was, the plans – produced by draftsmen on the basis of Olin Stephens's drawings – show a delicate-looking object that stretches easily and naturally between the fine points of the narrow, well-balanced bow and stern. Between the two ends, Stephens and his draftsmen produced a sweeping sheer line (the curve along the rail) that dips down from the stern to the cockpit, where, near the deckhouse, it starts a long, gradual ascent to the bow that makes the boat look both powerful and fine. The irony is that one of the features that give *Bolero* her distinctive appearance – the streamlined deckhouse located far aft – was a development of domestic concerns. As Olin Stephens (whose own preference was for *Baruna*'s more traditional deckhouse) would say, "The two boats have strong personalities, each in its own way."

In late October 1946, word came to stop work. John Nicholas Brown was going to Washington as Assistant Secretary of the Navy for Air in President Harry S. Truman's administration. He would serve in this delicate and highly charged position for almost two and a half years, resigning just as the Henry Nevins yard was completing work on his big black yawl – a boat that would be named, like all John and Anne Brown's boats, for a sensual dance, in this case one choreographed to the clicking of castanets and the strum of a guitar – the *Bolero*.

3 The Two Adventurers

When someone praised a sailing event put on by the Browns (seen here at *Bolero*'s launching) as "A naval operation with all the grimness left out and a great deal of beauty added," he put his finger on Anne and John Brown's blend of energetic focus, warm hospitality, and sheer personal gracefulness. (COURTESY JOHN NICHOLAS BROWN CENTER, BROWN UNIVERSITY)

After Edward Kane completed the restoration of *Bolero* in 2003, he was asked what had motivated him to go to all the effort and expense of returning her to her original condition. His answer hinted at a motivation that might be called spiritual. "There's something *mystical* about her," Kane said. As an example, he cited the striking "confluence of events" that brought together the team of individuals – each remarkable in his or her own right – who created the boat.

From a distance, the process seems simple enough. A man and a woman have a dream, which a designer translates into a two-dimensional plan, which a builder then translates into a three-dimensional reality. Yet any creation as intricate as building a large wood-and-metal sailing vessel is far more demanding than this skimpy narrative suggests. To cite just three statistics indicating the complexity of *Bolero*'s creation, she required almost three dozen minutely detailed scale drawings, some 37,000 hours of labor by her builders, and more than 100,000 bronze wood screws – all that (and much more besides) to produce an object whose reason for existence was to provide personal satisfaction to her owners and anyone who looked at her. When the maritime historian Samuel Eliot Morison observed that the creators of the most splendid clipper ships and Gothic cathedrals had two things in common, "visions transcending human experience" and "the power to transmute them into reality," he could also have been writing of the four men and one woman of contrasting temperaments and similar ideals who briefly came together to create *Bolero*. The path of such a complex act of creation is sufficiently long and winding to require that all the people involved be gifted in several ways. Of course they must be skilled, have high standards, and have and be able to express strong convictions. Yet at the same time they must be pragmatic and cooperative, willing to set aside their prejudices to make room for a common goal. Not least important, they must be flexible and ever open to the possibility of new solutions to old problems in the way suggested by the poet Theodore Roethke in the quote that serves as this chapter's epigraph: they must be prepared to "reject nothing, but re-order all."

> "My first interest has been my family. Then, second, has been the community. And third – the visual."

Two of the five who built *Bolero* were yacht designers. Olin J. Stephens II, was an artist-scientist with a vision of boats and life that he expressed as "balance between the ends, and, as far as possible, balance throughout." Because this philosophy was also his temperament, he often served as mediator between the extremes both in a boat's design and in the opinions of others involved in its creation. Working at his right hand was his extremely forceful brother, Roderick S. Stephens Jr., whose Holy Grail was "The Proper Yacht," every piece of which came through fierce concentration on the most minute details. A third *Bolero* collaborator was her builder, Henry B. Nevins, who over four decades had crafted the system that crafted her.

And at the beginning stood the remarkable couple who in their own forceful way provided the three things without which *Bolero* would not exist: a vision, a purpose, and the resources to make the collaboration possible. The owners and patrons of great objects are often left out of such stories, as though the only roles in creativity are played by the people with their hands on the object. But because *Bolero* began with John Nicholas and Anne Kinsolving Brown, so will we as we survey the beliefs, the skills, and the cultures that overlapped in the act of reordering that produced her.

"A Witness to the Act of Creation"

"Scholar, sailor, humanist who brought art into life and made of life an art." So reads John Nicholas Brown's tombstone. More specific was Brown's own description of his concerns: "My first interest has been my family. Then, second, has been the community. And third – the visual." Blood, public service, beauty – his secular trinity – led him to undertake three very different, grand, and complex building projects. In the 1920s there was a church in the towering medieval Gothic style. A decade later came Windshield, a striking summer house in the horizontal modern style. Brown's third great project was *Bolero*, which combines the vertical and the horizontal. For him, building a fine, useful object was a spiritual experience. "I felt that I had actually been a witness to the act of Creation," he wrote soon after watching the architect Ralph Adams Cram put the final touches on the plans for the Gothic chapel that Brown built at St. George's School.

Brown's path was neither straight nor easy. His bedrock was the Brown family fortune. As Edmund S. Morgan wrote of the Browns of Rhode Island, "Their candles lit the halls and assemblies of America's Colonial gentry. The cannon they cast had armed American ships in the War of Independence. Their trading vessels had carried the American flag to Canton and Batavia and St. Petersburg. Their cottons were worn in every state of the union." Alongside each other on College Hill in Providence are Brown University, named for John Nicholas Brown's great-grandfather, Nicholas, and Moses Brown School, named for his great-great uncle. Like many other Colonial American fortunes, theirs, lamentably, was intertwined with slavery, over which the family became deeply split. Nicholas and Moses pressed for abolition of the slave trade in the eighteenth and nineteenth centuries to the point of hauling another Brown, John, into court. (In the 1940s, John Nicholas Brown would oversee the racial integration of the United States Navy.)

With his name attached to such wealth and controversy, John Nicholas Brown would have been well known in any case, but the startling and sad circumstances of his inheritance made him an unwilling national joke. Within three months of his birth in January 1900, his father and then his uncle died, leaving him a fortune. The newspapers promptly called the boy "the world's richest baby," and this unfortunate label stuck throughout his long, highly productive life. When he was 47 and the new Assistant Secretary of the Navy for Air, with duties that included managing the navy's vast research program, a story about Brown in a popular magazine ran under the belittling headline, "World's Richest Baby Joins the Navy."

> "I grew up an American legend. Very little of it is true."

"I grew up an American legend. Very little of it is true," Brown would say. Rumors about his extensive travels, presumed romances, and recurring health problems (rheumatic fever left him with a weak heart) were regular fodder for the gossip columns. Lesser things have driven people to drink, drugs, or ruin; to quote a Vanderbilt, "Inherited wealth is a real handicap to happiness. It is as certain death to ambition as cocaine is to morality." But John Nicholas Brown succeeded in rising above the handicap with the help of a fiercely protective mother and his own strong character. When the president of Brown University offered him a slot in the freshman class and promised that the work would be easy, Brown chose Harvard. There, he was so reserved that his classmates at first believed he was an English aristocrat. His gravitas was lifelong and ubiquitous. "He was always a real gentleman," recalled one of his regular crew in *Bolero*, Dick Goennel. "He didn't give you orders. He *suggested*. He'd ask, 'Don't you think we should. . .?' 'Do you mind if I make a suggestion?' Nobody ever talked to me like that, especially on a boat."

After creating his own personal academic major in art history and the classics, he graduated with highest honors and was awarded a fellowship to study classical and medieval art in Europe. The quiet, unassuming life of a scholar and collector appealed far more to him than serving on boards of directors and managing real estate. When he was given a clerical position in the family business office, Brown was bored for the first and last time in his life. Even the company's name, The Counting House Corporation, was dusty. Still in his early twenties, he found an outlet in supervising the first of his three great building projects.

"One of the Greatest Educational Influences"

As a boy, Brown lived in his mother's Norman-style mansion, Harbour Court, in Newport, Rhode Island, and was a day student at a nearby Episcopal school, St. George's, where he was taken every morning and picked up every evening by one of his mother's servants. The school lacked a large chapel in which all the students and teachers could gather comfortably for daily services. Such an intense Anglo-Catholic – an Episcopalian who observed Roman Catholic rituals – that

(Above left) If 28-year-old John Nicholas Brown (right) seemed nervous at the consecration of the St. George's School chapel, it was because he had planned the ceremony down to the last ritual. The chapel's architect, Ralph Adams Cram, joined him at left. (COURTESY JOHN NICHOLAS BROWN CENTER, BROWN UNIVERSITY)

(Above right and opposite) Not merely a sponsor, John Nicholas Brown designed some of the chapel's pavement and collaborated on the building's visual symbolism. Cram considered the project to be "the source of one of the most valued friendships I have ever experienced." (COURTESY JOHN NICHOLAS BROWN CENTER, BROWN UNIVERSITY)

A Gothic Vision

Large enough for a congregation of 400, and 100 feet long under a 135-foot tower, the St. George's School chapel looks like a typical highly decorated fifteenth-century English church. Like any good church of that time it is part spiritual center, part art gallery, part commentary on contemporary life. It has a maze as a symbol of the search for truth and salvation. It also has a wealth of serious and lighthearted iconography that includes unicorns, St. George the dragon-slayer and many other saints, Don Quixote (the patron of passionate idealists), the 12 signs of the Zodiac, the four winds, and sailing ships (including Columbus's *Santa Maria* and a colonial-era trading vessel owned by the Browns). There also are an airplane, the architect Ralph Adams Cram, and two contemporary sports heroes, Babe Ruth and the football star Red Grange. Far up on the turret tower, just below a fierce gargoyle, is a bust of the energetic patron himself, John Nicholas Brown, shown by the sculptor Joseph Coletti in all the vigor that brought the chapel into existence. Brown often returned to the chapel, the last time in 1979, after his death, when his casket lay there overnight before his funeral in Providence.

After the chapel (which reportedly cost $1,000,000) was consecrated in 1928, Brown's only major frustration with it was his inability to retain absolute control from two opponents. One was the school's board of trustees, which refused to grant him a veto over its use as a religious institution. The other was what seems to have been his only life-long enemy, the common pigeon. Brown's nagging about what he called "those deplorable birds" became so incessant that one of the school's headmasters, tongue firmly in cheek, proposed that teachers be issued shotguns, cautioning that while the pigeon-shoot might eliminate most of the offending birds, it would also destroy the stained glass windows.

32 | THE TWO ADVENTURERS

> "Through what seems endless detail there runs joy in creation which is [the] *sine qua non* of great art."

he contemplated entering a monastery Brown was still a college undergraduate when he decided that if the school could not provide a proper church for services, he would build it. He began planning immediately even though he would not be able to pay for it until he came into his inheritance at the age of 21.

As architect, Brown retained Ralph Adams Cram, the country's leading specialist in the neo-medieval architectural style known as Gothic Revival. Cram had designed Harbour Court, many buildings at Princeton University and the United States Military Academy, and a large number of churches. Besides designing buildings, Cram was a social theorist who idealized the Middle Ages as the golden age of simple, perfect living. In his philosophical essays, historical novels, and supernatural stories, Cram laid out a critique of the twentieth century, which he darkly referred to as "the Nemesis of the Modern Age," and a program for bringing about America's spiritual regeneration through the revival of medieval values and forms. "Human society has become bloated into the wrong shape," he declared in his autobiography. He despised mass production, modern technology, mob psychology, alternative religions, secular humanism, and other features of his time that, he insisted, made up a "fabrication of a scheme of life and living that is ugly, arid, and divorced from the human scale." Cram believed that two revivals were crucial to the country's reform. One was the return of small social groups, like craft guilds; the other was the reintroduction of traditional understandings of beauty. For both, there was no need to look further than the medieval church.

Cram's organic view of art and the world appealed to the lonely, artistic, and religious young man. Brown believed in what he called "the importance of the visual" – the redeeming power of physical beauty to change lives if not the world itself. The St. George's School chapel was to be an example.

One of those fortunate people who love the steps of creation as much as the end itself, Brown was temperamentally incapable of being a hands-off patron. "Through what seems endless detail there runs joy in creation which is [the] *sine qua non* of great art," he declared. He had seen his mother press Cram hard when he designed Harbour Court – insisting, for instance, that the building be as fireproof as possible. After studying architecture and construction, Brown decided to introduce modern building techniques, like making the outer walls a granite sandwich around a brick core, which he believed would insulate the building from winter winds blowing off the Atlantic. (His open-mindedness about new technology would be exemplified a quarter century later in *Bolero*'s aluminum masts.) Brown insisted on reviewing every detail of the chapel design. Although there were many disagreements between the patron and the architect, Cram would write that Brown and the project combined to make "one of the greatest educational influences in my life, as well as the source of one of the most valued friendships I have ever experienced."

Not long after the chapel was finished, the stock market crash and a severe drought in the Midwest devastated the Browns' family business. He took charge of the vast real estate holdings of farms, meanwhile serving on the boards of other Brown holdings. As he helped steer the business back to recovery, he was a generous philanthropist. His favorite charities included a choir school he established at the Providence Episcopal cathedral, several museums and symphony orchestras, plus major universities and the cities of Providence and Newport. When Dutch Elm Disease swept through New England, he not only sprayed his own trees but arranged to have the trees of Brown University sprayed, too. His generosity extended to himself and his family, with travel, summer houses, yachts, and good cars. John Nicholas Brown, in short, was enjoying life.

"We Had Quite a Navy"

In 1930, after a whirlwind romance, Brown married Anne Seddon Kinsolving. They were an excellent match. As inquisitive and smart as her husband, and with a similarly broad range of interests, she also had a directness that balanced his shy courtliness. People who knew her invariably use the word "earthy" to describe Anne Brown. At least one middle-aged man's ears are still ringing from a scolding she administered after he was discovered sliding down Harbour Court's steep hill.

Raised in Baltimore in a family of clergymen and U. S. Senators, she had worked for a newspaper as a music critic and a reporter. Once, she chased down an elusive subject by leaping into a hotel's dumbwaiter. On another occasion, she flew upside down in a small airplane over the Washington Monument. Fascinated by military history, she co-founded the Company of Military Historians, became a world-respected authority on uniforms, and assembled a library and collection of lead soldiers so large that the walls of the Browns' Providence house began to sag. Anne helped translate the diaries of the Comte de Rochambeau, whose army (with the first Rousmaniere in America) landed in Newport in 1780 and helped beat the British in the American Revolution. She picked up sufficient Norwegian from the Scandinavians who crewed in the Brown yachts to have conversations with the man who lofted *Bolero*'s lines full-size at the Nevins yard, Nils Halvorsen.

Anne made John Nicholas Brown a sailor. He had cruised in large steam yachts, but while he was spending summers studying in European cathedrals, she was racing small boats at the vacation resort of Fishers Island, New York, where her father was the summer rector of the Episcopal church. When things became tense at Harbour Court with her commanding mother-in-law, the Browns started going to Fishers, where they bought a small racing boat. Like almost everything he tried, Brown came to sailing enthusiastically and on his own lively terms, which were most noticeable in the names he and his wife chose for their boats. Most boat names are inspired by birds or women. The Browns chose dances. Musical—Anne a violinist, John a cellist—they themselves were elegant dancers who won waltz contests, but a mere *Waltz* would not do for one of their boats. Their first boat was *Gavotte*. An electrifying ballet solo with plenty of *jetés*, it was perfect for the man who once enchanted a visitor to *Bolero* by bounding about on deck and ending the day with a jolly, "Were you converted to yachting?"

The Brown family's pre-*Bolero* 1947 Christmas card shows Nick's Quincy Adams 17 *Pavanne*, Carter's Bullseye *Conga*, their parents in the Wood Pussy *Polka*, and Angela's Weasel *Piroutte*. In the background is the family express cruiser *Hopak*. (COURTESY SARA PORTER)

In 1933 he acquired his first big yacht, a powerful 91-foot, steel schooner designed and built in Bristol, Rhode Island, by Brown's distant cousins John Brown Herreshoff and Nathanael Greene Herreshoff. Renaming her from a tepid *Princess* to *Saraband* (a sexy Spanish dance with African roots), Brown raced with some success and great joy.

As their three children grew, they sailed small boats at Fishers Island and Newport. "We had quite a navy," recalled Nick Brown of a time when the family Christmas card for 1947 was a photograph of five boats: the powerboat *Hopak* (a Russian peasant dance) and four small sailboats with the energetic names of *Conga*, *Polka*, *Piroutte*, and *Pavanne* (a Renaissance court dance of many flourishes). Other family boats included *Tango*, *Shag* (a bouncy student favorite of the 1930s), *Tarantella*, and the *Malagueña* (a type of Flamenco). A later boat was named for the *Volta*, a seductive court dance (featured in the film *Shakespeare in Love*) so complicated that an authority advises, "Do this dance with a partner you are familiar with!"

The ebullient partnership of Anne and John Brown fit the bill perfectly. Someone who saw them together in *Bolero* observed that they had "the serious yet excited air of adventurers about to adventure." Their handwriting was all but indistinguishable, and friends writing letters to them greeted them collectively as "Dear Johann." As a couple they regularly visited St. George's School and memorized the names of each of the school's 300 students with astonishing attentiveness, as one alumnus, Doug Logan, recalled: "I saw Mrs. Brown at Nantucket one day and she looked at me and said, 'You played football and sang in the choir.' She could have guessed one, but not two."

Anne brought a love of both sailing and music. Besides the family navy, there was a family string quartet of Nick, Carter, John, and Anne. Looking on is Angela, who would become a concert pianist. (COURTESY JOHN NICHOLAS BROWN CENTER, BROWN UNIVERSITY)

Over the years, Brown's natural sympathies mastered his shyness and aristocratic upbringing, and he sought people out in a way that brings to mind Kipling's words about the man who would be king: "Brother to a Prince and fellow to a beggar if he be found worthy." A small-d democrat, he was also a capital-D Democrat in his political allegiance. A reporter found him "affable but shy," with shoulders "perpetually stooped as if from bending over politely to talk with people of lesser stature." According to Dyer Jones, one of his successors as a New York Yacht Club commodore, "No matter who you were and how crowded the room was, he had the uncanny ability to make you believe that you were the only person there." After a cruising couple, Henry and Jo Strauss, dropped anchor in Brenton Cove one afternoon, they were entranced by the angular, dignified gentleman who rowed out from Harbour Court, doffed his cap, offered a hearty welcome to Newport, and rowed home.

Upon selling one of *Bolero*'s successors, *Tango*, Brown genially wrote the new owner a letter. "I want to wish you every good luck and hope that we may meet along the waterfront in the near future," he said. "If you should ever put into Newport, please let me know. My house is almost next to the Ida Lewis Yacht Club." With his characteristic absence of self-consciousness, Brown may not have been aware of the effect that "my house," a magnificent French chateau towering over Newport, would have on *Tango*'s new owner.

In the 1930s, at Fishers Island, the Browns built a very different sort of building than the chapel, cutting-edge modernistic in its low walls and its concrete and metal structure. The architect, Richard Neutra was described by the critic Norman Cousins as having a "cascading enthusiasm for life" (which could also be said of

Strikingly different in appearance from the St. George's chapel was Brown's modernistic water-view summer house called Windshield. The architect, Richard Neutra, enjoyed "mentally footloose" people and found them in the Browns. (RICHARD JOSEPH NEUTRA PAPERS (COLLECTION 1179), DEPARTMENT OF SPECIAL COLLECTIONS, CHARLES E. YOUNG RESEARCH LIBRARY, UCLA)

Brown). Neutra was as convinced as Cram and Brown that a proper building will always make the world a better place. "As an architect," Neutra wrote, "my life has been governed by the goal of building environmental harmony, functional efficiency, and human enhancement into the experience of everyday living." One of the more important architects of the modern style, Neutra had been born in Austria but did most of his work in southern California. There, he wrote in his diary, "I found what I had hoped for, a people who were more 'mentally footloose' than those elsewhere, who did not mind deviating opinions...where one can do most anything that comes to mind and is good fun."

To his surprise, Neutra found another two "mentally footloose" people among the two Eastern Establishment figures who approached him about designing a house for Fishers Island. He sent them a questionnaire concerning the family's tastes, habits, and interests. In his seven-page, single-spaced reply, Brown revealed the timetable of their daily routines, where they wanted to play music in their family ensembles, even what he and Anne laid out on their night tables. Asked what views they enjoyed in the morning, Brown wrote, "I like to see my boat and an open fire from bed and do not like early morning sun."

Schooling themselves in modern architecture, the Browns took major roles in the planning – she concentrating on the interior and furnishings, he on the structure that, he predicted, "will cause a tremendous stir." He was correct. The aluminum framed windows were so large that the house was nicknamed "Windshield," while the expanses of exposed cement and stainless steel led some neighbors in the conservative community to dismiss the place as "the soap factory." A few weeks after they moved in, the great 1938 hurricane blew off the roof, almost injured young Carter Brown, and so distressed John Nicholas

On a windy afternoon sail in 1936, with her towering owner at the helm in a blue blazer, *Saraband* knocks the tops off waves in front of Morris Rosenfeld's camera. She won Brown's first Astor Cup race.
(© MYSTIC SEAPORT, ROSENFELD COLLECTION)

Brown that he threw himself face-down on the ground and wept. Windshield was repaired, but the Browns only had three summers there before Pearl Harbor, when security measures restricted sailing and other joys of summer life. After the war the Browns returned to Fishers Island, where the children sailed, Brown was elected commodore of the small, informal island yacht club, and *Bolero* was moored within sight of the master bedroom. (Windshield later went into other hands and was destroyed in a fire in 1973.)

As for boats, after *Saraband* was wrecked in the 1938 hurricane, Brown waited until 1944 before he approached Drake Sparkman, Olin Stephens' partner, and expressed interest in buying an able large sailboat. Among the desirable ones on his list were several Sparkman & Stephens ocean racers, including the beautiful black 72-foot yawl *Baruna*, winner of the last Bermuda Race before World War II, and the teak 64-foot sloop *Orient*. Henry Taylor wanted to keep *Baruna*, but *Orient* was available, and so Brown bought and named her *Courante* (a dance of Italian origin).

One evidence of the affection that people held for John Nicholas Brown is this light-hearted caricature by editorial cartoonist Paule Stetson Loring. It is one of several Brown-related items now displayed at his former summer home, Harbour Court. Others include a formal bust of Brown, *Bolero*'s scale model, and artifacts in the *Bolero* Grill Room. (COURTESY NEW YORK YACHT CLUB)

"No Critics in Evidence"

There was little sailing in *Courante* due to Brown's two successful assignments to government work between 1943 and 1949 – one a mission of mercy for "the visual," the other a call to help modernize the country's navy.

Brown spent the first years of the war managing the family business and serving as a Newport town councilman, the only elective position he held. In 1944 he was appointed Special Cultural Advisor to the Supreme Allied Commander, General Dwight D. Eisenhower, with the mission of protecting cultural artifacts and works of art in war areas, including locating art that had been plundered by the Nazis. Holding the rank of major, Brown worked with the army and 80 professional art historians associated with the American Monuments Commission to locate and recover art. Among the many stunning successes was the discovery of most of the panels in Van Eyck's Ghent Altarpiece behind a false wall in an Austrian salt mine. Brown arranged for them to be flown to Belgium as the first cultural masterpiece returned to its owner after the war. The Belgian government promptly awarded him a high honor. Years later, in a church in Cracow, Poland, when Brown was identified as the man responsible for the return of its altarpiece, the applause was led by the priest, Karol Wojtyla, later Pope John Paul II.

The most difficult issue concerned artifacts taken from German collections or museums. While some officials believed these works should be seized as war reparations, Brown and the Monuments Commission argued strenuously that they be returned to their German homes. They won out in the end. More than 200 works of art were shipped to America, exhibited in the first "blockbuster" touring show, and later returned to Germany. For his part in preserving European art, Brown was admitted to the French Legion of Honor.

Back from the war, Brown began planning his new family boat. In late October 1946, as the initial plans for Sparkman & Stephens design number 711 were appearing, the boat was put on hold when the Truman administration asked Brown to serve in the Department of the Navy as Assistant Secretary for Air. As newspapers smugly chortled about the "world's richest baby" who named his yachts for dances, Brown effectively changed the subject by traveling 12,000 miles in his first month on the job, including landing on an aircraft carrier and becoming the first high government official to fly in a jet.

His job title was misleading; Brown had three responsibilities: aviation, personnel, and research. As the new U.S. Air Force attempted to take over the country's air power, he defended naval aviation in Congressional hearings. In the end, after senior navy officers went public with their concerns in the widely publicized "revolt of the admirals," Truman sided with the navy. As director of navy personnel, Brown eased burdens on seamen's families and supervised the navy's program to end its historic racial segregation. ("My father was as close to being color blind as anyone I have known," said his son Nicholas, himself a career navy officer.)

Brown also headed the Office of Navy Research, which developed new aircraft, ships, weapons, and meteorological systems. As a proud descendent of the builders of America's first textile mills, a habitual gadgeter, an amateur architect of cutting-edge buildings, and an officer of a family-owned high-tech company, Brown was fascinated. Nevertheless, as a humanist, he was inclined to keep technology in perspective. In a ribbon-cutting speech at a new $35,000,000 ordnance research facility early in 1949, he cautioned his audience of scientists that faith in weapons of mass destruction would only encourage unwinnable wars. "The ability of a human being to survive the blows of his enemies, in whatever form delivered, is immense," Brown went on. "His capacity not only to survive, but his faculty of continuing to fight, is amazing." In his own way he had identified the central paradox of the nuclear age, which is that a superpower can be humbled by a few true believers wearing sandals.

Brown won many admirers during his two and a half years in Washington. After he resigned in March 1949, the country's leading political columnist, Arthur Krock of the *New York Times*, lauded his "objectivity" and "deep humanitarianism against injustice," and said that Brown was leaving office "with no critics in evidence." In recognition of this contribution and his efforts to recover art in Europe, in 1950 he was elected to the prestigious National Academy of Arts and Sciences in a group that included the secretary general of the United Nations, Eleanor Roosevelt, the publisher of the *Times*, and prominent writers, musicians, theologians, and diplomats.

"With All the Grimness Left Out"

John Nicholas Brown at age 49 threw himself into family activities, philanthropy, and the sweet-lined new yawl nearing completion at City Island. The New York Yacht Club elected him vice commodore. Based in the middle of Manhattan, the club then was a formal, hierarchical, and purely masculine institution defined by tradition. In minutes of meetings, attending members were identified by the names of their yachts. *Bolero* rarely said a word before succeeding Henry S. Morgan in the top job of commodore in 1952. Then Brown's first concern was the state of the club's badly neglected half-century-old Beaux Arts clubhouse, a temple to boats as elaborate as a Gothic chapel. He introduced a preservation initiative that included a new war on pigeons, which had been depositing layers of dung on the building.

As a devotee of ritual, Brown delighted in the club's many meticulously prescribed routines. Messages were sent by code flags, not radio, and uniforms were specified for different times of day and night. Brown as usual had new ideas. Tired of the club's dowdy Prince Albert formal dinner outfits (called mess jackets), he and Anne designed a trim new one that might have been inspired by the Eisenhower army jacket. He also took the club's annual cruise of 50 yachts and 500 sailors to Maine for the first time in 30 years in order to escape

After a U.S. Navy task force steamed through the 1952 Bermuda Race fleet without picking up the boats on radar, John Nicholas Brown participated in an experiment to develop a reliable radar reflector for wooden boats. (NORRIS HOYT PHOTO)

the increasingly crowded waters off Southern New England. Anne, meanwhile, wrote press releases reporting race results.

As the club's commodore, Brown applied his active, pragmatic mind and interest in technology to a groundbreaking experiment involving radar. The technology for picking objects out of the night or fog was so new and so limited to military use that it was a mystery to average sailors. What was known was that while radar readily picked up metal objects, it was blind to the wooden hulls and masts of the typical sailboat. During the 1952 Bermuda Race, the officers of a nearby navy task force were so startled that their radar found none of the 58 racing boats that they ordered their ships to steam off in the other direction.

Hearing that story, Brown pulled strings at the Navy Department and arranged for a destroyer to accompany the New York Yacht Club Cruise in order to conduct some experiments. The ship's radar had only a few weak hits at close range until a sailor, George E. Roosevelt, hung a metal reflector in the rigging of his schooner, *Mistress*. The destroyer instantly picked *Mistress* up from a range of five miles. When Brown and a navy officer reported this breakthrough in an article in *Yachting* magazine, many sailors learned for the first time that there was a simple way to take advantage of radar, which soon became an essential aspect of normal seamanship.

Built by Brown's mother, Natalie Bayard Dresser Brown, and designed by Ralph Adams Cram as a version of a French chateau, Harbour Court is a striking presence on the Newport waterfront. Since 1987 it has been the New York Yacht Club's local clubhouse. (COURTESY DAN NERNEY)

"Coming Out Personally"

"A naval operation with all the grimness left out and a great deal of beauty added" was how a future club commodore, Chauncey Stillman, described a New York Yacht Club Cruise managed by the Browns. Among the many stories of their blend of efficiency and hospitality were two passed on by a sailor of that era, Bob Erskine.

Sailing aboard *Bolero* on a miserable April day, he was gratified when Anne Brown stuck her head up through a hatch and asked if the frigid crew would enjoy a cup of tea. "Yes, indeed, we did, and we all piled down below and sat around the cabin table. Out came the steward with a perfect silver tea service on a beautiful silver tray with a profile of *Bolero* etched on it." With no less relish Erskine remembered a cold, wet nor'easter at anchor in Brenton Cove as the New York Yacht Club fleet awaited Commodore and Mrs. Brown's clambake that night at Harbour Court. A launch appeared out of the mist. On board was their hostess, going from boat to boat to announce that there was no reason for the sailors to come ashore in anything more formal than sailing clothes. "Anyone else would have made the announcement by radio or sent out a professional sailor," Erskine recalled, "but Mrs. Brown insisted on coming out personally in a small powerboat in the pouring rain to tell the news to each crew individually."

THE TWO ADVENTURERS | 43

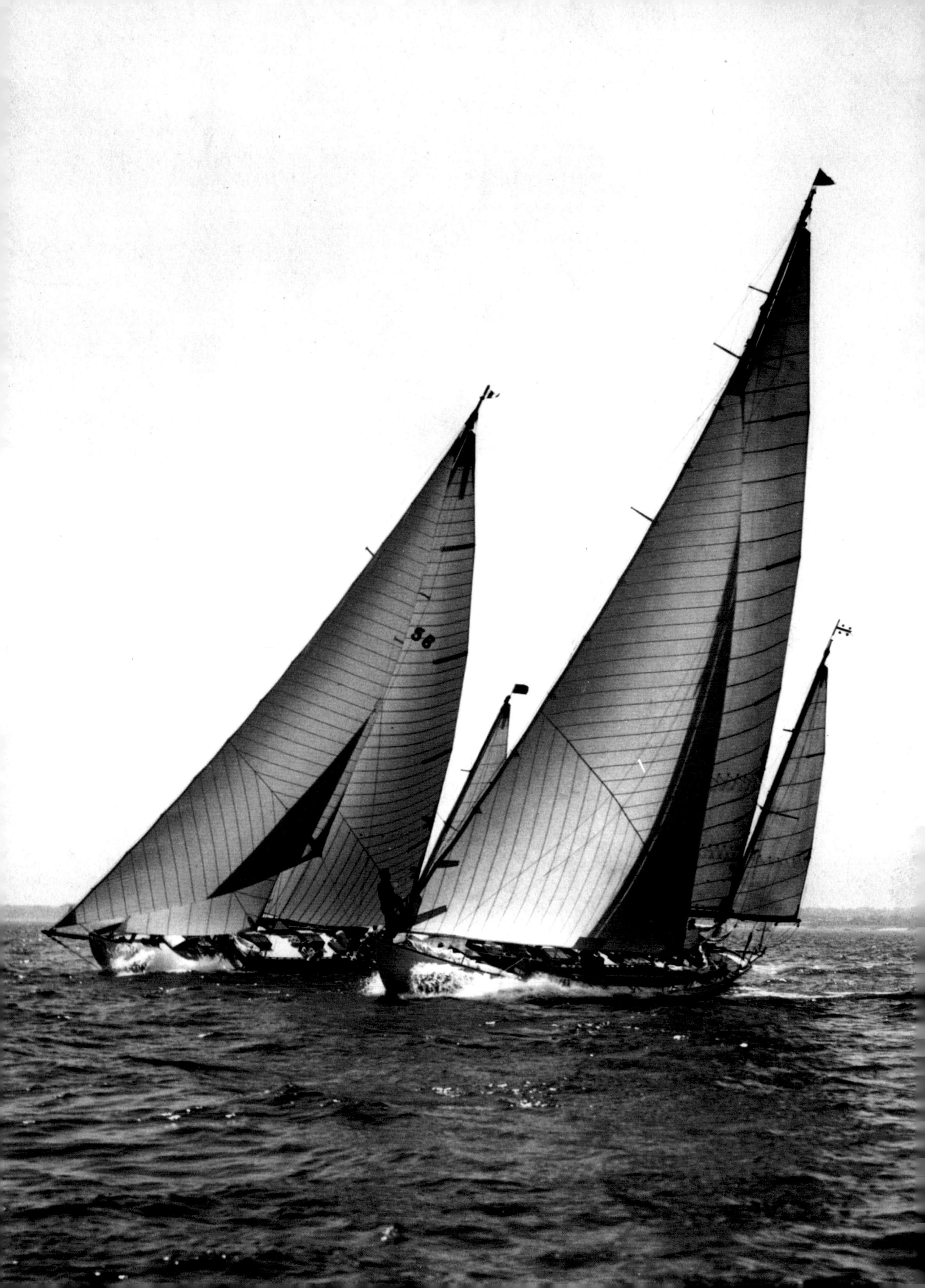
58

The best results do not always hinge on one characteristic but rather on a consistent combination.—Olin Stephens

Olin Stephens and the Matter of Balance

Olin Stephens' style of balanced ends and no extremes is exemplified in the yawls *Edlu* and *Stormy Weather*, seen sailing side-by-side in 1936. That is Rod Stephens on the bow, checking the set of the genoa jib. *Edlu* won the 1934 Bermuda Race, *Stormy Weather* the 1935 race to Norway. Stephens said of *Stormy* that she had a flare that is "always hard to define but universally recognized." (© MYSTIC SEAPORT, ROSENFELD COLLECTION)

As passionate as John Nicholas Brown was about "the visual," and as eager as he was to manage details, he left *Bolero*'s appearance largely in the hands of the designer, Olin Stephens. Brown knew what he would get. As distinctive in its own way as a Ralph Adams Cram Gothic church or a Richard Neutra home, a Stephens boat was instantly recognizable. The breed also had a legion of admirers. A few years after Stephens established his firm, Sparkman & Stephens in 1929, John Alden, then the leading American yacht designer, was examining the boats that were hauled out in the Henry B. Nevins Yacht Yard at City Island when he came upon Stephens's twenty-seventh design, the 54-foot yawl *Stormy Weather*. Looking her over carefully, Alden announced that it would be impossible to come up with a better design.

Alden knew Stephens personally; when the young designer was 20, he had sailed his first Bermuda race in 1928 on board one of Alden's schooners called *Malabar*. But Alden had objective standards that included seaworthiness, strength, speed, and, of course, beauty. Aesthetics weighs heavily in designing boats. Whether they were trained as engineers, mathematicians, or computer scientists, most people who design boats are artists at heart and want to make them beautiful. After all, they are *boats*. As Olin Stephens – himself an amateur painter, musician, and architect – once said, "It is a frequent mistake to assume that people with technical interests are likely to be short on the arts." The traditional view is that good looks are compatible with good performance. When Stephens was just starting out, he wrote in an essay about one of his first boats, "Though *per se* beauty is not a factor of speed, the easiest boats to look at seem the easiest to drive." Seventy-five years later, in 2003, when he was 95, he laid down another rule of thumb: "Thinking of appearance, I try to picture a boat running down and dirty. Would it still look right?"

Whether in a hard wind or a light breeze, what "looks right" means can be a mystery. *Stormy Weather*, Stephens wrote, has "a flair exhibited by few boats," and then he admitted with an artist's humility that this flare is "always hard to define but universally recognized."

For Stephens, no one characteristic made a good boat. It was a matter of balance between several features, beginning with a long, symmetrical, relatively slim hull over a deep keel. Such a boat looked good, sailed well, had a comfortable, seakindly motion in rough water, and – with plenty of lead ballast deep in the keel – was stable enough not just to resist capsize but to carry plenty of sail while other boats were reefed down.

That *Bolero* is a branch off the Stephens family tree is obvious in a composite drawing in Mystic Seaport's Ships' Plans collection that was made in 1948 by one of his draftsmen, Al Mason. On a sheet of paper, Mason compared the shapes of five of her predecessors between 50 and 72 feet in length. In many particulars, these boats were quite different. Some were sloops, some cutters, some yawls; accommodations varied widely; at an owner's request, or to satisfy a race measurement rule, a sheerline was drawn a little higher. But those differences aside, the boats might as well have been from the same design.

The key element, Stephens wrote, was balance: "balance between the ends, and, as far as possible, balance throughout." "Balance" here is a technical term meaning both that the bow and stern have similar shapes and proportions, and that there are no extremes there or in between. The boat must be regarded as a whole, no single feature standing out, and with all the features complementing each other. Balance was a rule that Stephens would carry into his own life, too, as a philosophical concept signifying moderation, proportionality, order, and equilibrium.

Born 16 months apart in 1908 and 1909, when Olin J. Stephens II and Roderick S. Stephens Jr., were boys, they fell for boats the way John Nicholas Brown was falling for the Middle Ages. Brought up in the Bronx and Westchester County, New York, and spending summers at Lake George, New York, and on Cape Cod, they were raised in a rigorous school of achievement and sports. Their grandfather, for whom Olin was named, had been a prize-winning single-sculler. He owned the family coal company. The boys' father, Roderick Sr., who worked there, was devoted to his boys, and because they wanted to sail he learned sailing with them in a gaff-rigged little tub with the inelegant name *Corker*. Each boy quickly found his own role in the boat. Gregarious young Rod handled the sheets and rigging, throwing himself around the deck and up and down the mast with such abandon that shipmates would call him "Tarzan." Olin, who was so shy that some people made the very serious mistake of underestimating him, took the more solitary and intellectual roles of helmsman, navigator, and close student of performance. "He was very quiet, so quiet that you sometimes wouldn't know he was aboard," said Dick Goennel, who sailed in his watch on *Bolero*. "He was always suggesting this or that to make the boat go faster or be a little more comfortable."

Olin Stephens gained his first recognition with the yawl *Dorade*, which he designed for his family in 1929. Here she is before the start of the 1930 Bermuda Race. Mr. Stephens is second from the left with his youngest son, Rod, to his left. On the far right is her 22-year-old designer and skipper. The next summer the Stephenses and *Dorade* won the race to England by two days. (© MYSTIC SEAPORT, ROSENFELD COLLECTION)

"I Was Lucky"

Even as a boy, Olin Stephens was fascinated by the problem of shaping a hull. He said as much in the opening words of his autobiography: "I was lucky: I had a goal. As far back as I can remember I wanted to design fast boats." He went to MIT to study naval architecture but was disappointed by the small interest there in yacht design. After illness forced him to drop out during his freshman year, he worked briefly for a few designers and then in the design office of the Nevins yard on City Island. Around that time an energetic, 30-year-old natural salesman named Drake Sparkman approached him about setting up a partnership, Sparkman to sell boats and Stephens to design them. Stephens was then 20. Just as John Brown had to wait until he was 21 to commit to building the St. George's School chapel, Stephens and Sparkman worked under an informal agreement until the documents could be signed in 1929. Brother Rod worked with him during a summer off from Cornell before Nevins recruited him to work in the yard. When Rod drove up to Ithaca to tell his football coach that he would be back in a year, the coach predicted that he would not return. He was correct; when young people are swept up by boats, their whole lives change. In 1935, after a thorough grounding in boat construction, Rod left Nevins to join Sparkman & Stephens.

Sailing often, looking around, and absorbing the literature of this still-new sport, young Olin Stephens decided that the best type of design was not the

When he posed stiffly with the tools of his trade for this photograph, Olin Stephens was still in his twenties. Reviving the ideas of designers of a half-century earlier and taking advantage of construction methods developed by Henry Nevins, he was rapidly becoming the most successful designer of racing boats, "You just try to maximize the stability of the boat and minimize the wetted area," he said. It was much more complicated than that. (© MYSTIC SEAPORT, ROSENFELD COLLECTION)

traditional wide American centerboard sloop but the narrow English cutter, with a cloud of sail and a deep keel carrying about 40 percent of the boat's weight in lead ballast. The narrow hull made for low resistance, the big sails produced speed in a light breeze, and the keel provided stability that allowed the boat to carry that sail in a fresh wind. A schooner or centerboarder might be faster on a reach, but the cutter was superior when sailing closehauled. The search for upwind stability and speed – or what the British maritime historian and naval architect Douglas Phillips-Birt called "the battle for weatherliness" – was obviously crucial to racing yachts because race courses were arranged with long legs into the wind, yet it was no less critical for cruising boats that had to beat their way off the rocky jaws of a threatening lee shore.

"You just try to maximize the stability of the boat and minimize the wetted area," was how Stephens summarized his approach. Although beamy centerboard boats did not pass either test, Stephens did design some of them, though not happily because, with their high center of gravity, they were known to capsize. He could not even conjure up much enthusiasm for *Finisterre*, a 38-foot yawl that looks like a pumpkin seed from overhead and that won a record three-straight Bermuda Races between 1956 and 1960. When *Finisterre*'s name came up in conversation, Stephens usually avoided discussing the design altogether, changing the subject to heap praise on her able owner, Carleton Mitchell.

Declining with characteristic modesty to take credit for the shape so closely identified with his name, Stephens said he was only standing on the shoulders of three giants. One was John Nicholas Brown's cousin Nathanael Greene Herreshoff, an American boatbuilder and naval architect who in the late 1800s pioneered in lightweight, strong yacht construction, which Henry Nevins later mastered with the assistance of one of Herreshoff's former assistants, Rufus Murray. Two other Stephens heroes were British yacht designers contemporary with Herreshoff: William Fife III and George L. Watson, each a specialist in fast boats that were some of the most beautiful vessels ever built. Stephens's own preference was Fife for sailboats and Watson for powerboats, but without any criticism of either. One of the most beloved Watson designs was the fast 121-footer *Britannia*, built in 1893 for the Prince of Wales. Four decades later, she was still being raced successfully by his son King George V when Stephens's wife, Susie, first saw her in 1931 and teasingly told her husband, "Buy me one of those."

Working in this school of design, Stephens tested his ideas in boats of about 35 feet that sailed in the Six-Meter class, the most important international racing boat from the 1920s through the 1950s. Because the measurement rules allowed experimentation in hull shapes, and new ideas could be quickly proved or disproved on the race course, the Six was the perfect school for an aspiring young designer.

One of his earliest projects was *Dorade*, Sparkman & Stephens design number 7 and essentially a 52-foot Six-Meter. His client was his father, the ever supportive Roderick Stephens Sr. Because the Nevins yard was booked solid, *Dorade* was built next door at the Minneford shipyard under young Rod's oversight. In 1931 the three Stephenses – 23-year-old Olin as skipper and navigator, 21-year-old Rod Jr. as first mate, and 45-year-old Rod Sr. (called "the Commodore" in deference to his seniority) – decided to race *Dorade* 3,000 miles across the Atlantic to England with four friends. This was the first-ever transatlantic race for normal-size boats and amateur crews, so it was not too surprising that, both in and outside the Stephens family, there was not little enthusiasm for the idea. After months of opposing the adventure, the senior Olin Stephens gave in and bought the boat a new mainsail. Still, on the day the crew left for the start at Newport, the boys' mother collected four-leaf clovers from the front yard to present to the sailors. Older yachtsmen in their hefty schooners and ketches praised the Stephenses for being "such good sports" for entering their little boat when they had no chance of winning. When these big boats arrived at the finish line at Plymouth, *Dorade* sailed out to greet them.

Olin and Rod – whom another shipmate, John Fox, referred to as "the imperturbable skipper" and "the hard-driving mate" – drove the boat so hard that even the cook was enthralled. Recalled Fox, "when we were piling down the side of a surging sea in a smother of milky foam, he would shout up through the half-closed companionway, 'Drive her, boys, drive her!'" After beating the next boat by an astonishingly large margin of two days, *Dorade* won England's 600-mile Fastnet Race in brutal weather that left several other boats in tatters and one sailor dead. "*Dorade* had no trouble winning the Fastnet race of 1931," wrote Alfred F. Loomis in his history of early ocean racing. "I say no trouble because the crew of this galloping yawl knew not what trouble was." When the crew returned to New York, they were greeted by a ticker-tape parade up Broadway.

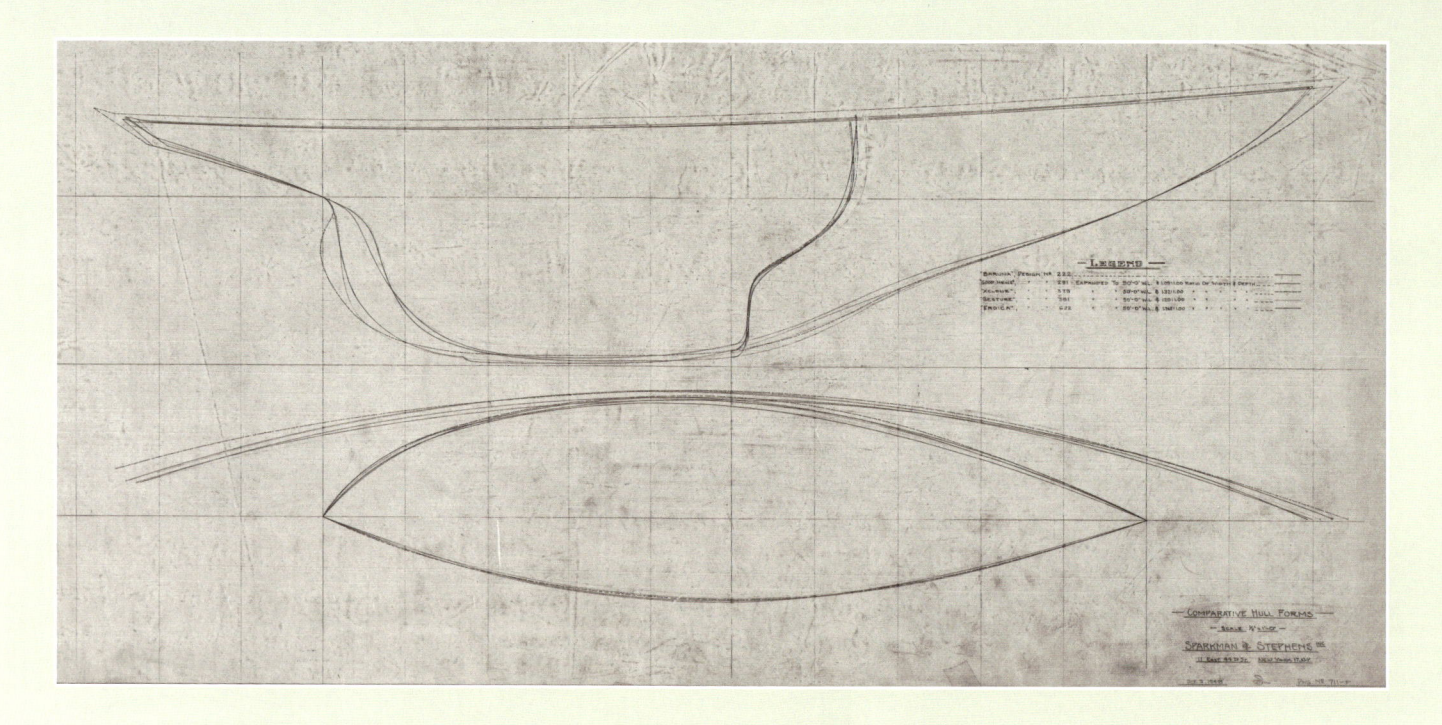

"Balance between the ends, and, as far as possible, balance throughout"

Replacing the old, heavy, ship-like appearance that made yachts almost indistinguishable from commercial vessels except for their polish, the new shape dominated yacht design for almost a century. In his extremely active and productive old age, Stephens at age 96, in an article in the magazine *Sailing World*, described their appearance this way, going almost foot by foot through the various design elements including the curve of the rail (called the sheer line). With a couple of exceptions, this could be a description of *Bolero*:

"The success and beauty of these new yachts" Stephens wrote, "gave the sailing public a long-lasting picture of the fast and handsome yacht with overhangs long and balanced, and a sheer line low somewhere aft of amidships and lifting more forward than aft.... The ends, particularly forward, were long and full, U-shaped. The extended length eased the degree of their bluffness against a sea. The after overhang was, to a degree, optional in length, but normally was proportioned to balance the bow. Freeboard was fairly low but lifted at the ends, more forward than aft, to keep water off the deck."

He wrote this with some sadness, for as he said elsewhere, "Somewhere along the line, the beauty has been lost," especially in exceptionally large modern superyachts. For this he placed responsibility on the modern-day fascination with complexity. Referring to other designers, he said, "Maybe if they thought about it, they'd realize that right back to the Greeks, directness and simplicity have been good."

50 | OLIN STEPHENS AND THE MATTER OF BALANCE

Amateur ocean racing in boats derived from racing designs was so novel an activity that some tradition-minded sailors expected disaster. The sailors, they believed, were too inexperienced to know when to stop pushing hard in a rough sea, and the new breed of boat was too delicate to take the pounding without heaving-to. These critics did not figure that the new sport would quickly school able seamen while simultaneously stimulating yacht designers and builders to develop boats that *could* beat into a gale without having to slow down. Olin Stephens was the most prominent designer in this new school, but Philip H. Rhodes, K. Aage Nielsen, James A. McCurdy, Charles E. Nicholson, and other designers also produced lovely, successful, seagoing boats of various types. The sheer volume of the Sparkman & Stephens design office (2,365 designs by the time of Stephens's retirement in 1980) and their successes (totaling some 250 trophies by 1957) made Olin Stephens the leader of the field.

"He Cared about How Things *Moved*"

"I found that observation and intuition were my best tools," Stephens wrote in his autobiography, *All This and Sailing, Too*. He was eager to discover and absorb new theories and novel technical and analytical tools. One was an indicator of a boat's relative slimness known as the prismatic coefficient, or the ratio between the volume of the real hull in the water, on one hand, and the volume of an imaginary rectangular block as long as the hull's waterline length and as wide as the widest part of the waterline. Over time, Stephens decided that this ratio should range between 0.500 and 0.535. A small prismatic indicates a low-resistance boat at her best in light winds; a high one a boat good in windy conditions, because increasing beam improves stability. He believed so much in the prismatic coefficient that his assistants, with whom he enjoyed remarkably collegial relations, kidded him about being a fanatic.

Stephens was drawn to skilled technical people in other fields, and they to him. In the early 1930s, he began collaboration with Kenneth S.M. Davidson, an engineer who improved on the method of testing designs by towing small models in tanks of water. Like Stephens, Davidson (who became *Bolero*'s navigator) was detail-focused and artistically inclined. "My father had that kind of musical-scientific mind that has a passionate interest in movement," his daughter, Anne, said "He cared about how things *moved*." As a boy he learned to play the piano and sail, and he later was a pilot in World War I. While studying mechanical engineering at MIT, in his spare time he built and raced model boats. Interested in gaining a scientific understanding of how sailboats worked, he towed models with dynamometers that measured resistance in swimming pools at Columbia University and the Stevens Institute of Technology, in Hoboken, New Jersey.

The method was not new, but Davidson sharpened it and made it possible with small, inexpensive models. Dissatisfied with his results, in 1932 he approached Olin Stephens for assistance. Seeing potential in Davidson's ideas, the Stephens

(Above) As Bolero was taking shape, Al Mason compared the very similar balanced lines of *Baruna*, *Ciclon*, *Eroica*, *Gesture*, and *Good News*. (DESIGN AND DRAWING BY SPARKMAN & STEPHENS, © 2005 BY SPARKMAN & STEPHENS, INC.)

(Below) Replacing the old, heavy, ship-like appearance that made yachts almost indistinguishable from commercial vessels except for their polish, the new shape was developed by William Fife and G.L Watson and continued by Stephens. It is seen here in the form of *Stormy Weather*, ready to be launched at the Nevins Yard. (© MYSTIC SEAPORT, ROSENFELD COLLECTION)

One of many members of the *Bolero* community who were amateur artists as well as professional technicians, Ken Davidson refined the science of predicting a vessel's performance by testing models in a towing tank. He was the boat's navigator under Brown and, like Olin Stephens, sailed with Sven Salen when *Bolero* broke the Bermuda Race record in 1956. (© MYSTIC SEAPORT, ROSENFELD COLLECTION)

brothers and Davidson tested a Sparkman & Stephens-designed, Henry Nevins-built sloop, *Gimcrack*, on Long Island Sound, and then compared her full-size performance data with the results of towing tests of her scale model. Out of this came mathematical coefficients that allowed any design's performance to be predicted. The design of almost every Stephens racing boat (and of the occasional cruiser, too) was tried out and refined in the test tank, including the ones for *Baruna* and *Bolero*.

Stephens estimated that Davidson advanced yacht design from 90 percent art and 10 percent science to something close to a 50-50 relationship. More was to come. When Stephens was asked in 2004 where he would focus his energy if he were starting out again as a yacht designer, he replied, "computer analysis."

Davidson's towing facility was financed in part by J. Seward Johnson, a member of the Johnson & Johnson pharmaceutical family who raced Stephens-designed, Nevins-built Six-Meters. Johnson was one of several well-heeled young amateur sailors who were regular Stephens clients and whose competitiveness at the top end of the sport furthered yacht design. Also numbered among them were Vanderbilts, Morgans, Rockefellers, and Whitneys, as well as heirs of major tobacco, mining, brewing, aviation, retailing, aluminum, computer, high-technology, and other companies. Some helped Stephens and other yacht designers by passing along their technology. The first extruded aluminum masts, for instance, were built by the Fuller Brush Company, whose president, A. Howard Fuller, owned the Sparkman & Stephens sloop *Gesture*.

One thing that did not rub off from Stephens's clients was their wealth. A yacht designer's fee is usually based on a percentage of the cost of the boat and

> "I found that observation and intuition were my best tools."

rarely covers much more than the time put into the design, although a successful one-design class (like the Sparkman & Stephens Swan and Tartan lines) does pay royalties. When I once asked Stephens if rumors were true that his work had made him rich, he replied somewhat testily that the most money he had ever made in his life came after his retirement when he sold his house in Scarsdale and moved to New Hampshire.

His and his colleagues' relations with clients tended to be strong. Rod Stephens in an oral history interview described them as "about 98 percent friendly." When Patrick Haggerty, of Texas Instruments, was asked why he had joined the syndicate behind the 1967 America's Cup defender *Intrepid*, he said flat out that it was his admiration for the designer, Olin Stephens. "He is not only something of a genius but as fine a human being as I've ever known. He's humble and quiet-spoken and it's a pleasure to work with people like that." Close personal bonds were often formed on the water during demanding races, when true character is hard to conceal. A regular client, Briggs Cunningham, the son of a founder of Procter & Gamble, sailed with the Stephenses often. In *Dorade* in the 1931 Fastnet Race, Olin recalled, "he did not sleep for three days, yet you cannot imagine anybody more keen or good natured." Stopping by the Nevins yard to check up on one or another of his Stephens-designed racing boats, Cunningham would lunch with the workers and talk about his other passion, racing sports cars. Cunningham won the America's Cup in 1958 as skipper of a Stephens-Nevins Twelve-Meter, *Columbia*, with the two brothers in the crew. For a time Cunningham owned one of Stephens's most unusual boats, the Nevins-built schooner *Brilliant*, which he later donated to Mystic Seaport where she remains extremely active.

"Boats, Boats, and More Boats"

Before the publication of his autobiography in 1999, it was not generally known that at the peak of his success, Olin Stephens had gone though a period of excruciating doubt.

By early 1939, when he turned 31, he had produced 286 designs in 11 years. Boats of his design had won the 1937 America's Cup and most of the major ocean races. In the 1938 Newport-Bermuda Race, five of the six prizewinners were Sparkman & Stephens designs. The new 72-foot yawl *Baruna* amazed everybody by winning all five trophies for which she was eligible, including finishing first both on elapsed time and, after handicaps were figured, on corrected time. People joked that Stephens had made *Baruna* so big so she could carry all that silverware. Putting their personal imprint on this achievement, the Stephens brothers sailed in the first- and second-place boats, Olin as navigator of *Baruna* and Rod as skipper of R.J. Reynolds's *Blitzen*.

By then the brothers were precursors to "Michael" and "Tiger" as stars known by their first names alone. The fastest way to silence a crowd around a yacht club bar

Tuning up a new rig, Rod Stephens adjusts the mainsail's leech line as Olin looks up from the tiller. Beginning when they were boys sailing with their father in little boats, Rod always took charge of rigging while Olin was at the helm.
(© MYSTIC SEAPORT, ROSENFELD COLLECTION)

was to declare, "Olin says" or "Rod wrote." Their athletic builds and tanned faces were as familiar to readers of sailing and general interest magazines as the sweeping sheer lines and fine bows of their race-winning boats in Rosenfeld photographs.

Yet Olin Stephens was flattened by depression. "For some time I had been exposed intensely to boats, boats, and more boats. All of a sudden it was just too much," he wrote in *All This and Sailing, Too*. He was seriously considering retirement before two new developments pulled him out of his despair. The first was challenging military work that included designs for torpedo boats, submarine chasers, minesweepers, an aluminum pontoon bridge, and (in a project headed by his brother) an ingenious U.S. Army amphibious vehicle – half-boat, half-truck – called the DUKW (pronounced "duck" – the name is a jumble of military officialese.) Rod was awarded the Medal of Freedom for leading the DUKW design effort.

The other new thing that revived Olin Stephens's spirits was his successful search for creative leisure away from salt water. In his spare hours, he played the piano, painted (his specialty was modern abstraction), kept up with exhibits in art museums and galleries, read widely and deeply in philosophy and history, and spent weekends and vacations far inland at his wife's family's farm in central Massachusetts. He had found a balance for his own life.

"Weights Were Fundamental"

A journalist who visited the Sparkman & Stephens office in 1938 found "shy and soft-spoken" Olin Stephens worked in the shadow of a mound of correspondence and drawings, while his brother, Rod sat "across the room, phoning incessantly and firing questions." And then, "In an adjoining office, seven assistant draftsmen were busy with pencils and rules." As we will see in chapter 6, Rod exerted enormous authority over construction, but the draftsmen were hardly lackeys. Young designers who arrived at Sparkman & Stephens expecting to do only scut work were surprised by how much authority they were granted.

The *Bolero* project was shared by several Sparkman & Stephens draftsmen, including Henry Uhle and Al Mason. Mason (who drew the intriguing comparison of profiles) was California-born and like the Stephens brothers was a fanatic about boats since youth. At 16 he designed a three-masted schooner. After graduating from Webb Institute of Naval Architecture, where many Sparkman & Stephens draftsmen were trained, he went to work for Olin Stephens in 1939. Over the years he left and returned several times, while also designing boats under his own name, including several well-regarded long-distance cruisers. While not fully committed to the office and its main calling to produce racing boats – Stephens remembered him as "a bit of a loner, more interested in how they looked than in how they went" – Mason was admired for his technical ability and especially for his skill as a draftsman.

To the world at large, the only evidence of the yacht designer's activity were the small, two-dimensional scale drawings showing the boat from the side and overhead that appeared in the boating magazines. These plans were supplemented by many detail drawings based on painstaking calculations that determined displacement, or total weight, from the weights of the thousands of items that would go into the boat. "Weights were fundamental, as they remain," Olin Stephens stated firmly. "By the careful and complete measurement of the volumes and densities of each part's weight and position, the weight and center of gravity of the entire boat was able to be determined. The key words are 'careful' and 'complete.'"

Nils Halvorsen, the head of the Nevins mold loft, summarized the challenge this way: "You compiled all the timbers, you compiled all the screws, you compiled all the bolts, and this is how much the boat is going to weigh." He might have added the engine, the main sheet, the sails, the anchor, the compass, the batteries, and even the galley sink.

Besides drawing plans and calculating weights, the draftsmen located each of the various "centers," which are for a boat what the pivot point is for a seesaw. Noting every step along the way, like a high school student working through a geometry proof, the draftsmen employed an engineering analysis called "moments and centers." After calculating the weights, they measured their distances from each other to find their moments, or leverage, before locating their pivots at the vertical and horizontal centers of gravity. The draftsmen also found

Boats that came out of Sparkman & Stephens were team efforts led by Olin Stephens (left) with the help of several draftsmen, his brother, Rod (in jacket), several construction and rigging experts, and consultants like Ken Davidson.
(© MYSTIC SEAPORT, ROSENFELD COLLECTION)

the balance points in the boat's underwater area and sail plans, called the center of lateral resistance and the center of effort. Some methods of calculation were wonderfully simple. The center of lateral resistance was often found by making a cutout of the boat's underwater profile and, through trial and error, placing it on the point of a pin until it was perfectly balanced.

If the boat was designed to weigh 88,000 pounds, there had better be 88,000 pounds worth of boat. Otherwise, she would float low or high and (at the least) the waterline would have to be repainted. Too much weight forward and the boat would float (or "trim") bow-down; too much on one side, she would have a permanent heel. The boat's trim could be adjusted slightly by moving around the small number of lead pigs consigned to the bilge as inside or trimming ballast. *Bolero* had 1,200 pounds of inside ballast, about one percent of her entire displacement.

Those were hardly the only calculations. Using a number of tables and manufacturers' specifications, all of which were filtered through the designers' collective experience, the draftsmen designed the masts and rigging, selected fittings, created a galley... on and on through the boat. To cite one example, seven pages of calculations went into determining the right propeller for *Bolero* (it was two-bladed with a diameter and pitch of 19 inches and 13 inches, respectively). All that time the draftsmen and the office's construction experts were creating

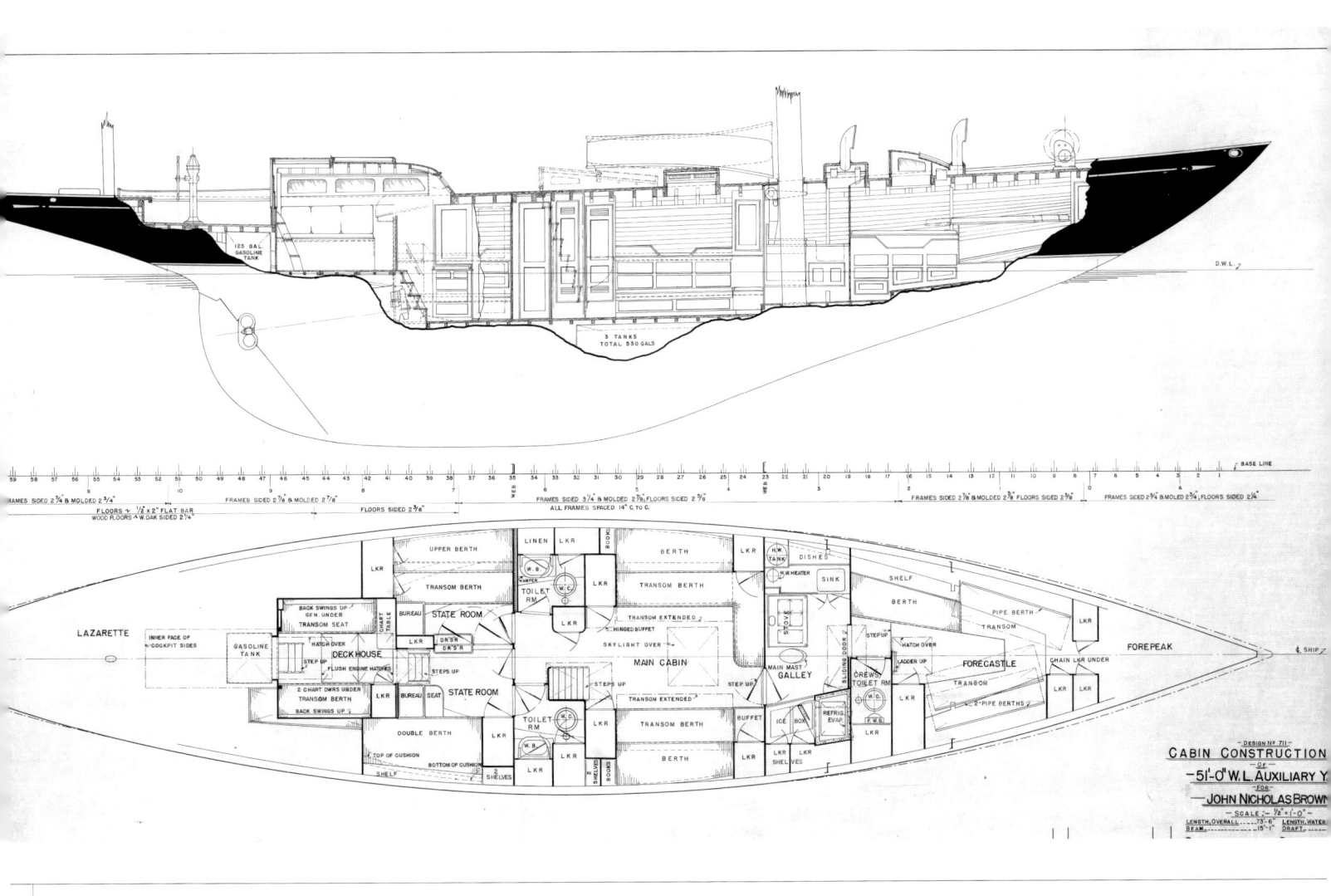

Bolero's final arrangement plans in February 1949 suggest the challenge of trying to fit bunks for as many as 12 into a configuration providing both privacy and flexibility. From left to right are the deckhouse, the owners' suite of cabins (with removable walls for racing), two toilets, the main saloon with four bunks, the galley, and the forecastle where the professional crew of three lived. Below the cabin sole are the engine, generator, and water and fuel tanks. (DESIGN AND DRAWING BY SPARKMAN & STEPHENS, © 2005 BY SPARKMAN & STEPHENS, INC.)

the elaborate plans and specifications that laid out how the boat would be built. One of the more important concerns was grounding and insulating all the metals, including the keel, engine, and electrical system, so that the boat would not turn into an immense, self-destructive battery.

Much of this work was instantly outdated in the fall of 1948 when the Browns decided to lengthen the boat's waterline from 50 to 51 feet. While the change was only 2 percent, lengthening a boat's waterline length is not like sticking a new wing on a house. Rather, it is like blowing more air into a balloon: the whole thing gets bigger. With more waterline length comes more boat in the water, which means more water to displace – in other words, more weight. More weight means larger, stronger sails, rigging, and sail-handling equipment. Those heavier loads demand greater stability to resist heeling so the boat will sail as well as in her original shape. This sudden change might have thrown a less organized firm topsy-turvy, but Sparkman & Stephens had the revised plans and calculations ready within a few days. In the interest of retaining the original appearance, with the same angle to the bow and stern profiles, the overall length was stretched from 72 feet to 73 feet 6 inches. (The length on deck remained 72 feet to meet the Bermuda Race maximum.) The beam, meanwhile, was widened from 14 feet, 10 inches to 15 feet, 1 inch. With these changes, *Bolero*'s displacement increased by 6,000 pounds to 94,000 pounds, with 39,000 pounds in lead ballast.

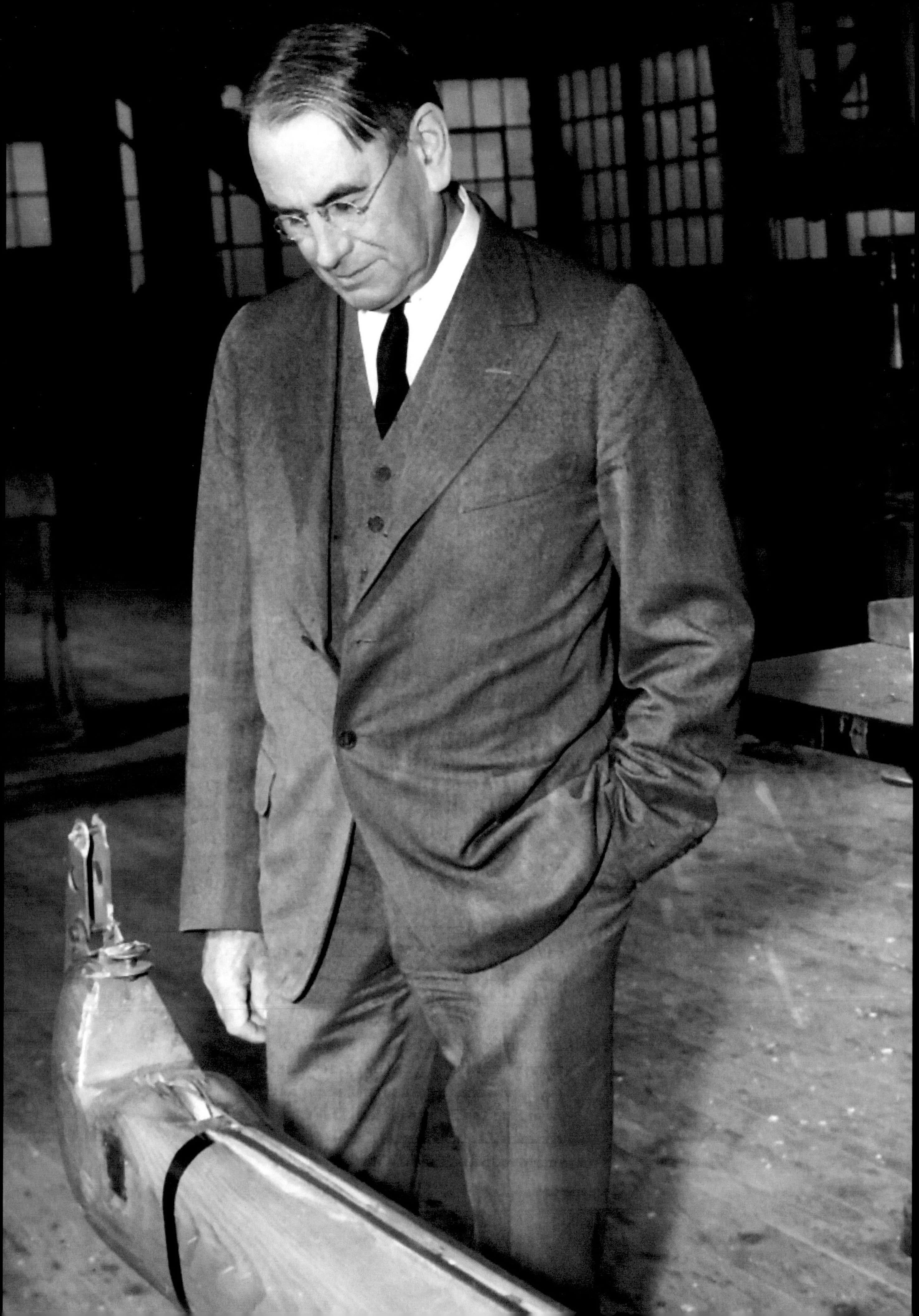

"He said, 'Number one, you do it the best way you know how to do it and do it right.' He said, 'I'll worry about getting paid for the job.'" —Rod Stephens on Henry Nevins

5 The Nevins Way

To Henry Nevins (here contemplating the details of a mast in the 1930s), yacht construction was not so much a test of technical ability as an expression of good character. Over four decades on City Island he insisted on building new boats even though it was less profitable than other work. (COURTESY CITY ISLAND HISTORICAL SOCIETY)

In the autumn of 1948, as John Nicholas Brown was making plans to leave the Navy Department and throwing cold water on efforts to get him to run for the U.S. Senate, he gave the go-ahead for his third great building project. As incoming vice commodore of the New York Yacht Club, he would need a boat to race in club events. Another source of urgency was concern about the future of the Henry B. Nevins Yacht Yard. Henry Nevins's two top assistants, head of construction Rufus Murray and general manager John Byrne, had died, and Nevins himself was so ill with heart and circulation problems that he could spend only a couple of hours a day in the place that he had ruled for 40 years. His eyesight, never strong, had declined so far that when he went out in his sloop *Polly*, he mournfully confided to the yachting writer W.P. Stephens, "I had to do so without being able to see the shiver in the luff of the mainsail or jib." Yet the Nevins system and many of his top people remained in place.

The eleventh-hour changes of dimensions did nothing to ruffle relations between *Bolero*'s designers and builders, who tended to get along much better than, say, the people behind the construction of a typical private home. There, as Tracy Kidder observed in his book *House*, "The relationship between architect and builders can explore the limits of sympathy in sympathetic people. It is not in either party's interest to understand the other's too well." After working together on more than 70 boats in 19 years, Sparkman & Stephens and the Nevins yard understood each other very well indeed.

THE NEVINS WAY | 59

Typical of the Nevins Yacht Yard's early work, Huntington Dancing Class sloops line the marine railway, ca. 1915. (COURTESY CITY ISLAND HISTORICAL SOCIETY)

"Very Carefully Fitted"

Born in 1878 in Rhode Island, Henry Brown Nevins (he apparently was not closely related to the Browns of Providence) was raised in New York City. The expectation that he would become a medical doctor, like his father, was done in by weak eyes and a profound love of sailing. He considered it an act of elemental creativity: "Sailing a boat to windward is perhaps the finest example of man's domination over the forces of nature." As the Stephens brothers would do, he made his career choice early. After building a 28-foot catboat at the age of 17, he worked in one of the shipyards that then lined the banks of the Harlem River until 1907, when he bought a little boatyard and pier on the east side of City Island, an earring dangling from the Bronx that was fast developing into New York's boatbuilding center. His early work gave no hint of his future as the builder of some of the country's finest yachts. The first boat off his ways was a common bumboat, a barge that delivered ice and water to anchored yachts. Later came some commercial vessels, the occasional rough-finished pleasure boat, and a great many cheap rowboats.

After his yard burned down in 1910, Nevins became so discouraged that he offered to sell out to the financier August Belmont, the latest of a long string of land developers who tried to turn City Island into another Manhattan Island. Belmont deemed his price too high. Taking a deep breath, Nevins expanded by buying a neighboring yard, filling in some marshes with rusted automobiles, and building a

> "Sailing a boat to windward is perhaps the finest example of man's domination over the forces of nature."

new pier, a marine railway, a sail loft, and a machine shop. Deciding to go into the business of building high-quality yachts, he hired Rufus Murray, John Byrne, and other veterans of the country's best yacht yards, who introduced new techniques for building racing sailboats and fast commuter powerboats.

At first many of the boats that came out of the yard were relatively small, but they won the loyalty of valuable friends who went on to buy larger custom boats. The 31-foot 6-inch Victory class, designed in 1919 by William Gardner (designer of the transatlantic record holder *Atlantic*) was one of the first one-design classes to sport the new, tall three-cornered Bermudian or Marconi rig in place of the traditional gaff rig. Demonstrating a knack for marketing, Nevins and the class sponsors chose a name inspired by the Allies' recent victory in the Great War and proceeded to give each of the 20 boats a well-known war-related name like *Ace*, *Spad*, and *Black Jack* (General Pershing's nickname). The Victory and another Nevins boat, the 29-foot 9-inch Sound Interclub class, designed by Charles D. Mower, were Western Long Island Sound's prestige classes in the 1920s, when they were sailed by some of the sport's future leaders. One was J. Pierpont Morgan's grandson Henry S. Morgan, who later founded the securities firm Morgan Stanley, owned larger several Nevins-Sparkman & Stephens boats, and preceded John Nicholas Brown as commodore of the New York Yacht Club. Another was Cornelius Shields, who would be *Bolero*'s racing skipper. A third was Herbert L. Stone, the editor and publisher of the sport's most influential magazine, *Yachting*.

Anne Brown learned sailing in a Nevins-built boat – the 24-foot centerboard Fishers Island One Design, designed by Charles D. Mower (who would later be the Nevins yard's in-house designer). The history of this class indicated Nevins's development as a yacht builder. When he built several Fishers Island One Designs between 1910 and 1913 for the burgeoning island resort of Fishers Island, his price was just $400 a boat, ready to sail. These boats were of uneven quality and wore out quickly, so the islanders came back for a second fleet in 1922. The new boats (many of which are still sailing today at Groton Long Point, Connecticut) were built to high standards for that day. Structural timbers – frames, keel, floors, stem, and mast step – were white oak and shaped not with a saw but by bending them after they were softened in a hot steam box ("The steaming time is an hour to an inch of thickness," commanded Nevins.) Mahogany, the prince of woods for a fine finish, was used in the new boat's trim and seats. Planking was white cedar that was (quoting the contract) "worked in long lengths and narrow strakes and very carefully fitted." Care was crucial. Once fastened into place with screws, the planks were "carefully planed, then caulked and puttied with white lead putty, then scraped and sandpapered until perfectly smooth."

To Nevins, the best proof of a boat's quality was not so much the wood used to build it but the metal used in the screws and bolts that held the wooden pieces together. "It cannot be too strongly emphasized that the ultimate strength of the structure depends on its fastenings," went one of Nevins's commandments. Iron, which was cheap, was the traditional material for fastenings. Iron spikes were acceptable to Nevins, but not iron screws, which corroded easily and whose rough burrs ripped the wood. "Don't ever let anyone put a galvanized iron screw in your boat anywhere," Nevins insisted in an article in *Yachting* magazine in 1935. "Such screws are no earthly good." The contract for the Fishers Island One Design specified more expensive brass – "yellow metal," it was sometimes called —which corroded more slowly than iron.

Ready to sail, the high-class, second-generation Fishers Island One Designs cost $985 each, over twice the first generation and then the equivalent of one year's college tuition. The contract guaranteed Nevins a profit of $500 each, which meant that for one of the few times in his long career, Henry Nevins actually made good money on a boat.

Responding to new technology, Nevins steadily raised his standards over the next quarter century as he developed ways to build strong, lightweight boats designed by Olin Stephens and other designers of the new school. Mahogany, stronger and more costly than cedar, went into planking; in larger boats, like *Bolero*, it formed the outer layer of double-planked topsides over a cedar inner layer. The

The America's Cup sloop *Vanitie*'s 168-foot mast stops traffic on City Island Avenue as two dozen men inch it out of the Nevins spar shop in 1928. The longest wooden mast ever built, at $30,000 it probably was the most expensive. (© MYSTIC SEAPORT, ROSENFELD COLLECTION)

Percy Orne installs fittings on a wooden mast. Like Rufus Murray, he had come down from Boothbay, Maine, and was at the cutting edge of boat construction. (COURTESY CITY ISLAND HISTORICAL SOCIETY)

Percy Orne and Masts

Nevins did not go along with every innovation. He took a pass, for example, on using the new glues to laminate strips of wood together to make frames and other structural elements, and except for a few small experimental aluminum craft for an aluminum company, he stuck with wood for hulls and spars because that was the material he knew best. When someone who hoped to sail for the America's Cup in a J-Class sloop, typically a metal boat, asked him in the 1920s to set up an operation to build metal hulls, Nevins turned him down.

He declined to build metal masts for the good reason that the yard was at the cutting edge of wooden spar construction. The head of the spar shop was Percy Orne, originally from East Boothbay, Maine (near where *Bolero* would be hauled on her first cruise to repair her centerboard). Orne was a master of the highly technical project of building strong, small-diameter, hollow wooden masts that could carry the great load of a modern racing rig while at the same time making the boat more stable through weight-savings aloft. In the 1800s, boatbuilders had hollowed-out masts by boring them or slicing them in half and scooping out the innards. Better than those crude methods was the intricate structure of long, narrow, Sitka spruce staves that Percy Orne shaped precisely with an adze and assembled in a box or oval shape, securing them in place with casein glue, an adhesive derived from milk protein that had been perfected during World War I by the infant aviation industry to build spruce fighter planes. (World War I aviation also taught designers how to make masts smaller and more aerodynamic in shape.) Legendary for his ingenuity—he once shortened a mast while dangling aloft from it in a bosun's chair—Orne was so good at his job that boats built by other yards came to Nevins for their spars, some so lengthy that teams of men were needed to cart them through the streets.

THE NEVINS WAY | 63

Among the procedures that Rufus Murray introduced to Nevins was the technique of planking smaller boats when they were upside-down and turning them over to install interiors. These are New York 32s in 1936. (© MYSTIC SEAPORT, ROSENFELD COLLECTION)

invention of waterproof glue in the early 1930s led to marine plywood, which the yard first tested in Nevins's sloop *Polly* and later used in areas requiring strong, flat panels, including the top of *Bolero*'s deckhouse and her bulkheads, the walls between cabins that provide structural support for the hull.

He kept up with modern metallurgy, which was producing new corrosion-resistant, strong, and smooth metals. In 1923 Du Pont and the American Brass Company developed a silicon bronze that they called Everdur for the manufacture of water tanks. With a tensile strength of 100,000 pounds to the square inch, it was exceptionally strong. There also was Monel, made by the International Nickel Company from nickel deposits discovered in northern Canada. Boatbuilders liked to use Monel in propeller shafts. Though both Everdur and Monel were expensive, they were used in Nevins-built boats — Everdur so frequently, in fact, that Nevins had his own foundry to make blocks, winches, structural supports, and especially screws and bolts. "Everdur-fastened" came to be almost synonymous with "Nevins-built."

"Always In a Good Humor"

"The man at the top deserves credit, just as I like credit," Olin Stephens once said, "but Nevins had a lot of good lieutenants." Nevins ruled the yard, but close at hand were top aides who included capable purchasing agents and knowledgeable supervisors. The best known was Rufus Murray. Born in East Boothbay, that cradle of boatbuilders, Murray dropped out of grammar school to work in a shipyard. In 1917 he was head of the wood shop at the great Herreshoff Manufacturing Co., in Bristol, Rhode Island, when the yard was reorganized following the death of John Brown Herreshoff. Then 52, Murray moved on to City Island, where Nevins made him vice-president and chief of construction, and allowed him the unique privilege of buying stock in the company. Murray brought a liveliness that did not come easily to Henry Nevins. He spent his lunch hours playing checkers with the stockroom janitor and was addicted to practical jokes (he was especially fond of tossing water balloons). "I loved this guy Murray," said Rod Stephens. "He was quiet, friendly, and everybody admired him. He taught me an awful lot. . . . He was such a nice man – quite elderly, but always in a good humor."

Murray was described by Olin Stephens as "unparalleled in his knowledge of the nature of wood and how it should be put together and fastened to form a yacht hull." One of the most difficult problems was identifying suitable oak. At Nevins, the only wood that would do for the frames, stem, deadwood, wooden keel, and other structural members was white oak, which was especially resistant to rot that spawns in the wet, poorly ventilated places where these members sit. White oak is not perfect; the acids in it can corrode metal fastenings ("Oak and metal don't like each other," Hans Zimmer, *Bolero*'s restorer in 2003, once said.) And yet white oak was desirable for a wooden boat's skeleton, from stem to forefoot to wooden keel to horn timber, plus the many frames and deck beams. Rod Stephens recalled with barely repressed horror the time that a half-built boat at another yard was tardily discovered to have a keel made of the wrong oak. The yard dutifully tore the boat apart, replaced the deadwood with white oak, and started over.

Such a mistake is not hard to make as there are several dozen species of oak, many of which look alike. Among guides to wood was a series of publications from the Forest Service's Forest Products Laboratory, which Olin Stephens called "the only branch of the U.S. Government deserving a star." Rufus Murray had a knack of being able to identify the right oak. "To most of us they all look about the same," Rod Stephens said in an oral history interview at Mystic Seaport. Not so to Rufus Murray. "From half a mile away, he could tell you what was white oak and what was yellow oak and what was black and what was piss oak and pin oak. I never knew how many kinds. . . . The only oak that he'd use was real white oak. And that's the only kind that should be used." Botanists distinguish species by inspecting them through a magnifying glass. Some oaks have large, open pores that absorb water and cause rot, but white oak pores are plugged. Murray needed

White oak members were shaped in the traditional, efficient way by adze and saw. The only personal safety equipment seems to have been the ubiquitous hat. (© MYSTIC SEAPORT, ROSENFELD COLLECTION)

Yard Minesweeper 6 is prepared to slide down the ways at the Nevins yard in 1942. During World War II and the early years of the Cold War, the Nevins yard concentrated on minesweepers of its own design, meanwhile building a few yachts, including *Bolero*. Problems with the navy almost destroyed the yard. (© MYSTIC SEAPORT, ROSENFELD COLLECTION)

no magnifying glass, just an improvised straw. Rod Stephens described his method this way: "He would take a small sprig of the wood about three inches long, put one end in a cup of water, and blow on the other end. If bubbles came out, it was not white oak."

Oak and other logs that Murray selected were hauled to City Island and cut into sections of so-called "green wood," meaning it was saturated with water. It was then left on racks to season, or air dry, for a year or more until the moisture content was reduced to an optimum. If insufficiently seasoned timber went into a hull, the boat would weigh more than the designer had calculated. Worse, the timber or plank might shrink or twist, causing it to craze or crack. For this reason, Murray would try to track seasoning with care, though mistakes were always possible.

By the late 1920s, Nevins had annual sales over a million dollars and a workforce as large as 150. The Great Depression ripped away much of that, and though the firm's auditors insisted that the only profit lay in servicing yachts, not constructing them, Henry Nevins insisted on continuing to build boats. Thanks to the new type of racing boat and to a financial deflation that made a dollar go much further than before, people with cash in their pockets and a yen for sailing came to Nevins with hopes of getting a good deal on a good boat. The yard remained open and was sometimes busy throughout the Depression, although Nevins had to make do with little if any profit.

Nevins understood marketing and cleverly promoted the yard as the top-of-the-line provider of boats for the most elite, most knowledgeable, and most safety-conscious seamen. The slogan "When they're breaking green over the bow, you're glad she's a Nevins" was repeated frequently in his advertisements, brochures, articles in *Yachting* magazine, speeches, and tours of the yard for visiting yachtsmen and yacht clubs. He railed against what he saw as the false economy of choosing a yard because its bid was the lowest. "Why is the American yachtsman so tolerant of, or indifferent to, a leaky yacht?" ran his opening sentence in an article titled "Economy Versus Cheapness," followed by a laundry list of horrors from leaking hulls to corroding keel bolts to toilets lifting off their bases – none of which, he wanted it known, would ever be found in a Nevins-built yacht.

The war transformed Nevins into a facility of almost 700 workers laboring in several shifts, night and day, to build warships. One was the navy's 136-foot Yard Class Minesweeper, designed by Nevins's then in-house designers, George Crouch (who had invented the three-point hydroplane) and R. O. Davis. Because a minesweeper had to be nonmagnetic, wooden construction was mandatory, and because shipbuilders had long ago moved on to metal construction, that meant construction in yacht yards. Under the supervision of the Nevins yard, 561 YMS ships were built at 25 yacht yards across the country during World War II and the early Cold War, 24 of them by Nevins. Military work kept the yard alive after the war, when the demand for new wooden yachts was initially slow (with a few exceptions like *Bolero*) and then all but vanished due to cheaper

European builders and to the rise of fiberglass and aluminum construction.

Henry Nevins died in January 1950. Four years later, the navy was insisting on so many costly modifications to minesweepers that his widow decided to shut the yard down. The announcement set off a blizzard of protests whose point was that a yacht yard could be a cultural landmark. Before the doors were closed, the yard was bought by Carl Hovgard, the owner of a successful Nevins yawl, *Circe*. (*Business Week* ran the story under the headline "All's Well Again for Yachtsmen.") With the infusion of new capital, the yard briefly enjoyed flashes of its old brilliance under a new name, Nevins Shipyard. Down the ways came a class of fast, wooden 40-foot centerboard yawls and the yard's first America's Cup boat, the 1958 Sparkman & Stephens Twelve-Meter *Columbia*.

Yet the knack of mastering new technology was history. Other builders had been using fiberglass since the late 1940s, but when the yard tried to make a fiberglass deck for a Nevins 40 yawl, all it got was a mass of uncured mush. An effort to use the modern technique of making strong, lightweight frames out of laminations of wood foundered when *Columbia*'s poorly funded syndicate neglected to pay the yard's oil bill, the heat was cut off, and the shed became so cold that the glue would not harden. The laminations had to be joined heavily with screws.

The last Nevins-built yacht was launched in 1959. Two years later, the yard failed for good at the age of 54. When the assets of the Nevins yard were sold off at auction in 1962, *Yachting* magazine editorialized: "The saddest day around the Sound in many a year was October 16 when the auctioneer's hammer, pounding out the disposal of a lifetime accumulation of equipment and supplies, tolled the death knell at Nevins Shipyard at City Island. We hear somebody's going to build an apartment development there, and all we hope is that it's properly haunted by the ghosts of vanished yacht builders."

In an aerial photograph of City Island taken around 1970, more than 30 piers and wharves can be counted, but the site of the Henry B. Nevins Yacht Yard is a black rectangle empty of buildings and boats. A few years later that void was filled with children.

"You're Glad She's a Nevins"

Henry Nevins had a house on City Island and was an important member of the Clammer community as an employer and in other ways. During the Depression he sponsored fundraisers for the relief of the families of unemployed neighbors (once, Olin and the two Rod Stephenses showed the movies they had taken during their winning race off England in *Dorade*). His primary home was on the mainland in Pelham, New York, and with his first wife and (after he was widowed) his second, he was active socially and in civic affairs. Though childless, he served as president of the Pelham Board of Education. For many years he served as treasurer of the country's oldest artists' and writers' retreat,

In 1939, Henry Nevins and his wife celebrate the launching of one of their sloops called *Polly*. When times were slow, Nevins sometimes built boats for himself in order to keep the yard busy. (© MYSTIC SEAPORT, ROSENFELD COLLECTION)

THE NEVINS WAY | 67

> "There was never a time when there wasn't a reference to 'The Nevins Way,' always with reverence."

the MacDowell Colony in Peterborough, New Hampshire. Named in memory of the composer Edward MacDowell, the colony was founded and run for many years by his widow and Nevins's aunt, Marian Nevins MacDowell. Aaron Copland, Leonard Bernstein, John Updike, Studs Terkel, and thousands of other composers, artists, and writers retreated to the colony to get away from the world and into inspiration. By 1949 MacDowell residents had won 20 Pulitzer prizes.

A quote ascribed to Marian Nevins MacDowell nicely summarizes the purpose of the MacDowell Colony: "It's what I've dedicated my life to prevent – the nonwriting of the great poem." Henry Nevins could have made the same affirmation about the nonbuilding of a great yacht. According to City Island's nautical historian, Tom Nye, "There was never a time when there wasn't a reference to 'The Nevins Way,' always with reverence, both during Henry Nevins's life and after his death when the yard was reorganizing. This was unusual for any business on City Island. He had a way about him. If his workmen had been a battalion and he were a general, they'd never lose. They'd follow him into hell." Nye likened the yard's reputation to the old advertising slogan for Hebrew National hot dogs that claimed they were from "a higher source."

Henry Nevins believed that building a boat was a fulsome act of conviction and an expression of character. Here he is, for example, on the subject of building masts: "Like many of the operations in the building of a boat, the proper making of a hollow spar depends largely on the integrity of the builder, and somewhat on his skill. After it is made, one cannot tell what it is like inside." Boatbuilding, then, was not no much a technical as a moral enterprise. "A good craftsman must have, first of all, a basic sense of integrity and pride in his work, or he is no good," he wrote in 1935 in an article in *Yachting* nominally about the correct techniques for building boats. "He is only secondarily materialistic, which is pretty foreign to the modern trend in all industry." By "no good" he clearly meant no good as a human being in a world whose standards, Nevins was convinced, were being lowered every day. No less than Ralph Adams Cram and Richard Neutra and John Nicholas Brown, Henry Nevins considered himself a prophet for a better world.

At first glance he would seem a highly unlikely general. A visitor from *The New Yorker* magazine in 1938 described him at age 60, in his tweed suit and with his soft gaze, as looking like a professor, "from high forehead to baggy trousers." Like a good professor, he refused to lock himself in an ivory tower, and like a good general he mixed with his men in order to reinforce his commands. The best work, Nevins preached, "can be accomplished only by skilled, painstaking workmen under conscientious and experienced supervision." The stress lay on the last word, for Henry Nevins was a man of rules: "An individual plank over five inches in width should have no less than three fastenings to each frame, and no plank less than two." "Caulking should be driven in neatly, smoothly, and tightly but not too tightly, or it may result in what is called 'wooded' seams." "The fundamental requirements of a yacht are that she shall be tight, strong, durable, and neat looking."

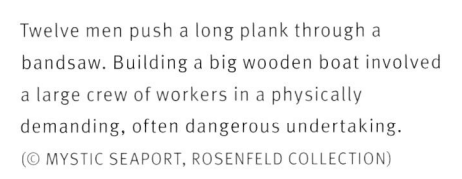

Twelve men push a long plank through a bandsaw. Building a big wooden boat involved a large crew of workers in a physically demanding, often dangerous undertaking. (© MYSTIC SEAPORT, ROSENFELD COLLECTION)

His routine was to spend the morning in his office, then stroll around the yard to check up and assert his authority in every department, greeting all his workers by name and sometimes joining them for lunch. After that, confident that his rules were being enforced, he returned to his office and took a nap. "No Nevins worker ever made a mistake," Herbert Lee, a retired Nevins machinist, said. "The first mistake that caused any embarrassment or anything like that, you were out the gate. There wasn't any room for that. On the other hand, nobody ever tried to hurry you, or tell you to hurry up or hurry on the job. If the job took six hours to do, you spent the six hours doing it. You didn't take any chance of messing it up." Asked if people got along, Lee replied with evident sarcasm, "Oh, everybody had to get along well at Nevins." When a labor union organizer started sniffing around the yard, Nevins gathered his employees and promised them that if they even attempted to unionize, he would shut down the yard, adding as a warning, "I think you'll all take me at my word."

Shaped from oak logs by adze and saw before being bolted together, the massive stem and forefoot then had a rabbet chiseled out to receive the ends of the planks. Even such heavy work was precise: "If you made a mark, you didn't do a rough mark," Rod Stephens recalled. (© MYSTIC SEAPORT, ROSENFELD COLLECTION)

He did not require his workers to be well educated, only that they fit into his system without too much friction. "You know, we who come from the other side, how much schooling did we have?" asked Nils Halvorsen in an oral history. "Very little. Simple arithmetic and so on. Then you come over here and you are willing to work hard and turn out a lot of work and do your best and learn by experience." That experience included (to Halvorsen's frustration) regular chiding by Henry Nevins, whose expectations of something like perfection were clear, precise, and dogmatically expressed. Unlike John Nicholas Brown, Nevins was not one to say "please." From time to time one of his workers would stand up to him. Halvorsen did. "Well, I'll tell you, he was a smart businessman. But we had a lot of" – Halvorsen paused – "I had a lot of problems with him when it came to doing things a little bit different. . . . He thought he knew it all. And I said one [day], 'I know as much as you do when it comes to boatbuilding.'" Stubborn as he was, Nils Halvorsen was not about to be let go. He remained at the Nevins yard until there was no more work for him to do there, and he then went next door to Minneford's, where, into the 1970s, he was still lofting boats, including several America's Cup defenders.

Despite occasional quarrels with the owner, Halvorsen and his colleagues understood their fortunate situation. "Nevins workers believed they were at the best boat yard on City Island," said Herbert Lee. "Nevins always went under that conclusion. Like their slogan was, 'When they're breaking green over the bow, you're glad she's a Nevins.' That was Nevins's only slogan, but anybody that had a boat built there, or anybody that took one there for repairs, they knew the price was going to be high, but they knew the work was going to be as good as it could be done."

"Benevolent Advisors"

To romanticize a boat is only human. To romanticize or even sentimentalize a boat made of wood is especially easy; most of us instinctively associate an authentic existence with natural fibers in the hands of traditional craftsmen. Yet it would be an error to deify Henry Nevins. "Nevins was not perfect," said Olin

Stephens, "but he was so much better than he could have been." He was a businessman as well as a craftsman, his business was complex, and, like anybody, he could make the occasional mistake, whether financial or technical.

Marjorie Gladding Young, a 27-year-old former librarian, was vibrant and pretty, and she was enchanted with sailing. In 1937 she found a job as a secretary for W. Starling Burgess, a 60-year-old brilliant but eccentric yacht designer whose boats included the three most recent winners of the America's Cup (the last of which, *Ranger*, he had designed with Olin Stephens). Taking a fancy to the young woman, Burgess tutored her in yacht design, advising her, a little mysteriously, "let every line have a beauty of its own." His friend Elihu Root Jr., a lawyer, sailor, and accomplished painter, offered to buy her a boat costing up to $2,500 on the condition that she design it. Taking the idea to Henry Nevins, Marjorie at first found him with his business face on – "austere and perhaps distant," as she would tell her sister, Constance Andrews. But he soon warmed to her proposal. "I want to build this boat," Nevins told Marjorie. "Draw exactly what you want, and we'll make the price come within your means." Having been approached by many other dreamers, Nevins had plenty of experience with handing out encouragement without pinning himself down to the exact cost.

Working evenings, with Burgess and Root serving as her "benevolent advisors," she produced the plans and specifications for a 25-foot cruising sloop. In the interest of low cost, she insisted that there be nothing fancy about the boat – no brightwork or teak, and not even a toilet (a bucket would do). Nils Halvorsen allowed Marjorie to work alongside him as he lofted the lines, and he and his wife provided her with free room and board at City Island as the boat was under construction, and also with a decorative ribbon for the bottle of Champagne that she smashed across *Pomelion*'s bow at the launching. By then she knew that Nevins had ignored her instructions and had provided teak cockpit slats and plenty of gleaming brightwork so *Pomelion* would be a proper yacht. (The name refers to a part of a cannon but was chosen for its pretty sound.)

Nevins's bill was 10 percent over Marjorie's budget. He gave her easy terms, but by the time she paid off her bill, she had discovered that the boat was leaking and the frames had hairline cracks. Nevins responded as most businessmen would, with some embarrassment and elusiveness. Perhaps, he suggested, the

Marjorie Young was the central figure in a story illustrating both the strengths and the weaknesses of the Nevins yard, which built a sloop of her design.
(© MYSTIC SEAPORT, ROSENFELD COLLECTION)

designer had made the scantlings too light or the keel too heavy. One of his staff members later told Marjorie Young that somehow or other, the wrong wood had been used in the frames. Other people theorized that the hard mahogany planks might have pulled the frames apart (there is a school of thought that favors planks made of softwoods, like pine or cedar). Whatever the cause, Nevins reinforced the frames with Everdur straps, but when the cracking continued after the boat was moved to Chesapeake Bay, a yard there sistered the frames by installing more of them alongside the originals.

As with most boats that are not as perfect as hoped, the flaw was not fatal to the owner's dream. Marjorie and Burgess married and cruised in *Pomelion* for several years until his death. She kept sailing for years and eventually gave the boat to her stepdaughter. The little sloop was still active in 1988, her 49th year. Her owner then put her in a barn and began a restoration, the first step of which was to replace those cracked frames.

"You Do It the Best Way"

"It is about as expensive a metal as one can afford to put into a boat," Henry Nevins once said of Everdur bronze, but he could easily have substituted "my boatbuilding method" for "metal." Mahogany was pricey and so was double-planking, which by Nevins's estimate cost about 75 percent more than single-planking. Even with labor running at less than $1 an hour, Nevins's system was not cheap, and he was the regular target of displays of astonishment and even outrage over his prices. He had a complaint of his own, which was that too many potential clients had "a Champagne appetite and a sour beer purse," as he told W.P. Stephens. Rather than tactfully keeping this concern secret, Nevins could spout off at the least prompting. "The 'kicking' about cost has risen by God knows how much," he wrote in *Yachting*. "It doesn't make sense – that's all."

Olin Stephens later put this tension in perspective: "He certainly did not blow himself up in any way. He was very articulate about the difficulty of the job he was about to do. Once a person decided to go with him, he was fair prey." The fact was that the competition was fierce. When the 88-foot Sparkman & Stephens yawl *Odyssey* was built in 1938, Nevins billed the owner, a Whitney heiress, exactly $99,841.26 (the equivalent of almost $1,000,000 today). Just six years earlier, Donald Starr, a young Boston lawyer aiming to sail around the world, paid only $35,000 for his 85-foot, John Alden-designed, clipper-bowed, gaff-rigged schooner *Pilgrim*, which an old Maine commercial yard built with little lead in the keel, with the hull fastened with bronze spikes, and with a minimum of polish. (Nevins might have chosen *Pilgrim* as an object lesson. Due to construction errors, she leaked so badly that the voyage almost ended at Panama before repairs were made.)

Nevins's business model was, very simply, to do the best possible work by his standards and charge enough so the yard did not have to shut down. Rod

Young's pretty little *Pomelion* sails near City Island after her launching but before troubles appeared. (© MYSTIC SEAPORT, ROSENFELD COLLECTION)

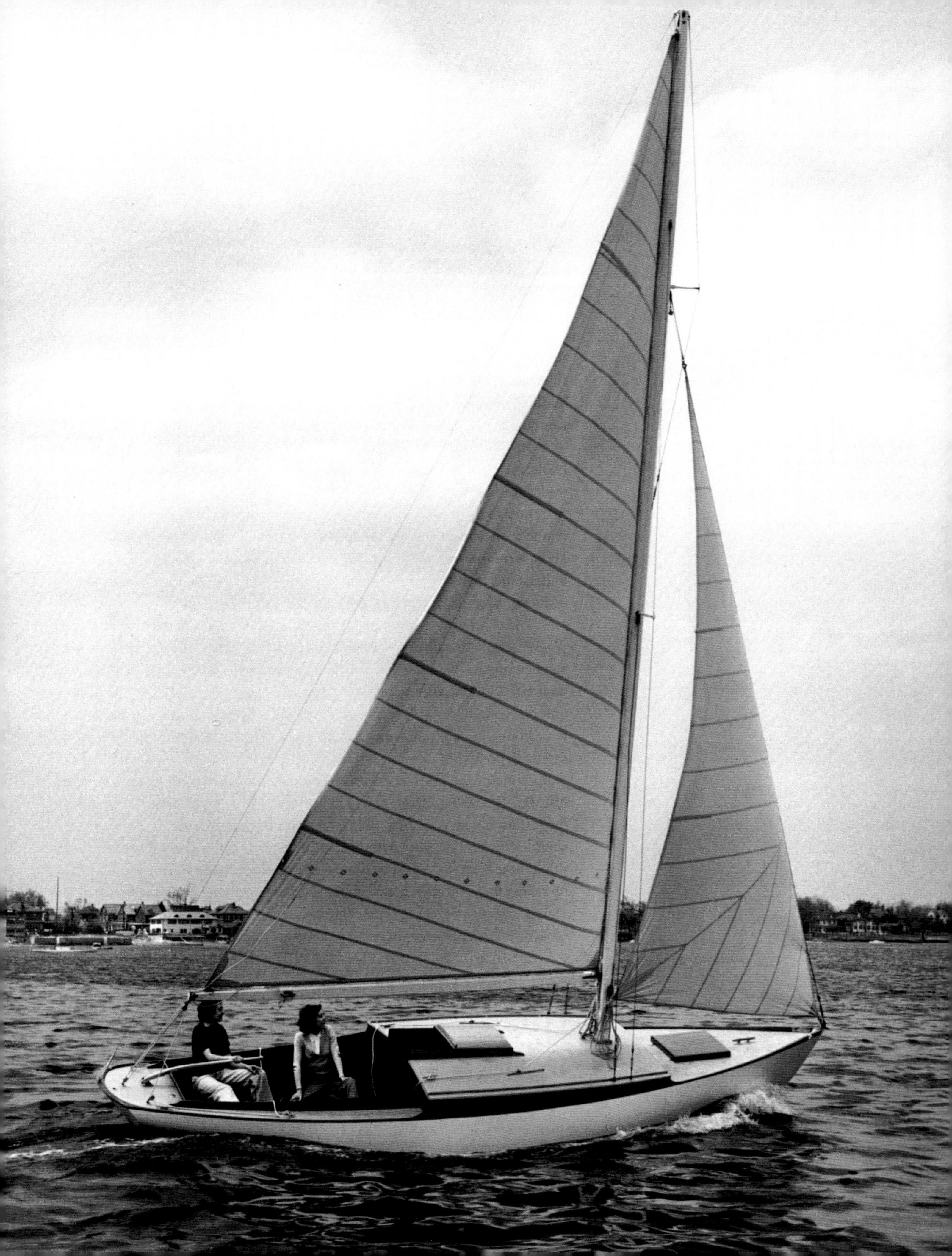

> "When the millionaire men had the money they came to Nevins."

Stephens described the policy from an employee's point of view: "His rates were high. Everybody thought they were terribly high and unreasonable, but it didn't bother him at all. He said [to his workers], 'You do it right, do it carefully.' If you made a mark, you didn't do a rough mark. He wanted a very accurate line. You don't just write a quick mark and cut near it, but you make an accurate line and cut to it. A little thing, but he was right about that, of course."

"So," said Nils Halvorsen, "he did good and he made good money and we had the best men and we had the finest work.... When the millionaire men had the money they came to Nevins. We built the *Bolero* for these men." It was widely supposed that Henry Nevins himself was one of Halvorsen's "millionaire men." Auditors' reports for the Nevins yard prove otherwise. Often, his only income from the yard was the rent he charged as the owner of the property it sat on.

His problems began with the wildly fluctuating economy (boom in the 1920s, bust in the '30s) and continued through the very nature of a carriage-trade business, with its small clientele that may be more concerned about price than they at first let on. His many competitors promised high quality and low cost to clients who were fundamentally unqualified to judge the merits of either. There were internal problems, too. Nevins and his bookkeepers were slow to understand the new requirements that arose in the 1930s for making payroll deductions for Social Security and other New Deal programs.

The chief problem was the inherent contradiction of the "Nevins way." When the only thing workers are told is that they have to do the job well – as Rod Stephens put it, "Number one, you do it the best way you know how to do it and do it right" – time sheets are likely to be sloppy at best. Stephens remembered how one wiseguy left this entry in a time sheet: "Four hours, looking for ladder. Four hours, couldn't find the ladder." Even without such built-in difficulties, profits in boatbuilding were as hard to come by then as they are now. In 1925 – amid one of the greatest booms in boating and the economy in American history – Nevins's accountant issued him the following scolding: "Reflected by the results of your company, the average annual net profit for the past six years would indicate that the boatbuilding industry is not a profitable one." Such things have been said about boatbuilding ever since Noah. Nevins's auditor kept on saying them through good times, when the yard's net profit rarely ran more than 3 percent of gross income, and bad, when Nevins often took on work at cost (or even below cost) in order to keep his men busy and to satisfy his urge to keep building good boats. If (as some believe) the schooner *Brilliant* is one of the best boats Henry Nevins ever built, it is partly because orders were so few in 1932 that his top people were able to work on her without hurry. When he built two substantial boats for himself named *Polly*, it was in part because he loved to sail good boats – and in part to keep his workforce intact.

The marvel, then, is not that Henry Nevins made so little money at boatbuilding. It is that he was able to keep the Nevins way of boatbuilding alive long enough for *Bolero* to be built there.

City Island was so closely identified with boats in the mid-twentieth century that a leading maritime insurer used an aerial photograph of the island in an advertisement. The Nevins yard was located just beyond the bulge in the island on the left (east) side. Its pier was the long one with the white boats at the end. (COURTESY CITY ISLAND HISTORICAL SOCIETY)

"The Clammers"

The ghost of Henry Nevins eventually could go happily to its rest because, instead of apartments, the island's new public elementary school was put up where he once built yachts. This evolution was appropriate for a place where, for centuries, to say "City Island" was to mean "boats."

Today's City Islanders still call themselves "Clamdiggers" or "Clammers" in honor of the shellfishermen who worked the nearby mud flats in the 1800s, before yacht-building came to the island. Clammers need not be native-born. Leonard Halvorsen, son of a long-time Nevins worker, Nils Halvorsen, described the island in the 1930s and '40s as "a very congenial, very closed community. Irish, Scotchmen, Scandinavian, German. It was the League of Nations. They all had that one goal: turn out the best boat you can." He remembered his father's strolling home daily for a hot lunch, then grabbing a snack and walking back to the yard, carrot greens poking out of the back pockets of his overalls. Most jobs at the yard were done by full-time workers like Halvorsen, who ran the mold loft, but outside contractors might appear for special projects. According to Leonard Halvorsen, a team of Italians caulked teak decks, and some French Canadians would appear to prepare a hull for painting by delicately planing the planks fair and smooth.

The maritime trades were well represented on City Island for 350 years, since whites took over from Indians who called the island "Minneford." Peter Cooper tried to create a glue

THE NEVINS WAY | 75

From the Nevins yard on the right to the Minniford yard in the center and the Consolidated yard on the left, this stretch of the City Island waterfront was devoted to high-quality yacht construction, maintenance, and storage. The yards employed craftsmen from so many countries that City Island was compared to the League of Nations. (© MYSTIC SEAPORT, ROSENFELD COLLECTION)

factory there in 1830s but was discouraged by the absence of a bridge to the mainland. Somebody else tried to make bricks except that there was not much clay on hand, and the fellow who tried to use it to make pottery went blind before the clay ran out. One land speculator or another was regularly scheming to make the island a commercial center, with no success.

So it was farming and the sea. As the mud flats became polluted after the Civil War, the shellfishermen became pilots, sailmakers, and boatbuilders. It was a fine site for shipyards – well protected both by other islands and by the law; thanks to generous riparian rights granted long ago to a developer, wharves and piers could be built almost at will. Shipwrights from rural places liked the island because it was so much like a New England or European saltwater village. When a new Episcopal church was needed, the boatbuilder Robert Jacob sent his carpenters over to fashion the pews. When the Nevins yard needed a spare hand or two, boys were pulled off the street, handed a sheet of sandpaper, and instructed to smooth a racing boat's bottom.

City Island was insular in every way. "These 'Clammers' have really been a race in themselves," a New York paper reported in 1902, five years before Henry Nevins arrived.

"For more than a century the intrusion of the urban resident or the man of commerce was resented. The native City Islander was content with his little world, measuring a half-mile in width by a mile in length, and he hoped, as his ancestors had hoped before him, that the invasion, now at flood time, would never come. Within sight and almost within sound of the glare and tumult of the great city, the 'Clammer' had lived from generation to generation happy and undisturbed."

That culture remained throughout the first half of the 1900s. The island retained this village feel into the early 2000s, at least on a quiet weekday when the seafood restaurants were not packed with people starving for surf 'n turf. Charles Ulmer, a City Island sailmaker in his early sixties whose nickname, "Butch," reflected his direct, genial personality, was raised and still worked on the island, and carried a Clammer's tangible sense of place. On a cool day in late March 2004, from his chair in his sail loft across the street from the waterfront, just down City Island Avenue from the old Nevins Yacht Yard site, Ulmer undertook a vigorous narrative of the island's maritime history, which for him was as much a story of geography and families as of boats.

"Arthur Gauss worked for Nevins, and his brother Phil ran the Minneford yard," Butch Ulmer started out, waving toward the waterfront. "I used to date Phil's daughter. They were an old City Island family. I think they lived on Buckley Street [a wave south]. When Nevins closed, Nils Halvorsen went over to Minneford's. They all did, when Nevins closed. Nils lived here on Earley Street [a wave northwest]. I grew up on Pell Street. Henry Nevins had a house on Pell Street [Ulmer waved southwest] and Mrs. Nevins allowed us to play football in their yard running down to Eastchester Bay. This building burned down in '45 and that was when my father bought it—'46—and that was when my mother stopped working as Henry Nevins's secretary and came over here."

In those days, City Island was so confident of its place as the center of American yachting that the largest sailmaker, Ratsey & Lapthorn, shut down every August. "Ratsey used to close in the summer for *two weeks for vacation* and send people over here for repair work." Ulmer's voice rose with the amazement of a sailmaker of the modern age who could not wrangle a day off from April through November.

One of Ulmer's associates in the UK sail loft, Tom Nye, was (in ascending order of importance) a sailmaker, the volunteer curator of the City Island Nautical Museum, and a fifth-generation Clammer. His great-grandfather played a part in the original sale of the site of Henry Nevins's yard. The Nautical Museum dated to the day in 1982 when Minneford's shipyard, which had built several America's Cup winners with the help of Nils Halvorsen and other former Nevins employees, stopped building new boats and began concentrating on the more profitable and predictable work of providing repairs and other services. Over a cup of coffee, Tom Nye and a long-time City Island yacht broker named Gerry Ford sadly agreed that the island's long, colorful, and important history of boatbuilding was coming to an end. To keep that history from disappearing from memory, they founded a museum in the island's former elementary school on Fordham Street. Over the years Nye filled his museum with historic photographs and pieces of old ships, little boats, and collections of documents from the major shipyards, including nine volumes pertaining to the Henry B. Nevins Yacht Yard. One treasure that was donated in 2003 was a portion of *Bolero*'s old wooden keel, which had been ripped out during the boat's restoration at the Pilots Point yard in Connecticut. At the elementary school, there was a contest for the best project on local history; first prize was a copy of Olin Stephens's autobiography, which included many pages on City Island boatbuilding.

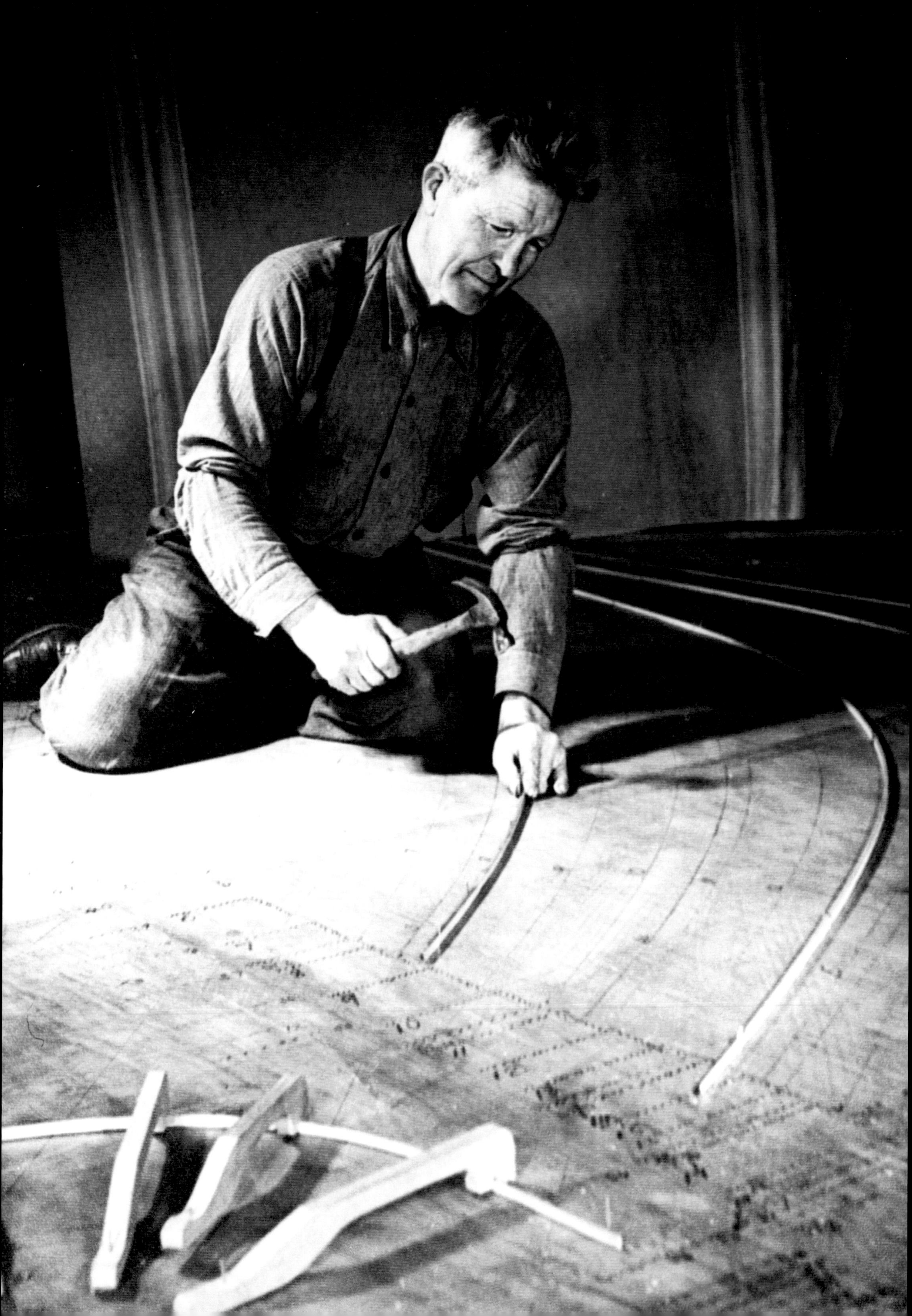

"I like windsurfing because it's difficult." ~ Rod Stephens

Shown through Heaven: Building *Bolero*

In the early stages of a new boat's construction, Nils Halvorsen tacks a batten down over one of the boat's lines on the mold loft floor so he can check the design's fairness before making the wooden molds to define the shapes of the boat's timbers. Born and raised in Norway, Halvorsen lofted boats on City Island for over half a century despite poor eyesight and a crippled left hand. His relationship with Henry Nevins was long and sometimes stormy. (COURTESY LEONARD HALVORSEN)

John Nicholas Brown and Arthur Gauss, the acting president of the Nevins yard, signed the contract for the boat on November 8, 1948. Brown put down $25,000, promised to pay an equal amount (described as the yard's profit) when the job was completed, and agreed to pay all expenses at the yard's rates. The contract called for a maximum of 37,000 hours of labor, the equivalent of 27 men working full-time, six days a week for seven months.

Yet when work began, only one person was needed to start converting Brown's dream and Olin Stephens's design into a real boat. In a vast loft on the top floor of a brick building in the Nevins yard, a partially blind and somewhat crippled Norwegian unrolled the plans of design number 711 and with an inventory of seemingly incompatible tools – chalk, string, nails, and long, flexible spruce battens – proceeded to recreate the little drawing full-size across a floor so vast and smooth that Henry Nevins called it "nothing more than a big drawing board." As the boat's shape gradually was revealed full-size, Nils Halvorsen constantly tested its fairness. After tacking down the battens over the lines, he squinted along them through his damaged eyes, searching for a bump or a hollow in the chalk line. Though Halvorsen was a crusty fellow, when he came across a small kink he had no hard words for the designer. "A pencil width on a blueprint can mean a quarter inch on the full-size plans of a boat," he would say. When he found unfairness or an inconsistency, he went to the telephone and reported it to the Sparkman & Stephens office in Manhattan, where someone worked out a solution.

The long-time manager of the Nevins yard's mold loft department, Nils Halvorsen had been working closely with the Stephens brothers ever since the days when, as teenagers, they had followed their love of boats onto City Island.

Rod Stephens's first job had been on the lofting floor. Halvorsen had known them so long, in fact, that he referred to them as "the sons of the old Stephens Coal Company." "I know them so well," he would say in his retirement. "And they've been very nice boys to work with, and you could talk things over with them and you come up with new ideas and say, 'Yeah, maybe this is the way to do it,' and they were very nice people to work with." The respect was mutual. Said Rod Stephens, "We had admiration for [Rufus] Murray and Nils Halvorsen, and weren't against getting a phone call from them and saying, 'You called for a three-quarter-inch bolt. The stem scarf would be much better three-eights or half-inch or something like that.' We'd listen to that and were pleased to get that input. It helped the quality of the boats."

> "A missing finger was the badge of a great many shipyard men."

Halvorsen had been honing his craft for 44 of his 56 years, since before he fled Norway in 1913 to avoid military service. "I was a boatbuilder when I came over here. I started with my father on the other side when I was 12 years old," he would say, making it clear that no American, not even Henry Nevins, had an edge on him. He expertly handled the precise steps of getting a construction process started despite two handicaps that might have disqualified anyone else. Halvorsen had lost one and a half of his fingers to a bandsaw – a common enough accident when, as another boatbuilder said, "A missing finger was the badge of a great many shipyard men." Even more problematical was the damage to his eyes that resulted when, as a boy in Norway, Halvorsen stared directly into a solar eclipse. The hand may have been mangled, but it manipulated battens on the lofting floor and (in yet another example of a technician's aptitude for the arts) managed the strings when Halvorsen played his violin. The half-blind eyes were barely able to read newsprint, but they were sharp enough to pinpoint an error of a fraction of an inch in a designer's lines.

His job, as Henry Nevins described it, was "laying her down and picking her up." Once the design's lines were "laid down" and faired full-size on the loft floor, Halvorsen "picked up" the design for construction by building wooden patterns, called molds, on top of the drawings – a mold for the stem, more for frames, and so on. The molds were then carried down to the construction shed where they became patterns for the boat herself.

In mid-November, design number 711 began to take three-dimensional shape. Using Halvorsen's molds as guides, carpenters shaped a log of white oak into the wooden keel, 30 feet long, three feet wide, and nine inches thick. By Christmas this massive board was lying between the lead keel below and a wood and metal skeleton above. In due course the boat was planked, the structure was reinforced with long Everdur straps and Monel ring frames, the interior was installed, the cedar deck was laid over a web of beams, and thousands of other details were addressed as the yard, the designers, and the Browns counted down toward the launching scheduled for June 9.

Using an elaborate jig, two Nevins boatbuilders bend a steamed oak frame to its designed shape. In due course the frames will set into the keel to form the ribs of the vessel's skeleton. (© MYSTIC SEPAORT, ROSENFELD COLLECTION)

The long, focused, and friendly wrestling match with those details was defined in *Bolero*'s three dozen plans and the 36-page mimeographed Final Specifications, which summarized Sparkman & Stephens's institutional knowledge concerning the building of what Rod Stephens reverently referred to as "the Proper Yacht." Sometimes the specifications and the accompanying plans instructed the shipwrights to copy details from other boats (the capstan, for handling anchor rodes, was to be a "Nevins' *Mistress* type"). Occasionally they freed workers to use their best judgment ("Stern deck framing, lodging knees, etc., arranged to suit structure as required"). But usually the Final Specifications gave strict orders based on published rules for boatbuilding that establish types, scantlings (sizes), and placement of wood and fastenings for boats of different size and displacement. While the best way to test a boat's strength is after construction (the idiosyncratic New York builder-designer Bob Derecktor favored dropping any new boat 15 or

Almost hidden by elaborate scaffolding, *Bolero* stands planked in March of 1949. It must be the end of the workday because not a shaving is visible. Two of Henry Nevins's many rules were that each work area be swept up daily and that the cleanup be noted in the construction log. (© MYSTIC SEAPORT, ROSENFELD COLLECTION)

20 feet onto hard cement to simulate falling off a wave at high speed), builders and designers followed scantlings developed by respected builders based on their own experience with the severe racking, twisting, pitching, rolling, and pounding forces on a hard-pressed boat in a confused sea.

The scantling rule that dominated in modern yacht racing – largely because it was adopted by the New York Yacht Club – was drafted in 1928 by Nathanael Greene Herreshoff, who for almost 60 years had been designing and building relatively lightly constructed boats. In the 1930s Henry Nevins developed his own Scantling Rules for Wooden Yachts for use in his yard and to advise Sparkman & Stephens and other designers who had boats built by him. The Nevins rules called for somewhat heavier construction than the Herreshoff rule. For example, *Bolero*'s oak stem piece was 8.12 inches square instead of the 7.27 inches square mandated by the Herreshoff rule, while her frames were 14 inches apart instead of 19.66 inches.

Bolero's wood was selected from a large inventory assembled from many parts of North America. The white oak for structural members came from upstate New York. Cleats for sheets and halyards were shaped from New England black locust, which is rot-resistant and hard as metal. From the Pacific Northwest came Sitka

By spring the lightweight cedar deck was being laid. We are looking forward from near the stern, over the cockpit and the half-completed mahogany deckhouse, and to the distant bow. (COURTESY JOHN NICHOLAS BROWN CENTER, BROWN UNIVERSITY)

spruce for the booms (wooden because John Nicholas Brown could not stand the *ping-ping* of sail slides against metal), Douglas fir for the clamp (the long timber at the rail supporting the deck beams), and Port Orford cedar for the inner of the two layers of planking on the upper part of the hull.

Cedar also was chosen for the deck. Sailors often prefer decks made of Asian teak, whose rough grain provides a secure tread for feet even when wet and slanting. But at over 40 pounds a cubic foot, teak was far too heavy a material to place high above the center of gravity in a Sparkman & Stephens racing boat. A cedar deck saved 1,500 pounds. (Some teak, however, was laid on the soles, or floors, of the cabin and the cockpit.)

And then there was mahogany – rather *mahoganies. Bolero* had two of them that were close cousins from the then vast hardwood forests of Central America. Not so easy to find today, mahogany was as beloved by high-quality boatbuilders as by furniture makers because it is strong, easily worked, and beautiful with its long, pink, straight grain. Nevins reserved especially fine-grained Mexican mahogany for rails, decorative features, cockpit seats, and other varnished areas, and for the planking in the rare boats that were "finished bright." For uses that were painted, there was Honduras mahogany. *Bolero*'s bottom was planked with a single layer

SHOWN THROUGH HEAVEN: BUILDING *BOLERO* | 83

(Above left) Weighing more than 37,000 pounds, *Bolero*'s cast lead keel is securely bolted to the oak keel. With the planking of the hull completed, a shipwright uses a grinding wheel to fair the surface of the lead keel.
(© MYSTIC SEAPORT, ROSENFELD COLLECTION)

(Above right) Since the mainmast would act like a pile driver, much thought went into designing the mast step so it would distribute the massive load around the hull. In the end an immense Monel girder was installed. With so much metal, it is more accurate to call *Bolero* a composite yacht than a wooden one. (COURTESY JOHN NICHOLAS BROWN CENTER, BROWN UNIVERSITY)

of mahogany, above which, up to the rail, ran more than two dozen double planks – mahogany on the outside, cedar on the inside. Though more expensive than single-planking, the two layers spread the great stresses that ran through the hull so well that there was no need to caulk the seams in the outer mahogany layer. The hull of one double-planked Nevins boat was so smooth, a *Yachting* magazine writer observed, that it seemed to have been carved out of a single block of wood. Such perfection even under great strain was a good thing for any boat, but especially for a black hull like *Bolero*'s, which can be a billboard for every spat-out seam or other blemish.

After some talk of aluminum construction, wood was decided upon. But to call *Bolero* a wooden boat is inaccurate. "Composite" is the better adjective. Of her almost 94,000 pounds, at least half is metal. The lead keel weighed almost 40,000 pounds, and at the other end of the spectrum came the boat's 100,000 (or so) Everdur wood screws, each weighing a couple of ounces. In between were bolts as long as five feet and the many floors, straps, knees, and other Everdur or Monel elements produced in the yard's foundry and shaped in its machine shop.

Monel, rustproof nickel alloy, found several homes in *Bolero*. The tangs, the small metal plates connecting the stays to the mast, are Monel, as are the five large ring frames that encircle the hull at highly stressed points near the mast or between it and the bow (a sixth ring frame intended at the after end of the cockpit was not built). Then there is the mast step, the mast's support in the bilge. The compression of any mast is always great, but in a big, heavy, extremely stable racing yacht, there is a pile-driver effect that Rod Stephens referred to as the "tendency for the shrouds to push the mast down through the bottom of the boat." A Sparkman & Stephens draftsman calculated that at a 30-degree angle of heel, the downward thrust would be 14,700 pounds a square inch – sufficient to deflect *Bolero*'s bottom by 6 inches unless the loading could be spread. The designers settled on a 12-foot girder of welded Monel, with a few holes cut in it to save weight.

Other than the engine, the only major components that were not built at the Nevins yard were the aluminum masts. The war had rapidly advanced the technology of working with aluminum, which, since it was 25 percent lighter than wood of the same compressive strength, had great appeal as a material for masts. Save one pound at the top of *Bolero*'s 90-foot mainmast and a valuable one pound of lead could be added to the bottom of the nine-foot, six-inch keel. Brown, who had used aluminum in his summer home, Windshield, was easily persuaded. Because Nevins built spars only of wood, the masts were made elsewhere. Since no spar remotely as long as *Bolero*'s mainmast had ever been made using the new method of extrusion, it was welded together from five sections of aluminum plate at the Bath Iron Works, in Maine, while the much smaller mizzenmast was extruded at the Fuller Brush Company.

"He Knew the Whole Thing"

By the end of November, *Bolero* was far enough along for Rod Stephens to begin making regular inspections. When he came out to the Nevins yard, he officially represented Sparkman & Stephens, but there were people who believed that Rod's higher calling was to the Church of The Proper Yacht in which he was at least a prophet and perhaps even its deity. After Stephens led the Canadian journalist and yacht designer Bruce Kirby on a tour of the 1958 America's Cup defender, *Columbia*, Kirby told his wife, "I've just been shown through Heaven by God."

Whatever he was called, his authority was unquestioned for many years. "Rod would get the best out of a boat better than anyone I've ever known," said his frequent shipmate and client Briggs Cunningham, "and he knew the whole thing, from building and keeping them up and taking care of them." His reputation was enhanced by his seriousness and intensity. A shipmate in the 1931 Transatlantic Race, John Fox, wrote of him, "The hard-driving mate brought into play those personal forces which figured so prominently in *Dorade*'s success, namely speed, expert knowledge, and a keen determination to keep the boat going at all costs." When Henry Nevins first laid eyes on teenage Rod Stephens, he must have thought he was seeing himself as a young man. Both were the sort of people who are convinced that life's most important parable is the one about the kingdom that was lost for want of a horseshoe nail.

Though Rod Stephens was only 39 when *Bolero*'s keel was laid, his knowledge, focus, and convictions were already legendary. Over the past 21 years, while working either for Nevins or for his brother, he had helped build, supervise the construction of, or write the specifications for hundreds of boats. Anecdotes about his devotion to miniscule details were legion. His shipmates in *Columbia* joked that he not only knew the weight of all the screws in the hull but could provide a name for every single one of them. One of his obsessions was the proper preparation of a cotter pin, the tiny hairpin-like device that secures a fitting in place, so it could be removed quickly. He could (and did) give lectures on a proper

Working with the precision of furniture builders, plankers spring the narrow cedar deck planks into place, screw them down, and seal the screw holes with wooden bungs. (COURTESY JOHN NICHOLAS BROWN CENTER, BROWN UNIVERSITY)

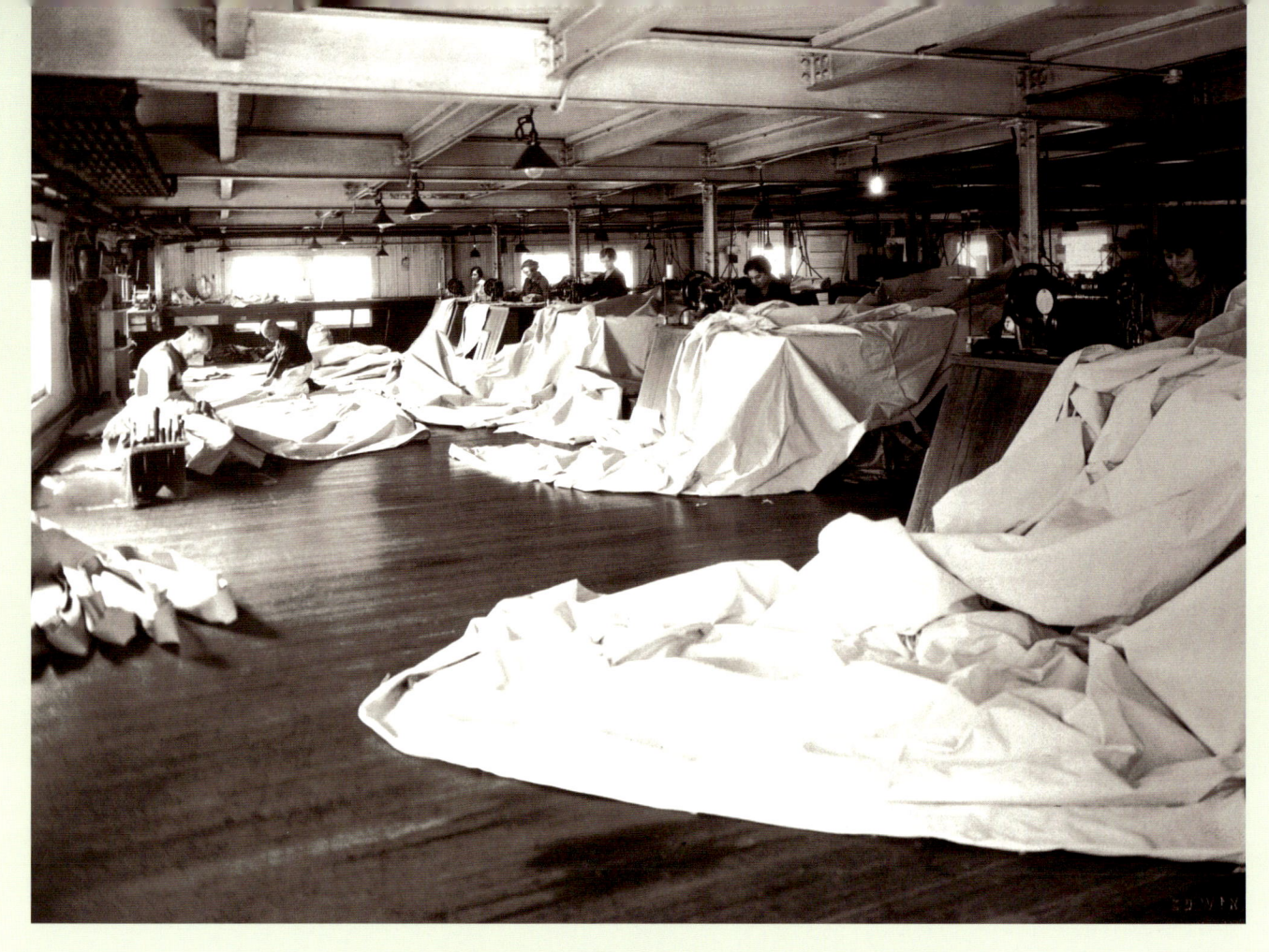

Like Sheet Metal

The vast Ratsey & Lapthorn loft near the Nevins yard could handle the largest sails, some sewn by women at machines, some so heavy that they had to be sewn by hand on traditional sailmakers' benches.
(EDWIN LEVICK PHOTO, MYSTIC SEAPORT)

Thirteen sails were cut for the boat the first year, all of them cotton except a spinnaker and two jibs of the relatively novel synthetic material nylon. All were made in the loft adjacent to the Nevins yard that was the American headquarters for the ancient English sailmaker Ratsey & Lapthorn. Like Nevins, Ratsey's was at the cutting edge of the technology of that day. Ernest Ratsey's close relationships with textile companies guaranteed that the loft had access to the very best low-stretch cotton fabric.

Having cut sails for America's Cup boats almost twice *Bolero*'s length, the loft was up to the job of making large sails from fabrics as stiff as sheet metal. While most of the sails weighed between five and 12 ounces a sailmaker's yard and could be sewn by machines, the mainsail and storm jib were each made of 17.5-ounce cotton whose panels, boltropes, and reinforcements had to be handstitched. It was said that the sailmakers worked so fast that their sewing needles glowed red hot. Rod Stephens protested that 17.5 ounces was too heavy for a mainsail and that the boat's stability would suffer, but a 14-ounce mainsail built for the 1952 season stretched out of shape and *Bolero* had her worst racing season under the Browns. When Dacron was introduced in the early 1950s, the weight could be decreased.

Everybody thought she would fly two jibs in a cutter rig when sailing to

SHOWN THROUGH HEAVEN: BUILDING *BOLERO*

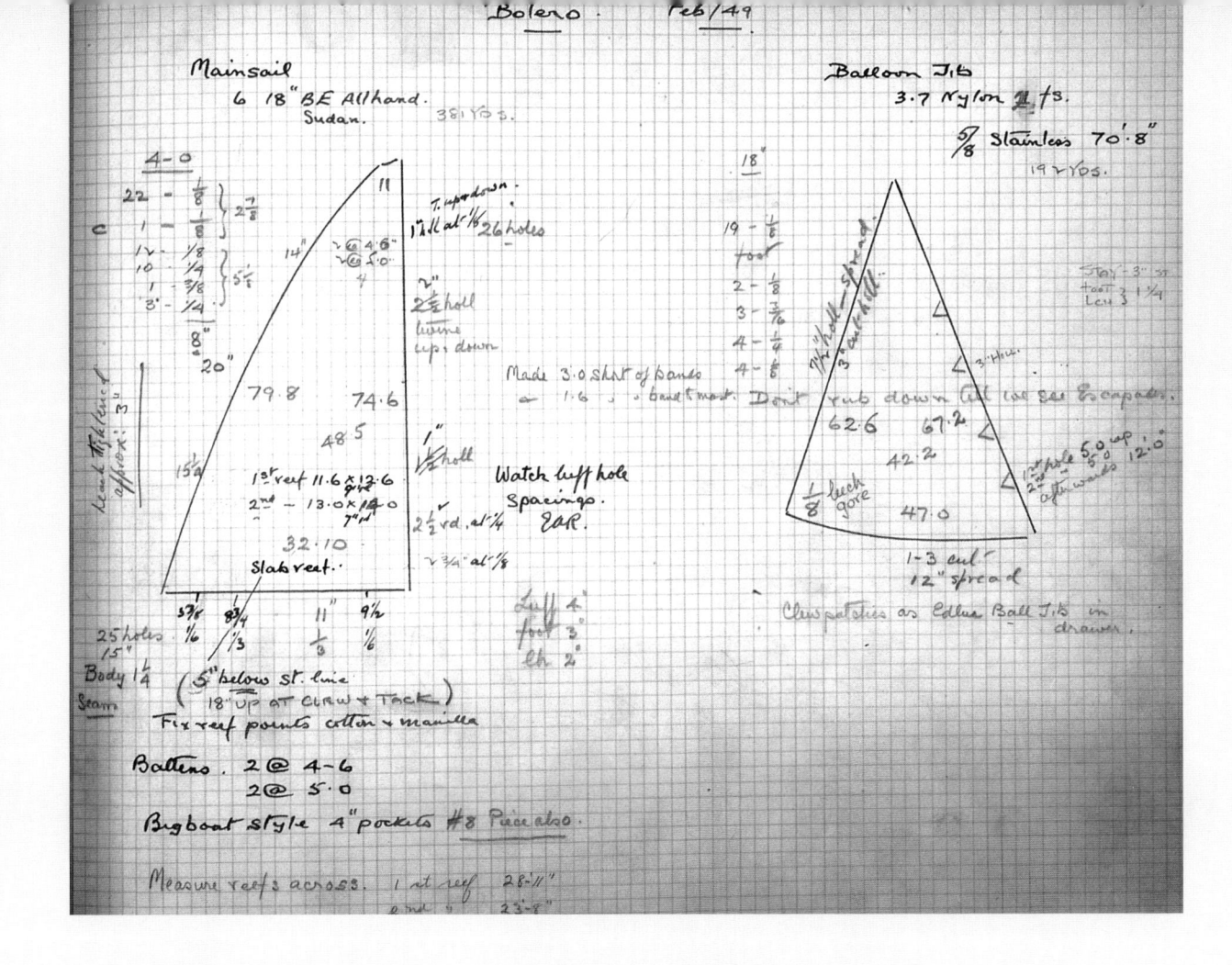

Recorded in one of the Ratsey & Lapthorn gore books, the plans for *Bolero*'s sails combine precise measurements with references to standard practices. The Sudan cotton mainsail had a luff precisely 74 feet six inches long—"Watch luff hole spacings" noted Ernest Ratsey—and "Big boat style" batten pockets. Her nylon balloon jib had clew patches like those on *Edlu*. (COLL. 53, SHIPS PLANS LIBRARY, MYSTIC SEAPORT)

windward; cotton then stretched too much to allow a single overlapping genoa jib to be carried upwind on such a large boat in anything more than a light breeze. By 1949, however, *Baruna*'s crew was satisfied that the latest genoas held their shape. Henry Taylor could have kept that breakthrough a secret, but with characteristic sportsmanship he told John Nicholas Brown about it, and except in a hard breeze and when cruising, *Bolero* generally carried a big genoa.

To trim those powerful sails there were 17 winches, each chosen by Rod Stephens for its purpose. The jib and spinnaker sheets and the other heavily loaded lines and wires were managed amidships by two tall, powerful, custom-built pedestal winches called coffee grinders, each demanding the full attention and considerable muscle power of two or three sailors who often labored in blinding spray.

One problem was the winch for the main halyard. To make the great load manageable, the main halyard had two parts, which meant that almost 200 feet of wire was exposed when the sail was hoisted all the way. Using the usual solution of that day, the halyard went to a reel winch that, like a fishing reel, wound up all the wire on a drum that was then locked. The load on the winch was so great that reefing the mainsail in windy conditions was difficult if not impossible.

SHOWN THROUGH HEAVEN: BUILDING *BOLERO* | 87

Rod Stephens inspects the tension in the running backstays on the 12-Meter America's Cup defender *Columbia* in 1958. Athletic, intense, demanding, and fond of challenges, Rod Stephens was a master of boats and rigging. The only detail that he was not a fanatic about in his long, breathless memoranda was the comma. (CARLETON MITCHELL COLLECTION, MYSTIC SEAPORT)

cotter pin, and also on a proper limber hole, the drain in a structural member in the bilge that funnels water to the bilge pump. In *Bolero*'s Final Specifications, the entry for "Limber Holes" runs 60 words – longer than the ones for "Planking" or "Lead Keel." Another of his concerns was ventilation. For his family's yawl he designed and built an ingenious ventilator that separated out water so only air came below. This device became so well known that people who came upon the yawl *Dorade* commented that she must have been named for the ventilator.

If most of the work of the world is accomplished by people who are competent, the best work is done by people who are fanatical, and fanatics are not famous for flexibility. As time passed, Rod's convictions tended to become more conservative, firmly held, and intensely defended. He was known to be personally offended if a boat was built or used in ways he thought improper – if, for example, the sailors of a Sparkman & Stephens-designed 12-Meter cut away furnishings in order to save weight. Sometimes his brother stepped in to mediate disputes between him and boatyards.

The Proper Yacht was his oxygen, his life's blood. Olin as a young man learned that, if he were to thrive, he required a balanced life that provided physical and intellectual distance from boats and salt water. When Rod was asked if he ever needed a break from sailing, he declared, with characteristic energy verging on defiance, "Never. Never, never, never a second or a moment. Nope."

"I feel things are progressing most satisfactorily," Rod Stephens reported to John Nicholas Brown in late January 1949, when over one-third of the planking was on. Yet many questions needed to be resolved. His notes and regular memorandums indicate that every subject was fair game, even the common paper towel: "I am a great believer in paper towels and certainly would have a roll in the galley and in the forward washroom." One day he became focused on a skylight that was intended to provide fresh air in the crew's quarters forward but whose arrangement stuck him as inefficient. He advised: "It occurs to me that the presence of the forecastle and toilet room bulkheads in this skylight considerably reduces its effectiveness and that we should study this problem carefully and see what steps can be taken to make adequate provision possibly including a permanent shielded air outlet to carry off the hot air and smells from the galley."

As that typically breathless memorandum indicates, one detail about which Rod Stephens was not a fanatic was the comma.

Presented with several possible solutions to a problem, he usually chose the simplest. The 41-inch, 600-pound bronze centerboard, for example, was raised and lowered in its slot deep in the keel not with an electronic system or complicated tackle, but with a long threaded rod leading to a worm gear in the cabin. One hundred turns on a crank and the board was either down or up. While not foolproof, as the problem on the boat's initial cruise demonstrated, it provided a straightforward, reliable solution to a complicated problem.

Stephens had learned to keep things simple through his own lengthy and intense sailing experience. His outer ring of paradise was to design and build a good boat and then sail it hard with a band of enthusiastic brothers. Between 1931 and 1933, he raced or cruised across the Atlantic three times in *Dorade*, along the way winning a transatlantic race and two Fastnets. After he helped build the 54-foot Sparkman & Stephens yawl *Stormy Weather* for Philip LeBoutillier, the president of the New York department store Best & Co. – this was the vessel that John Alden declared was beyond improvement – in 1935 he commanded her in the 3,200-mile race from Newport to Norway with a crew that included the owner's son and Kenneth Davidson, who was developing the towing tank at the Stevens Institute of Technology. They won that race and then Rod's third Fastnet in a row. On leaving the boat, Davidson wrote in the log, "It has been a great privilege to sail in *Stormy Weather* and to share, very humbly, the spirit of seamanship which has always prevailed."

For Rod Stephens, the spirit of seamanship did not preclude high spirits. On deck, the seven sailors drove themselves and the boat hard. In the cabin, they listened to classical music over the short-wave radio and formed a ship's orchestra

With his brother sighting up from the cockpit, Rod Stephens walks the boom, assessing the set of *Bolero*'s mainsail as the wind freshens during her shakedown sail. Captain Fred Lawton stands ready on the foredeck. (© MYSTIC SEAPORT, ROSENFELD COLLECTION)

consisting of three harmonicas, a clarinet, guitar, and two accordions (one of them the skipper's). At parties ashore, he was the fellow with the squeezebox and the repertoire of sea chanteys and silly monologues like "The Lion and Albert."

He kept himself in superb condition by, among other things, declining to take elevators. "He always challenged me to climb the 12 flights of stairs to the office after lunch," recalled Diana Russell, who worked at Sparkman & Stephens in the 1970s, setting up its computer system. The sports he played favored individual athleticism and grace – competitive ice dancing, skiing, and windsurfing, which he took up when in his sixties because it was "difficult." In a community in which a normal activity after a day's sail was to gather around a cabin table with some bottles of clear or amber fluids, Stephens was a rare non-drinker. Yet as Halsey Herreshoff, Nathanael Herreshoff's grandson and a regular crew in Rod's racing sloop, *Mustang*, made clear in a telling and humorous story, he was able to wrap his practical intelligence around even a bottle of gin: "Rod was a total teetotaler but his wife, Marge, liked a drink and would occasionally sneak one to us. One evening, sitting about the cabin, Rod noted a mysterious liquid emanating from the hanging and boot locker. Upon investigation it was discovered that a boot or something had cracked one of Marge's hidden gin bottles and that it was gin seeping out and covering the cabin sole. After cleaning all this up, we retired for the night. Next morning at breakfast, we were all astounded to observe a sparkling bright cabin sole. Rod observed that we had finally found a constructive use for gin."

Rod Stephens's life revolved around preparing, inspecting, and sailing boats. Commuting from his home in Westchester County, he was in the design office in midtown Manhattan early every morning, except when he was off in Finland inspecting a yacht in the Swan line, in Ohio looking at a new Tartan, or in California, Japan, or wherever else a Sparkman & Stephens boat was built or undergoing builders' trials. "I always fly tourist class, of course," he assured people, as if anybody believed Rod Stephens would do anything luxurious. His authority was commanding. Hans Zimmer, who would restore *Bolero*, saw some of this when Rod came aboard a boat he was sailing in Sweden in 1970 that had proved a little slow. "He was in very good physical condition. I also remember that he was a gentleman. He was very good, very thoughtful. He asked lots of questions. *But he had his way*."

He drove himself hard, and he drove others hard – sometimes a little too much so, and some people objected and a few even rebelled. He kept up his punishing routine into his early eighties, when a serious stroke almost took him down. Through rigorous rehabilitation he regained enough strength and agility to return to limited activity. A sailing friend who was a medical doctor, Susan Kline, was on hand on his 85th birthday when he was hauled aloft in a bosun's chair. "He went up and found a cotter pin that was not properly covered with rigging tape, and he fixed it. When he came down, he looked at me with a huge smile and said, 'That's the first time I felt normal since I had my stroke!'" He died several months later.

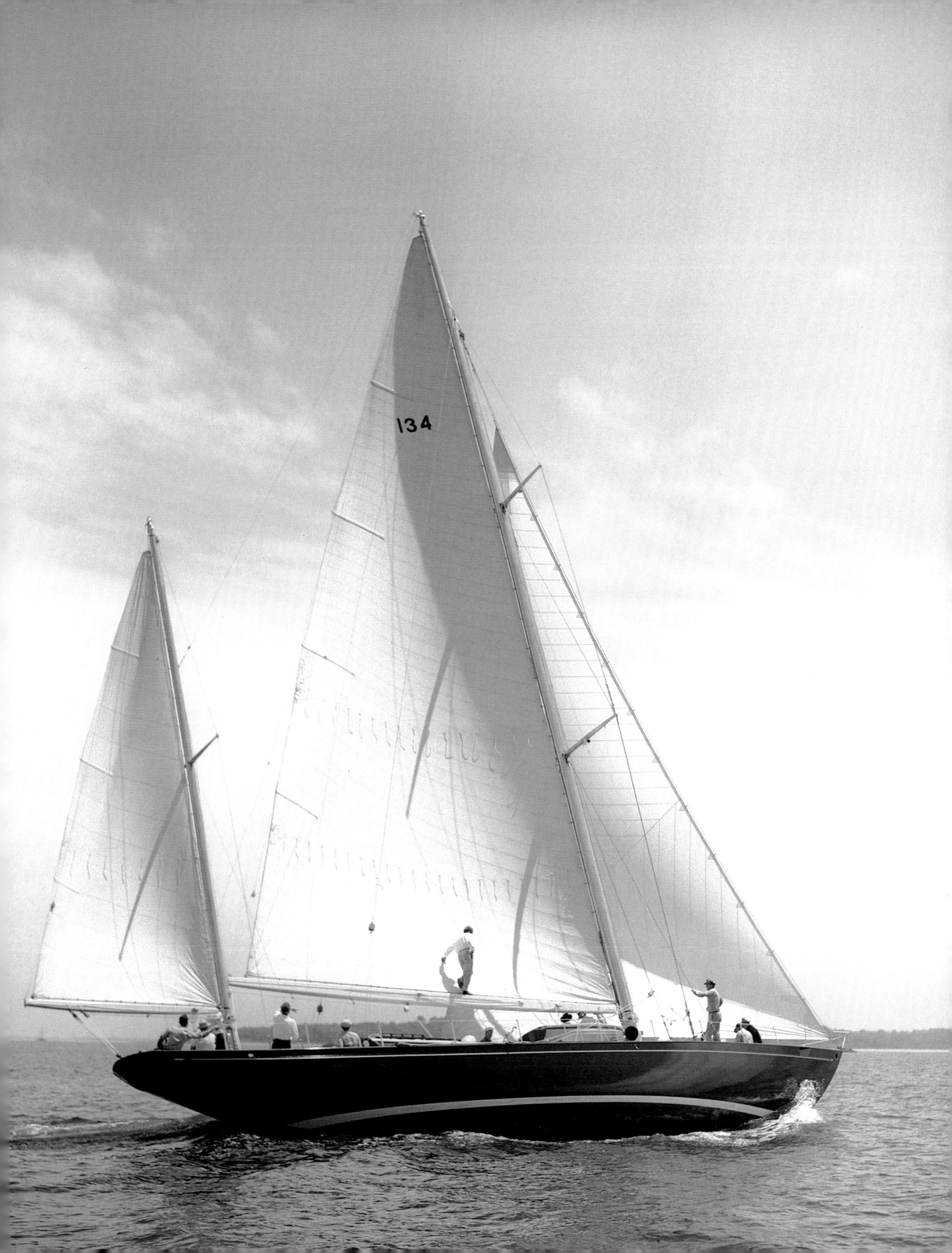
134

During the final rush of outfitting one of the Nevins yard's painters concentrates on an out of the way square of wood in the forecastle (above left). Although the Browns made some unusual choices for the color scheme on deck, down below *Bolero* had a simple, traditional look as seen in the view from the saloon into the galley (right). (COURTESY JOHN NICHOLAS BROWN CENTER, BROWN UNIVERSITY)

At left, the Nevins yard riggers prepare the boat's heavy turnbuckles as the mainmast is stepped after launch (© MYSTIC SEAPORT, ROSENFELD COLLECTION)

"Not Yet"

Rod Stephens was not the only one of *Bolero*'s creators who was a fanatic about detail. Anne Brown's critical mind seized on any possible problem, and John, as with all his building projects, seemed bored when things were easy. A decade earlier he had complimented Richard Neutra on the plans for Windshield, writing "I feel the beauty of the design to be entirely satisfying," before proceeding to chide him that some areas still left room for improvement.

Although the Browns were busy in early 1949 – he was still at the Navy Department, she was founding the Company of Military Historians – they stayed on top of the boat's progress and came to City Island frequently for inspection tours with Stephens and their professional captain, Fred Lawton. Where to fit the compressor for the electric refrigerator, what size to make the lockers in the stateroom, what sails to buy – all these and more became the subjects of fevered correspondence. Nick Brown, at Groton School, was especially concerned about the design of the mainsail and exchanged energetic letters with Rod Stephens. When Sparkman & Stephens sent out the Final Specifications, John Brown studied it as carefully as he would a medieval manuscript and left it covered with queries. The ship's bell would be six inches in diameter: "*Where? Too small? 10 inches.*" There would be a Mexican mahogany hatch over the lazarette, a stowage area aft of the cockpit: "*Hinged?*" As in all his building projects, sometimes Brown got what he wanted, sometimes he got an argument and then got what he wanted, and every now and then he was left with the satisfaction of having been presented with a reasonable explanation for the status quo.

When Sparkman & Stephens amended the lengthy Final Specifications, it grew from 36 to 49 pages. There were so many suggestions and questions that even Rod Stephens became confused. At the end of a page-and-a-half, single-spaced memorandum reviewing the options for exactly the right wash basin to go in the professional crew's quarters, he admitted, "I have had so much information on so many different papers that it is more than possible that I may have missed something. If I have, it is not intentional." At one point his usually patient brother, Olin, threw up his hands and announced, "We are getting down to rather fine points, but I guess we all agree that this will be worth while in the end." Now and then the inspectors permitted themselves to step back from the details and rediscover the gorgeous object that was rising around them. One day the Browns were shown the magnificent steering wheel, carved from a single piece of mahogany and inlaid with ebony and white holly. Anne discovered that the workers's standards exceeded even hers. "When you went aboard while it was being built," she wrote a few years later, "you had to pick your way over workmen. Nobody would stop. Even when the whistle blew, you had to tear them away. Once I happened to run my hand over a smooth plank, and it seemed to me so nicely finished that I said, 'Good. Fine.' But one of the workmen looked up, and said, 'Not yet.' He was shocked. We were always satisfied long before the workmen were. And they finished her on time. That's almost unheard of for a ship." She added about Henry Nevin's workers, "They were wonderful."

Bolero Blue

"Nothing Miami Beach About This Yacht"

As lovers of "the visual," the Browns of course had strong feelings about the boat's appearance. Some touches were standard, like the five coats of varnish that, once every mote of dust was cleared away, were brushed painstakingly onto the Mexican mahogany rails, seats, and other brightwork. When Brown read in the Final Specifications that the hull would be painted with "two coats semi-gloss, best grade yacht black," he crossed out "semi-gloss" and inserted "high gloss." The correction must have been instinctive with Brown. It died when someone warned him that a glossy finish would show every splotch of dried salt and every pat by the fender of a launch coming alongside.

Already some thought had gone into protecting the topsides with double-planking and with a scupper system that drained water from deck not over the side (which would stain the paint) but through non-corroding lead pipes running inside the hull from the deck to the waterline.

The traditional pattern of black hull, brown brightwork, and white masts and sails was broken by a profusion of bright colors chosen by the Browns. When Sparkman & Stephens specified the usual bronze bottom paint and white ventilator cowls, John insisted on a green bottom and cowls that were red inside and oyster white outside. ("Color samples to be approved by owner," sternly commanded the amended specifications.) And for canvas awnings, sail covers, and the crew's shirts, in place of the usual workmanlike khaki Anne chose a bright turquoise so unusual that Ratsey & Lapthorn gave it a custom name – "*Bolero* Blue."

This theme of traditional colors enlivened by swatches of brightness was carried throughout the boat. Down below, the cabin sides and ceilings were painted with a white enamel that nicely set off the brightwork and the teak cabin sole, which glowed with a single coat of varnish that had been rubbed in with a rag so the footing would not be slippery. *Bolero* Blue canvas pillows with white rope piping were on all the bunks. Painted on each of the blue canvas

94 | SHOWN THROUGH HEAVEN: BUILDING *BOLERO*

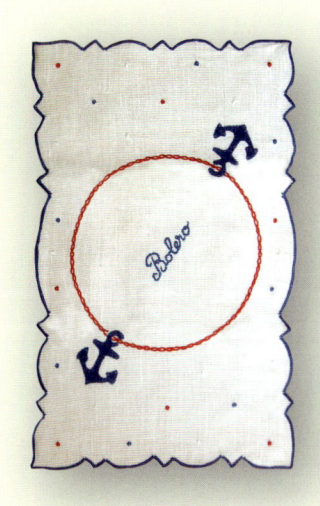

The Browns's traditionalism was anything but rigid and unimaginative. For the boat's fabrics, Anne Brown worked with the sailmaker Ratsey & Lapthorn to develop a vivid color so unique that it came to be called "*Bolero* Blue." It is seen here in a cushion, which (like the dark blue blanket and many other items) carried John Nicholas Brown's own stamp – his private signal crossed with the New York Yacht Club burgee. (COURTESY ANGELA BROWN FISCHER)

seat cushions was Brown's private signal. In pattern, his personal flag was similar to the ones used by his father and their ancestors, and his wife's and children's house flags also were recognizable as Brown private signals. Crossed flags were everywhere – on the table linens, bath towels, the corners of the cashmere throw blankets, and the boat's white, blue-rimmed chinaware and glassware. Sometimes the New York Yacht Club burgee was paired with Brown's house flag, and sometimes it was with his flag as a club officer. When Brown was elected commodore in 1952, all the dishes and glasses carrying the vice commodore's flag were replaced by a new set with the commodore's.

Typical of a Brown production, practicality went hand in hand with formality. Bed linens were color-coded to identify the cabin where they belonged, and the red and blue bath towels were embroidered with Roman numerals so they could be quickly identified by their users. In the cockpit, Angela recalled: "The cushions were made of something like Naugahyde, white on one side which reflected the heat of the sun, and a deep shade of *Bolero* Blue on the other side which retained the heat. So on hot days we'd have the white side up, and on chilly days my mother would say, 'time to flip to the fanny-warmers,' and the blue side was turned up. It was very practical." Water-resistant Naugahyde was used on the cushions in the deckhouse, too. The only problem was that this was Angela's usual sleeping cabin and the cushions were so slippery she sometimes woke up on the floor.

The boat's distinctive style long survived the Browns' ownership. "She is not posh, but is simple, efficient, and an example of fine nautical taste inside," reported an artist-sailor named Bob Smith after sailing in *Bolero* in 1965. When Smith added that there was "nothing Miami Beach about this yacht," Anne Brown would have shouted, "Amen!"

SHOWN THROUGH HEAVEN: BUILDING *BOLERO* | 95

96 | GRAND AND GLORIOUS SENSATIONS

"I do not believe I would ever be happy with a sluggish boat, even though she might have admirable accommodations."
—John Nicholas Brown

7
Grand and Glorious Sensations

When the Browns first went to see Olin Stephens, they asked for a family cruising boat. Implicit in all they said, however, was that she also be impressive to look at, rewarding to sail, and able to win races. This meant only one thing in 1946: a boat like the queen of East Coast yacht racing, *Baruna*.

Months before *Bolero* went into the water, newspaper and magazine reporters were already gauging her against *Baruna* as though the two boats were heavyweight prizefighters preparing for a championship bout. Since her launching in 1938 at the Quincy Adams shipyard in Massachusetts, Henry Taylor's Sparkman & Stephens 72-foot yawl had compiled a superb record, including finishing first in each of the three Bermuda Races she had sailed, winning two of them outright. Neither Brown nor Taylor was the sort of person to issue public challenges, yet their competitiveness was real. It also was sporting. When Brown learned that *Baruna*'s spinnaker had been ripped on the 1947 New York Yacht Club Cruise, he loaned Taylor one of *Courante*'s. When the Browns and Sparkman & Stephens were planning *Bolero*, Taylor generously passed on a few lessons learned about sailing these big boats.

Friendly opponents and also social friends, the two owners had several things in common. Both were patrician businessmen who owed their fortunes to the textile industry, both were bibliophiles who specialized in books on early American exploration (sometimes they competed for the same volumes), both built their boats for family sailing, and both kept their boats active from early spring to late fall. "Out

Carter Brown (above) and his brother, Nick, sailed in many of the family boat's ocean races. Carter was in charge of the mizzen, and Nick served on the foredeck with the man he called "the incomparable Fred Lawton." (NORRIS HOYT PHOTO)

(Opposite) *Bolero* in typical close quarters with a competitor as the starting gun nears. Even on a light day like this one, the boat's power is obvious in her stout rigging and heavy wire jib sheets. (NORRIS HOYT PHOTO)

(Previous Page) *Bolero* (sail number 134) pulls away from the 72-footer *Windigo* after the start of a New York Yacht Club race in 1954, her last year of racing under the Browns. Upwind are two 12-Meters. Flying from *Bolero*'s mizzen masthead is John Nicholas Brown's private signal (or house flag) derived from the ones flown by vessels in his colonial ancestors' shipping line. The jib is made of the new low-stretch sailmaking material Dacron. (© MYSTIC SEAPORT, ROSENFELD COLLECTION)

of commission after grand 1949 season," ran a typical last log entry (in this case in *Baruna*'s log on Columbus Day, 1949). Racing comprised only a small portion of their time, with two weeks for the New York Yacht Club Cruise, two weeks in even-numbered years for the race to Bermuda and the return voyage, a little less time for the race in odd-numbered years from Newport to Annapolis, Maryland, and then several overnight or day races. Otherwise, the boats' six-month sailing seasons were devoted to cruising or day sailing. Almost always there was a family crew. Carter and Nicholas Brown often raced on *Bolero*, while *Baruna* (the name of a Balinese sea god) raced with Taylor's three sons and son-in-law. Stillman Taylor, *Baruna*'s racing skipper, had won a Silver Star for sinking a Japanese destroyer from a PT boat.

"The Lure of the Big Boat"

Bolero and *Baruna* first went bow to bow in early August 1949 on the New York Yacht Club Cruise in a race from New London, Connecticut, to Newport. Despite its name, the cruise was in fact a series of 20- to 40-mile races for what was then America's largest, most cutting-edge fleet of big boats. Besides *Baruna*, her main competition among the cruising-racing "maxis" around 70 feet included *Ticonderoga*, *Black Watch*, *Escapade*, and *Cotton Blossom IV*. Also in her racing division were slightly smaller boats like New York Yacht Club Commodore Henry S. Morgan's Sparkman & Stephens *Djinn*, the idiosyncratic Starling Burgess schooner *Niña*, and a few of the largest all-out racers, the International Twelve-Meter Class, many of them designed by Sparkman & Stephens and built by Henry Nevins. The better Twelves sometimes beat *Bolero* and the other maxis around the course but, since they were not designed to the prevailing measurement rule, had to give them time on handicap.

Bolero's first important race did not go well for her. She led at the start but *Baruna* caught a favorable puff off Block Island and overtook her and won. After that disappointment, things improved considerably, and by the end of the cruise the standings on corrected time, after handicaps were calculated, had *Baruna* with three first places, two fifths, and a withdrawal due to calm, and *Bolero* with a more consistent two firsts, three seconds, and a fourth.

In the best wind of the regatta, rising over 15 knots, the new boat beat *Baruna* by almost seven minutes to win the race for the Astor Cup. Donated by the financier John Jacob Astor in 1898, this was one of the club's two most prestigious trophies. In her six years under Brown, *Bolero* would win three Astor Cups as well as three races for the club's other major trophy, which was presented by the reigning monarch of Great Britain. Winning a King's or Queen's Cup was sweet reward for any Anglophile, especially since there later came a letter from Buckingham Palace stating that "His Majesty was most interested" in the results and sent his personal congratulations to the winner. It does not take much imagination to picture the pleasure this brought John Nicholas Brown.

"The Tension Was There"

The racing was often thrilling. Take the following account of the pre-start maneuvers in the 1950 Astor Cup race, written by a sailor in the Twelve-Meter *Vim*, Engelina Dickerson, sister-in-law of *Vim*'s skipper, W. Mahlon Dickerson. In a southwest blow, *Vim*, *Bolero*, *Baruna*, and 17 other boats between 50 and 73 feet in length – over a million pounds of oak, mahogany, and lead – fought for inches of advantage during the second-by-second countdown to the starting gun as the crews' excitement intermixed with anxiety.

> *A minute and a half to our start and suddenly the tension was there! Every headstay carried its largest genoa; every hull approached its top speed; every skipper was dedicated to be on the line as the gun went off. Not more than a boat length, and in many cases less, separated boat from boat. The absolute silence was broken only by the surge of the seas past the shining topsides, the harping of the wind in the rigging, and an occasional, "Room! Room! You've got to give me room…" But there was no room. One mistake at the helm, one sheet let go too soon, one instant's loss of control could precipitate an unimaginable tangle of rigging, crashing spars, crumbled topsides, and crushed bodies – disaster. In the minute and a half I suddenly understood the lure of the big boat and the thrill of knowing that you have under you the fastest of them all.*

Vim was the fastest boat that day, but *Bolero* saved her time on handicap to win the Astor Cup for the second straight year. She won three more races in the New York Yacht Club Cruise (including the King's Cup) and was awarded the trophy for best overall performance on the cruise. In the Bermuda Race (her first) she was first to finish and second on corrected time. In her first full season of racing, *Bolero* had found her legs.

GRAND AND GLORIOUS SENSATIONS | 99

Corny Shields said that when he first steered a sailboat, "Never, before or since, has anything opened up to me so spectacularly." One of the top sailors on Long Island Sound, he was *Bolero*'s racing skipper. His only idiosyncrasy was an unquestioning faith in weather signs. (NORRIS HOYT PHOTO)

Her regular crew included Anne Brown, Carter and Nicholas Brown, Olin Stephens, and the boat's amateur racing skipper, Cornelius "Corny" Shields, who would command *Bolero* in many races for six summers.

Born in Minnesota in 1895, Shields was the son of a former water boy for a western railroad who had risen to run railroads and industries in the United States and Canada. After his father's death in 1904, the family moved to New Rochelle, a few miles from City Island. Corny, who had learned some sailing in Nova Scotia, began crewing for other boys with more dutifulness than joy until the day someone handed him the tiller. That was when he discovered his bliss. "It didn't take 20 seconds before I was hit by a welling-up of emotion so strong it's almost indescribable," Shields wrote of that moment in his memoirs. "It was like a theater curtain going up. Suddenly, I was tremendously happy.... I felt a great exhilaration, and for the first time really sensed the full joy of sailing, rather than the mere motion of the boat.... Never, before or since, has anything opened up to me so spectacularly." In time, Corny Shields became so good at racing sailboats that he acquired an iconic nickname, "the Gray Fox of Long Island Sound." He spent his weekends working for his brother, Paul, in real estate and later in the investment business, and his weekdays racing small boats, often against the Stephens brothers, who recommended him to Brown.

He was not infallible. After racing small boats for so many years, he needed some time to accustom himself to the 94,000-pound behemoth that was *Bolero*. In one early race sailed in tidal current, he mistimed the start and barged, or forced an opening, on Henry Morgan's *Djinn*. Morgan filed a protest. Because the racing rule was not entirely clear, there were hearings and appeals rising to the national level before *Bolero* finally suffered something that a Corny Shields boat rarely endured – disqualification.

Ashore, Shields seemed a dry, unemotional Wall Street executive. But going afloat drew out a romantic streak. In painterly terms, his canvas was the racecourse, his brush was his boat, and his colors were the elements of the changing environment, to which he was acutely sensitive. "No matter how many hundreds of times in your life you have sailed," he told a reporter for the *New York Times*, "each trip is a brand new adventure and there's something new to learn. The wind and the water always help make it so." He had a deep, sometimes quirky faith in weather signs. Everybody is familiar with one or two signs, like "red sky at morning, sailor take warning." Shields called upon on an entire inventory of them – dew on the morning grass, spiders in the rigging, the changing routes of migrating birds. Some of these rules have scientific merit. Morning dew is a reliable predictor of a sea breeze – air sucked in from the water by land that is heated on a cloudless day – because the dew is evidence of a cool, cloudless night. (The Indian writer Rabindranath Tagore expressed this principle in a poetic saying: "'I have lost my dewdrop,' cries the flower to the morning sky that has lost all its stars.") More obscure, however, was Shields' fascination with porpoises, which he believed were portents of a northeast wind, though he admitted he had no idea why. His best guess was that "like me, they just love that sparkly northeast air." In other words, porpoises, too, were romantics.

"No Bloody Secrets"

The only person who was on board *Bolero* for every mile she sailed under the Browns was Fred Lawton, her captain and sailing master, who headed a professional crew of three. The importance of a competent captain in a boat this size – especially a wooden boat – cannot be overstated. Besides keeping the boat sparkling and the electrical systems operating properly, assiduous attention ensured a dry bilge and a well-ventilated interior, both of which kept rot at bay. People were known to hold off buying boats until a suitable captain could be hired. Henry Taylor sold *Baruna* in no small part because his professional captain, Lars Myrdal, decided to go back home to Norway.

Many professionals aboard yachts before the 1970s were big, decisive, square-jawed Scandinavians with hands the size of hams. All of this was true of the professional captain of *Bolero* except that he was an American. After early training in a yacht that was a full-rigged ship, he worked for the demanding Harold S. Vanderbilt for many years, managing powerboats and racing sailboats. Lawton had a distinguished war record in command of a destroyer escort, then went back into the yachting trade. At Shields's recommendation, John Nicholas Brown hired him when *Bolero* was under construction. His chosen title was "sailing master"; he cared for the boat both at the mooring and under sail. He would fill this joint mission again in 1958 in the America's Cup defender *Columbia*, designed by Olin Stephens, built by Nevins, and sometimes sailed by Corny Shields.

A consummate seaman, Lawton could and did pick up a mooring while *Bolero* was under sail, make perfect wire-to-rope splices, keep the boat spotless (he scrubbed the deck so hard with sand that the cedar wore down), and, in the off season in his basement workshop in Newport, lubricate each of the boat's many sea cocks and varnish each of her wooden-shelled blocks.

Loyal Fred Lawton was, but not to a fault. On one windy day, Brown carelessly put *Bolero* about without alerting the crew. This was no small thing on a boat so big and complicated. Once Lawton had scrambled to get the sheets and running backstays set up correctly, he stomped aft to the cockpit and half-shouted, "*Commodore! Leave us have no bloody secrets from the foredeck!*" Recognizing the

Nobody knew the boat better than her sturdy professional captain, Fred Lawton, seen here with his cap on and studying an instrument with navigator Ken Davidson. After John Nicholas Brown made a careless tack, Lawton said enough to guarantee it would never happen again. (NORRIS HOYT PHOTO)

Bolero pauses for a crew photograph before the start of the 1952 Bermuda Race. (*Left to right*) Cook Joe Gorton, Sailing Master Fred Lawton, Mate Bucky Reardon, Norris Hoyt, Carter Brown, Arnie Gay, Olin Stephens, Ken Davidson, Corny Shields, John Nicholas Brown, Dick Goennel, Redwood Wright, and Jerry Fagan. (© MYSTIC SEAPORT, ROSENFELD COLLECTION)

trouble he had got himself into, Brown handed the steering wheel to another sailor and went forward to make peace with the one individual without whom *Bolero* could not function. Such thoughtfulness pleased Lawton. One day when Lawton was busy with a messy mechanical problem, a visitor who chanced by the boat heard him growl, "I wish I worked for a so-and-so! I'd quit right now."

Fleshing out the racing crew of 14 were two other professionals (including a first-class cook, Joe Gorton, who refused to lower his standards just because he happened to be sailing) plus several amateur sailors. One regular was Norris D. Hoyt, who during the winter taught English at St. George's School and the rest of the time followed his obsession, which was sailing (Hoyt titled his memoirs *Addicted to Sail*). Hoyt won Fred Lawton's respect on his first day in *Bolero* when, after the race, instead of going below for drinks he remained on deck to help the professionals with the hard work of folding sails and cleaning up. Hoyt also was the boat's photographer. After each long-distance race, he assembled handsome albums of his candid photographs and gave them to his shipmates.

"The boat was big and powerful and stately. She had a *dignity* about her."

Dick Goennel was amazed that John Nicholas Brown came personally to invite him to sail in *Bolero*. He was in her crew throughout the Brown years.
(NORRIS HOYT PHOTO)

Another regular crewmember was Richard Goennel, a young, financially insecure magazine advertising space salesman. He had raced with Corny Shields and Olin Stephens, who remembered his talent and enthusiasm and recommended his name to Brown. Many owners would have asked one of them to call up Goennel and ask him to appear for a race at such and such a time. Not John Nicholas Brown. Nobody was to come aboard his yacht except by his personal invitation. One day after a race, Goennel (whose name is pronounced "Go-nel") was helping to put another boat away when he heard an aristocratic voice call out, "Is Mr. Goennel aboard?" Turning around, he discovered Vice Commodore John Nicholas Brown standing tall in his motorboat, *Hopak*. With the formality of a King of England, he invited Goennel to come aboard and proceeded to request the favor of his company in an upcoming race. Goennel's astonishment remained fresh half a century later. "You come back from sailing and you don't know if you have a job. My wife later told me that my butt was sticking out of a big hole in my shorts. But John Nicholas Brown himself asks me with a 'would you please' to go sailing in *Bolero*!"

Of course, Goennel answered yes. A few days later he drove to City Island to check *Bolero* out. "I went down to the Nevins yard to see the boat. Fred Lawton came on deck. He was very nice, a gentleman, very smart, and I later learned he had a good instinct about the sea. The boat was big and powerful and stately. She had a *dignity* about her. She was always neat. There were no lights left on, no wrinkles in the sail covers. And she looked like she could *go*."

Goennel raced in *Bolero* for six years with the Browns, then sailed his fourth Bermuda Race in her with the new owner, Sven Salen, in 1956, when she set the course elapsed-time record. He became close friends of the Browns and their children; as he approached 80 he was still sailing across oceans with Garry Fischer, Angela Brown's husband.

"Like Hunting Tigers"

In the long-distance races to Bermuda or Annapolis, Corny Shields headed one watch of five or six men and Olin Stephens the other, while Kenneth Davidson called "Doc" by his shipmates in admiration of his intellect, though he did not have a Ph.D., did the navigation. John Nicholas Brown floated from watch to watch. He steered competently in fair weather, and commanded and navigated the boat on the pleasant cruises home from Bermuda. Nick Brown worked on the foredeck with the man he called "the incomparable Fred Lawton," and Carter ran the extreme back of the boat, setting and trimming the mizzen and, when the boat was reaching, the mizzen staysail.

Wherever a sailor was positioned, there was plenty of hard work. It took three strong men just to lug around the storm jib, known as "the double-hernia jib."

Sailing *Bolero* had its risks. Norry Hoyt compared her with his own much smaller boat: "The difference between *Bolero* and my *Wagtail* was like hunting tigers instead of making a daisy chain." One sailor new to *Bolero*, Bob Smith, was only half joking when he observed that people were the smallest objects on a boat this size, and that the only thing he could lift without the help of a winch was a sandwich. "It dawned on me that *anything that flapped on this yacht could kill you on contact*," Smith exclaimed with a wonder he stressed with italics. He was exaggerating, but not by much. When hoisting *Bolero*'s mainsail in a hard breeze, said another former deckhand, Bob Keefe, a sailor could be knocked down by the whack of a batten.

After the end of the first, short racing season in 1949, Brown and his crew decided that the best preparation for the next year's Newport-Bermuda Race was to test gear immediately and make improvements over the winter. One thing they learned during several sails in dirty weather was that *Bolero* was a floating chain reaction ready to happen.

When a wire jib sheet snapped, it was replaced with a heavier-gauge wire. The new sheet held, but one of the blocks it ran through blew apart and the wire sliced right through one of the stainless steel stanchions supporting the lifelines. When the sheets were not self-destructing or tearing up the boat, their turns were overriding on the drums of the two powerful pedestal winches, jamming so tight that the only solution was to snap the wire with bolt-cutters. That winter Fred Lawton strengthened all the blocks in his basement workshop, and he took the two pedestal winches to a machine shop where custom gears were installed to allow the drums to be backed off in order to free those dangerous overrides.

GRAND AND GLORIOUS SENSATIONS

Bolero's first ocean race, the 635-mile slog across the Gulf Stream from Newport to Bermuda in 1950, had little damage, but more than its share of excitement. As the wind gusted up to 40 knots, and the water flowed knee-deep across the deck, *Bolero* charged along at 10 knots under the double-hernia jib and full mainsail. (According to Dick Goennel, in the six years he raced on the boat, the mainsail was never reefed, even in a hard blow. *Bolero* was unusually stable, the main halyard winch difficult to operate, and the crew worried about blowing out the sail.)

Discomfort turned to fear when a wire jib sheet caught one of the professional sailors, a Norwegian named Arvid Arnheim, behind the knees and tossed him over the rail. Arnheim succeeded in grabbing the sheet, which flogged him about violently as Olin Stephens, at the wheel, luffed into the wind to stop *Bolero* and Corny Shields reached out, grabbed him, and hauled him aboard, his head bleeding profusely. Arnheim slumped on deck, muttering, "Ay taut ay vas gone."

(Above and left) With her heavy gear, this powerful boat was always physically demanding. When the wind and sea came up (as here in the Gulf Stream), she could even be dangerous. (NORRIS HOYT PHOTOS)

Bolero ended up first to finish in 75 hours, 32 minutes, beating *Baruna* by four hours and placing second on corrected time in the 54-boat fleet, only an hour behind a 57-foot Sparkman & Stephens yawl, *Argyll*. The main story out of Bermuda, however, was Arvid Arnheim's close call. Other owners have hushed up such accidents out of concern for their reputations, ordering their crews to stay tightlipped. Once *Bolero* reached Bermuda, however, Anne Brown told the story to reporters, while John, whose youthful notoriety had made him painfully suspicious of journalists, granted interviews.

"Big-Time Stuff"

As grueling as these long races were, there were compensations. One was success. Under the Browns, *Bolero* competed in five Bermuda or Annapolis races plus six shorter overnight races –11 races in all totaling some 2,500 miles. She was first to finish seven times and second to finish twice. On corrected time she had four wins and two seconds. The many elapsed-time wins are not all that surprising for a boat her size (although she did have the fast, well-sailed *Baruna* to deal with for three years). But because big boats are harder to sail to optimum performance than smaller boats, it is unusual for a maxi to do that well on handicaps.

If the hard work that went into achieving this record was not widely known, it was due to John Nicholas Brown's habitual modesty and grace. Any praise that came his way was waved aside with a good word for the designer and builder. "It's a boat one can be proud of," he said after almost winning the 1950 Bermuda Race.

Not one to take all the credit for Bolero's successes, John Nicholas Brown shares some silverware with Norris Hoyt after the 1952 Bermuda Race. Hoyt kept up a regular account of Bolero's doings in his photographs taken during the big races. (NORIS HOYT PHOTO)

"She sails herself." Sometimes he would add a word or two about the importance of luck in ocean racing; no lottery, he said, was as big as the Bermuda Race, with the fast-moving currents of the Gulf Stream meandering across the course. Yet it is striking how in ocean racing, somehow or other the same well-prepared, well-sailed boats seem to be lucky, time after time.

One reward for the crews' hard labors was the Browns' first-class hospitality, with an excellent cook and well-provisioned larder. As Dick Goennel recalled, "We had pretty fancy food." Once, however, the high living was self-defeating. As *Baruna* trailed her great rival, Stillman Taylor did his best to follow in *Bolero*'s track so the two boats would sail in the same wind. Losing sight of *Bolero*, he was getting a little desperate when a trail of green suddenly appeared on the water, heading off in a new direction. On further inspection, the green substance was identified as leaves from artichokes. Realizing that only one boat maintained such high culinary standards in the middle of an ocean race, Taylor altered course and continued the stern chase.

"When I told friends what boat I was racing, they always thought that it was big-time stuff," Goennel said. One of the finest tributes came from Henry Taylor after the 1950 Bermuda Race. Leaving *Baruna* in the hands of his sons, he had gone off on a long fishing trip and returned to learn that *Bolero* had been first to finish. While he may have been disappointed, he surely was not peevish, having been first to finish the race three times in his own boat. Taylor sent Brown this generously worded telegram: "Ain't it a grand and glorious sensation to cross the finish line first and get the wonderful welcome which they give you off St. David's Head, and then to be anchored alone in your glory in Hamilton Harbor?"

The message's value lay in the fact that it was so informal and private. Neither man would have said such a thing in public because it might seem like bragging, but between two friendly competitors, it carried special importance.

Models

Much of *Bolero*'s intricacy is revealed in Joseph Appleton's scale model of *Bolero*, completed in 1951. In the cockpit are exact miniatures of winch handles and engine controls. The deckhouse hatch can be pulled back to reveal ash trays, binoculars, a radio, and a bunk with the sheet perfectly turned down. Each block, with its own spinning sheave, is a miniature of the one that Rod Stephens had chosen specifically for the job from the inventory of fittings available from Nevins and hardware suppliers.

Appleton half-complained about such customizing. "The Stephens brothers in particular," he told Anne Brown, "seem to take delight in using practically everything in Merriman's catalogue and then some that perhaps Nevins has thought up." Appleton built models the same way good boatbuilders constructed yachts, laying them up plank by plank and employing joinerwork on the details. It took him a year and a half to make the miniature *Bolero*, almost three times longer than it took to build the original. The model is now on display in Harbour Court, the former Brown home and the New York Yacht Club's Newport clubhouse.

Appleton's was only one of several models built of *Bolero*, but in some ways the most interesting was a sailing scale model made by Albert Lemos, a Rhode Island shipwright who had come over from the Cape Verde Islands in a trading schooner and, though illiterate, could read plans well enough to build some handsome boats. Two of them were scale models of *Bolero* and the Sparkman & Stephens, Nevins-built Twelve-Meter *Vim*, each about 20 feet long, which Lemos would sail in Newport Harbor.

Besides the beautiful Appleton scale model now in the New York Yacht Club's Harbour Court clubhouse (top), a 20-foot sailing model of *Bolero* was made by a Rhode Island boatbuilder, Albert Lemos. (TOP COURTESY NEW YORK YACHT CLUB; BOTTOM NORRIS HOYT PHOTO)

GRAND AND GLORIOUS SENSATIONS

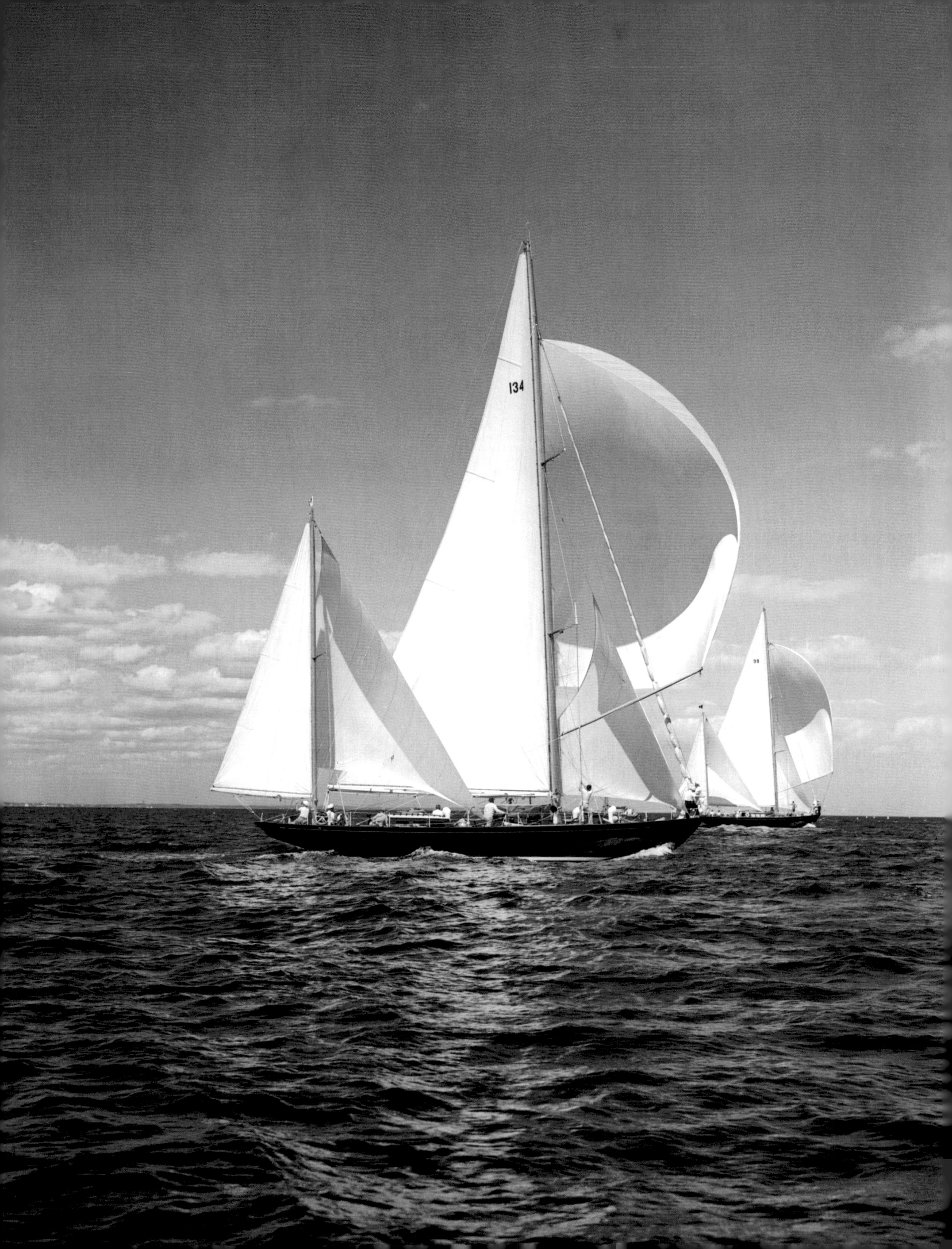
134

Henry Taylor's family and their friends, many of them from Cold Spring Harbor, New York, put together a remarkable record in *Baruna*, with two Bermuda Race overall victories and, in one of the closest races in history, a win in the 1951 Annapolis Race. The difference in the deckhouse arrangements is obvious here. Another difference was that while *Bolero* had two powerful pedestal (or coffee grinder) winches for quick sail handling in a fresh breeze, *Baruna* had just one, under the mizzen boom. (© MYSTIC SEAPORT, ROSENFELD COLLECTION)

Competition among the big boats was close, but none was tighter than that between *Bolero* and *Baruna*, here leading her newer near-sister by a typically small margin. *Bolero* was usually a little faster when sailing upwind and in strong breezes, *Baruna* when off the wind and in light breezes. After they raced almost bow-to-bow for four years between 1949 and 1952, *Barun*a went west to San Francisco, only to be have their duel renewed there. (© MYSTIC SEAPORT, ROSENFELD COLLECTION)

"There Never was Such a Race."

Although *Bolero* was newer, bigger, and had greater stability due to her lighter metal masts, she and *Baruna* were evenly matched, with the new boat usually enjoying a slight edge when the wind came up, both on the East Coast and later in San Francisco Bay. Anne Brown calculated that before *Baruna* went west at the end of 1952, the two boats raced each other 20 times, and the results lay in *Bolero*'s favor. In those 20 races, she beat *Baruna* to the finish line 13 times, and won on handicap 12 times. Anne was the first to admit that winning was never easy. "She could sail with us boat for boat and would pass us if we relaxed for a single instant. I can truthfully say that at no time during those four years did *Bolero* engage *Baruna* with any certainty of victory."

Such was the case in one of the closest and most famous races in yachting history. Racing 466 miles over three and a half days from Newport to Annapolis, Maryland, in 1951, *Bolero* and *Baruna* were within sight of each other almost continuously and often were overlapped. "It was as close as a little day race on Long Island Sound," Dick Goennel looked back. (The race was a journalist's dream; newspapers across the country followed it closely, running photographs taken from spotter planes and chase boats.) Although the light conditions favored *Baruna*, *Bolero* led narrowly almost throughout the race. She could not get away when *Baruna* ripped her mainsail soon after the start and had it down for several hours for sewing. When Corny Shields spotted a school of porpoises, altered course, and, just as he predicted, found a northeast wind, even that did not pry *Bolero* into a big lead. In conditions so mild that one of the sailors said the race was "just a pleasant early summer cruise," the boats sailed along as though tethered by a rubber band, *Bolero* pulling slowly away in daylight and *Baruna* gaining in the dark, when Stillman Taylor had a knack for clever tactics.

The flavor of the terrific duel comes across vividly in the two crews' log entries on the two boats raced, miles ahead of the rest of the fleet, often only yards away from each other.

The 1951 Annapolis Race Duel

(The times are in the 24-hour clock)

DAY 1, JUNE 17
BARUNA: "1900, *Bolero* is the only boat near us, 2 miles to windward."

DAY 2, JUNE 18
BARUNA: "1830, *Bolero* 5-6 miles ahead and slightly to leeward – no other boats in sight!"

DAY 3, JUNE 19
BARUNA: "0500, Gained 2 miles in night."
BOLERO: "1400, We are slowly dropping *Baruna*, but she is somewhat to leeward."
BOLERO: "1930, *Baruna* dead astern – gaining."
BOLERO: "2330, *Baruna* – astern & much closer. Fine night. Moon."

DAY 4, JUNE 20
BARUNA: "0030, Every night we have gained on *Bolero*, but this is the payoff."
BOLERO: "0515, *Baruna* passes close aboard to starboard."
BARUNA: "0737, Rounded Chesapeake Lightship behind but overlapped on the *Bolero*. We are the 1st boats around. Have come 228 miles and have only lost sight of the *Bolero* at night. Could observe her by moonlight most of last night."

Turning the lightship side by side at the mouth of the Chesapeake Bay, they headed north for the finish 180 miles ahead. *Baruna* slowly took the lead for the first time, but lost it when her cotton spinnaker came apart. She fell back and set a new spinnaker, but as often happens the wind filled in from behind and *Baruna* brought up a better breeze and came even again.

DAY 4, JUNE 20
BOLERO: "1016, *Baruna* abeam to leeward. She comes up astern, reaching."
BOLERO: "1300, Reaching, still with our spinnaker. *Baruna* close astern."
BOLERO: "2251, *Baruna* quite close, to windward."

(Top to bottom) *Bolero* won the start of the 1951 Newport-Annapolis Race and was inching away when *Baruna*'s mainsail ripped. While her crew sewed away, the newer boat pulled farther ahead to a lead of almost six miles. Then *Baruna* began to gain, and they rounded the Chesapeake Bay lightship overlapped. (NORRIS HOYT PHOTOS)

GRAND AND GLORIOUS SENSATIONS

With Nick Brown trimming *Bolero*'s spinnaker in an erratic, light southerly breeze, the two crews jibed and jibed again to find puffs or a tactical advantage. They were sailing so close that the skippers kept up a running dialogue across the water about the racing rules. Stillman Taylor recalled, "At this point, none of us on the boat had had any sleep for at least 36 hours, the race had been so exciting. Every time I would go below I'd hear Bus Hovey, who was the mate on the other watch, say, 'We're gaining a little on her,' or, 'She's gaining on us,' and I'd have to get up and see what was going on."

DAY 5, JUNE 21

BARUNA: "0045, Abeam Sharps Island 20 miles from finish – *Bolero* finally passed us."

BOLERO: "0130, *Baruna* close aboard lee quarter – running slightly by lee."

BOLERO: "0230, *Baruna* close on our lee beam."

In the predawn hours of the year's longest day, everybody was on their toes. In *Bolero* only Doc Davidson was below, in the navigator's station in the deckhouse studying the chart, tide tables, and depth sounder. A quarter mile from the finish, both boats were on starboard tack, steering just east of the line. Although *Bolero* was just ahead, *Baruna* held the advantage because she was slightly overlapped to leeward, and the rules barred *Bolero* from jibing onto the port tack toward the finish and forcing *Baruna* to give way. Using a classic tactic, Taylor would try to sail on until both boats were beyond the finish line, then jibe and reach fast back to the buoy with *Bolero* trailing in his wake. But perhaps due to exhaustion, Taylor underestimated the speed of the strong head current and jibed early. As the frustrated *Baruna* ran slowly to the finish, *Bolero* was free to go for the line at her own pleasure.

BOLERO: "0401, Finish 04-01-17."

BARUNA: "Finish 24 seconds after *Bolero* after spinnaker duel and jibe. Most thrilling race ever."

Bolero got the gun at Annapolis, yet the slightly smaller *Baruna* won the race on corrected time. The last word came from John Nicholas Brown: "It left me so groggy that I hardly know what day it is. There never was such a race."

Baruna constantly attacked from astern before *Bolero* finally eked out a paper-thin victory, though her rival won on handicap. John Nicholas Brown was left wondering if *Bolero* would ever be a bride on a long-distance race. (NORRIS HOYT PHOTOS)

GRAND AND GLORIOUS SENSATIONS | 111

The end of the "always a bridesmaid, never a bride" streak finally came in 1953, when (with *Baruna* 3,000 miles away in San Francisco) *Bolero* finished first on both corrected and elapsed time in the Annapolis Race. At the awards ceremony, the crew suitably recognized the occasion by marching in to the strains of Mendelssohn's "Wedding March" and presenting John Nicholas Brown with a wedding veil, which Anne Brown proceeded to place on the head of her beaming husband, his arms spread in triumph.

"The *Bolero* Feeling"

The 1951 Newport-Annapolis race was sailed in light winds – conditions in which *Bolero* can seem as bored as Marilyn Monroe at a PTA meeting. Give her wind and the hull pulses with energy and a warm glow surrounds the helmsman. Remarkably for a boat so heavy, *Bolero* almost steers herself. In a fresh wind, when most boats pull like a pit bull on a leash, if *Bolero* is trimmed just right she feels like a feather and tracks like a plow. Walter H. Wheeler III, a Connecticut sailor, steered her during a windy distance race in the 1960s: "Early one morning on Block Island Sound I had the boat all to myself. She had a very light weather helm, so light I could almost take my hand off the wheel. She was also very sensitive and responsive to sail trim. Not all boats are equally so."

When racing in *Bolero* in several Classic Yacht regattas in 2004, we discovered that when sailing close-hauled or on a reach, the crucial sail was the tiny mizzen, aft of the steering wheel. No matter how well the big mainsail and jib were trimmed, if the mizzen sheet was too tight, the speed flattened and the helm stiffened. When we eased the mizzen sheet two or three inches, the speed invariably leapt half a knot. That is true even when the leeward deck is knee-deep in water, which is often the case in a rough sea. As Dick Goennel remembered, "*Bolero* was a *wet* boat. She would lay over quickly and put her bow into it and throw a lot of water." He paused and a big smile spread across his face. "But that was because we were going so *fast*."

When running before a fresh breeze, *Bolero*'s narrow hull quickly finds and surges beyond her theoretical maximum speed, as the adrenalin (boosted by a little anxiety) pumps through the watch on deck. Someone who sailed in these conditions in a race in the 1960s, when the speedometer was pegged at its maximum reading of 12 knots, reported: "A loud, ear-splitting scream let loose from our excited crew. This 1949-vintage boat was alive, straining to go even faster. Backstays, sheets, and guys were like rod steel. . . . There were three boats ahead of us after passing the buoy, and within half an hour we were leading the pack."

In one of the last serious races under the Browns' ownership, in August 1954, there was 30-knot blow for the New York Yacht Club's annual Astor Cup race. Over a course of 20 miles, *Bolero* was first to finish by over 20 minutes and won easily on corrected time. As the yachting journalist Everett Morris observed, the

"*Bolero* was a wet boat," Dick Goennel said. "But that was because we were going so fast." Too powerful and heavy to rise over waves, she rolled right through them, throwing water everywhere as the crew scrambled in search of the elusive dry spot. When she raced offshore, the pretty lapstrake dinghy was turned bottom up so there was less windage, and no place for water to settle. (NORRIS HOYT PHOTO)

On this cruising day during her first season, *Bolero* contentedly snores along on an easy reach. Carter Brown coils lines aft, his father steers, his mother trims the mainsheet, and another shipmate sprawls comfortably in the dinghy's shadow. All is content. Everybody is experiencing what John Nicholas Brown called, "the greatest of all sensations." (© MYSTIC SEAPORT, ROSENFELD COLLECTION)

conditions "were made to order for big, powerful boats, and *Bolero* is all of that and more, too."

The memory of such thrills remained with anybody who sailed in *Bolero*, but no more profoundly than with the man who first owned her. Years later, long after he had moved on to smaller 40- to 50-foot cruising boats that he and Anne could handle without a big crew, Brown wrote his old shipmate Olin Stephens to ask for advice about his next acquisition. He told Stephens he wanted a comfortable boat, but there was an overriding condition: The boat must not be slow or sluggish. "What I am looking for," he insisted, "is the greatest of all sensations, namely, the *Bolero* feeling under sail."

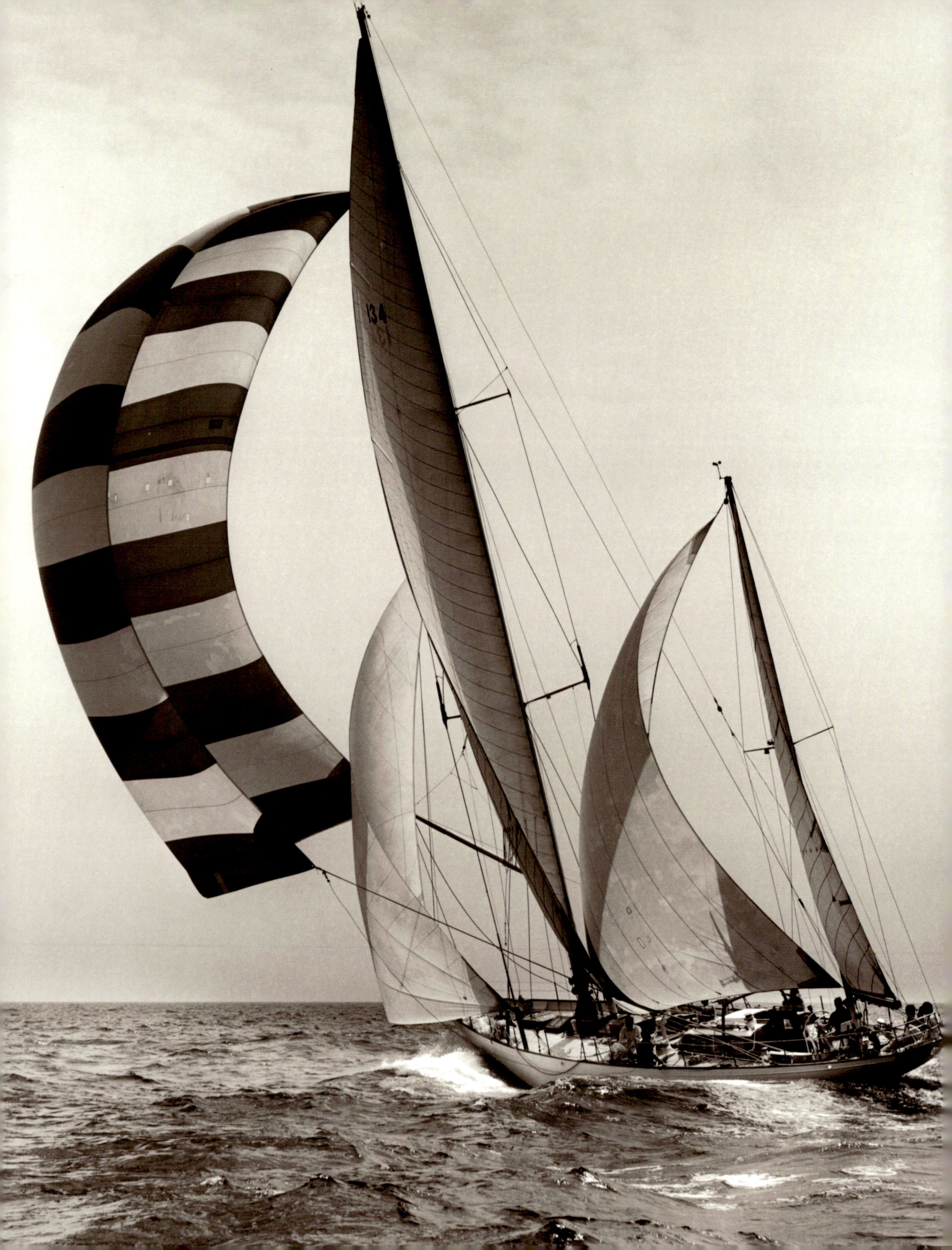
134

"The kids today… will never know what it was like to see the two great yawls overlapped at a weather mark with one captain doffing his cap to the other." ~ Robert C. Keefe

8 The Queen, Four Owners, and Ted Turner

After the Browns sold her in 1955, *Bolero* (painted a more easily maintained white) became the sailing queen first of Sweden, then of San Francisco, and finally of Long Island Sound. (© MYSTIC SEAPORT, ROSENFELD COLLECTION)

"Last Sail, Newport to Fairhaven." As *Bolero* was being delivered to her winter home in southern Massachusetts on October, 24, 1954, the log entry had a double meaning. Everybody knew it was the last sail both for the year and for the Brown ownership. John Nicholas Brown's six years as a New York Yacht Club commodore were almost over, his health (never robust) was uneven, and with her large professional crew and insatiable thirst for varnish, paint, and new sails, the price of maintaining the boat to the expected high standard was large enough to concern even a Rhode Island Brown. Years later, when his son Nick was tempted to buy *Bolero* and return her to her former luster, he suppressed the impulse by reminding himself of the obligation that comes with owning an icon. *Bolero*, he said, "would have so ruled my life, as it did my father's life." In any case, the Browns had other things on their expansive plates. John was an Overseer at Harvard and was chairing an important committee reforming the college's programs in the fine arts. Anne was busy with military history. Carter was training as an art historian; he would become director of the National Gallery of Art in Washington and one of the country's cultural leaders. Nick, a Naval Academy graduate, was starting a successful naval career; after retiring, he would head the National Aquarium at Baltimore. Angela was developing as a concert pianist.

With not much of a market for such a demanding yacht, *Bolero* sat in her cradle for over a year. Among the people who expressed interest in her was Carleton Mitchell, a gifted sailor, photographer, and writer who had often raced against the Browns in his yawl *Caribbee*. Ready to move on, Mitchell juggled two possibilities – build a new yawl or acquire the well-tested *Bolero*. He recalled, "I was thinking that instead of building a new boat, I'd buy *Bolero* and race it everywhere with my regular crew. I thought it would be a wonderful thing to race *Bolero* until your money ran out." In the end, he opted for a new boat and had Sparkman & Stephens design him a beamy 38-foot yawl called *Finisterre*, which put together one of the very finest records in ocean racing history, including winning three straight Bermuda Races.

With the navy escort standing by and worried about reefs, Sven Salen steers *Bolero* to the finish of the 1956 Bermuda Race, the first stage of her voyage to Sweden. (NORRIS HOYT PHOTO)

When Brown encountered the respected Swedish yachtsman Sven Salen and proposed he buy *Bolero*, Salen protested that she was too expensive. Brown replied (as Salen recalled), "How can you know before you have asked the price?" They settled on $100,000. After the deal closed in December, 1956, Brown sent one of his generous messages in a telegram to Stockholm: "Seasons warmest greetings from your *Bolero*, Brown."

News of the sale was received like the obituary of a movie star. *Time* magazine mourned the loss of "the trim queen of modern U.S. racing yachts," and the customs official who handled her paperwork told Brown, "I am sorry to see the famous *Bolero* go. She certainly was in a class by herself." The separation was a hard one for Brown. "He missed *Bolero*," said Dick Goennel, who saw him frequently. "He missed her hugeness and her glamour. He missed those times when people were always circling around her with their cameras." After years of politely declining invitations by later owners to return aboard, one day in the early 1960s Brown paid a visit only to discover that she was not being kept up to his standards. Later that day, Goennel saw John Nicholas Brown in tears. From 1956 until 1970, four owners – two men and two women – raced and cruised in *Bolero* far and wide in the Atlantic, the Pacific, and the Caribbean. The first was Sven Salen. The head of an international shipping line, he was one of Sweden's most successful racing sailors (he had often raced against the Stephens brothers and Corny Shields) and was credited with developing the modern, overlapping genoa jib for sailing to windward by flattening a reaching balloon jib. (The name "genoa" came from the Italian town off which Salen first set the sail in the late 1920s. Henry Nevins, who was working on the same idea, might have called it the "City Island jib.") A former vice commodore of the Royal Swedish Yacht Club, Salen had headed his country's national sailing federation and played an important role in the development of the Folkboat, one of Scandinavia's most popular sailing classes.

As the first leg of the transatlantic delivery to her new home, Salen entered *Bolero* in the 1956 Newport-Bermuda Race with a Swedish-American crew that included Olin Stephens, Ken Davidson, Fred Lawton, and Dick Goennel. The latest Sparkman & Stephens maxi-boat, *Venturer*, sailing her first race, held the lead until less than 25 miles from the finish, when a gale blew in and her crew made some sail-selection and navigational mistakes. *Bolero*, meanwhile, was wrestling with her own troubles. Two jibs blew out; the main halyard winch slipped twice, letting the sail down a few feet; and – most frighteningly – the turnbuckle on the headstay broke. Losing a headstay will take the mast out of most boats, but *Bolero*'s welded spar held up until a new stay was jury-rigged from wire jib halyards.

> "Nobody was hurt, but flying bronze fragments got everybody's attention along with an accelerated heart beat."

Her headstay gone but the rig still standing, *Bolero* smashes through a big one near the finish at St. David's Head to set a new elapsed time record. (BERMUDA NEWS BUREAU, COURTESY RICHARD GOENNEL)

Bursting out of the rain squalls at almost 11 knots, *Bolero* skirted Bermuda's dangerous reefs so closely that a skittish nearby navy crew fired warning flares and signaled, "You are standing into danger." *Bolero* was first to finish, beating *Venturer* by 75 minutes. Her elapsed time of 70 hours, 11 minutes, 37 seconds broke the 27-year-old record by one hour, 24 minutes. (The record held for 18 years until the 79-foot ketch *Ondine* broke it by two hours, 19 minutes in 1974.)

After collecting their prize, the Swedes sailed *Bolero* across the Atlantic to her new home, where she cruised and raced for three summers, winning several important trophies and many friends. After three years in Scandinavia, Salen decided she was too big for easy handling in the narrow channels of the Baltic islands and put her up for sale.

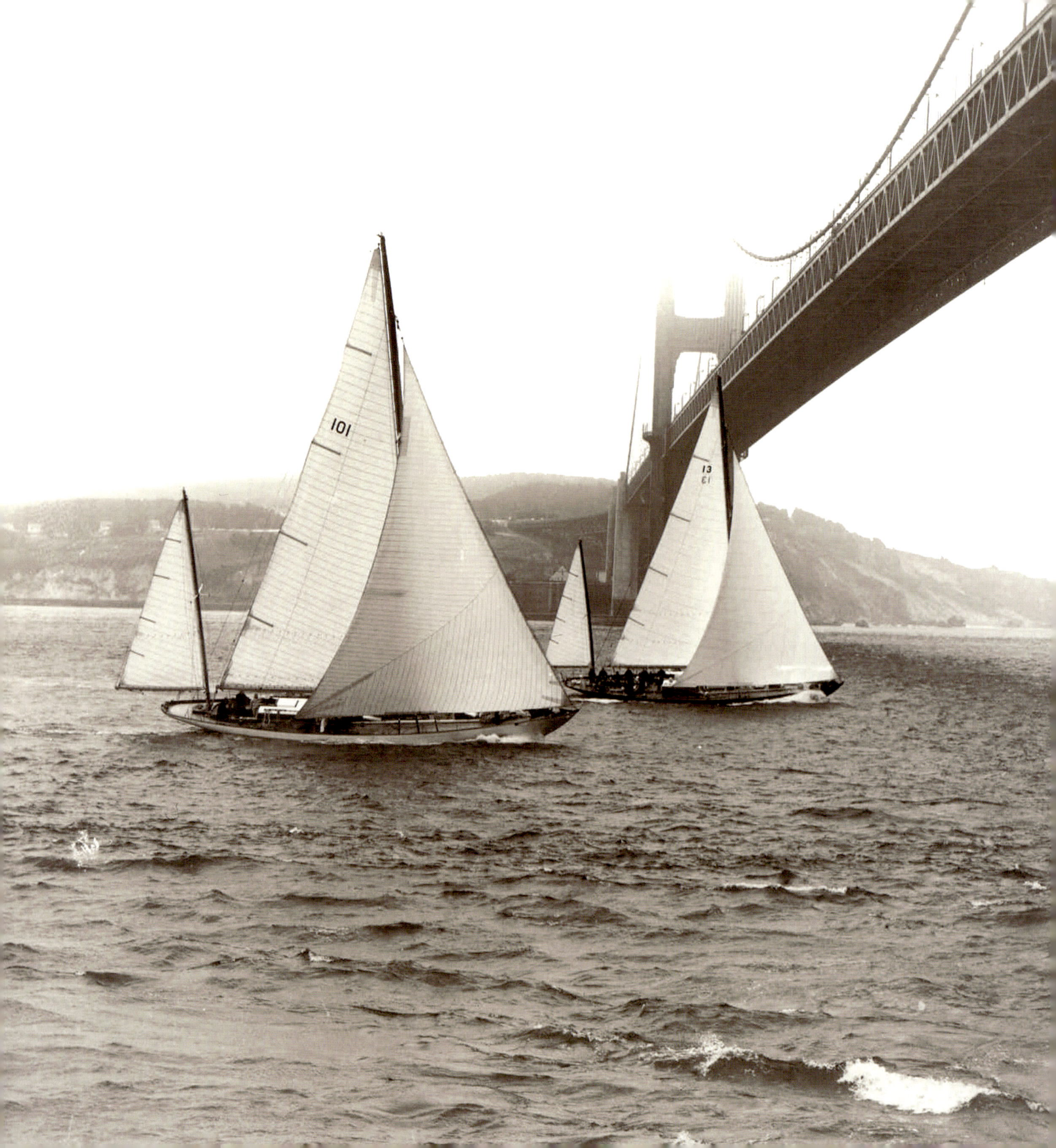
101
13

Denny Jordan plays the drums with his usual brio during the first St. Francis Yacht Club stag cruise in 1958. (COURTESY ST. FRANCIS YACHT CLUB ARCHIVES)

A familiar sight on San Francisco Bay in the early 1960s was the two Bs—*Bolero* (left) and *Baruna*—matching up in the Golden Gate in the renewal of their old competition. Their sail numbers have changed; in those days, owners could choose their own numbers. (COURTESY ST. FRANCIS YACHT CLUB)

The Queen of the Bay

Interest in *Bolero* instantly sprang up in San Francisco, which had been a center for westward-migrating Sparkman & Stephens boats since the Stephens family sold their *Dorade* there in 1935. In her crew when she won the 1936 race to Honolulu was a 17-year-old named James Michael, whose mother later gave him *Dorade* as a 21st birthday present. After Michael bought *Baruna* from Henry Taylor in 1953, she became so well known, Michael would say, that even San Francisco taxi drivers recognized her name. When Michael persuaded his old friend Dennis Jordan, commodore of the St. Francis Yacht Club, to buy *Bolero*, bring her out to San Francisco Bay, and resume the great rivalry, she became the flagship of one of the world's great yacht clubs for the second time in six years.

In the first race for the title of Queen of the Bay, on April 10, 1960, *Baruna* and *Bolero* (her formerly black topsides now painted a more easily maintained white) sailed in a typical hard westerly. When *Bolero*'s mainsail – no reef as usual – first filled, the boat went over so far that the leeward deck was submerged. A crew member that day, Bob Keefe, recalled, "I stood in the lee of the mast and watched her life lines disappear into white foam. Pete Sutter was down there doing something and immediately was swept aft about 25 feet, bouncing along each stanchion before he fetched up on one of the coffee grinder winches." When the jib was set, the sheet block blew up. "Nobody was hurt, but flying bronze fragments got everybody's attention along with an accelerated heart beat."

With thousands of spectators looking on from the cityfront, *Baruna* inched ahead through the square sea and rounded the first turning mark with a 25-second lead. Although the breeze was then whistling at over 40 knots through the Golden Gate, both crews set spinnakers on the run before the wind to a buoy east of Alcatraz Island *Bolero*'s tiny cotton sail quickly blew to shreds, and while the crew of 15 was setting another spinnaker, *Baruna* lurched out of control, broached, and lay on her side, dead in the water with her spinnaker streaming its full length from her mast. In the 20 minutes it took to get *Baruna* back in order, *Bolero* opened up an insurmountable lead.

Physically imposing, fiercely combative, and extremely colorful, Denny Jordan once explained why a boat sank under him by saying, "We were going so fast we just caught on fire." Like the Browns he was a fan of flashy colors, though his preference ran to red, white, and blue. His lifelong friend and rival Jim Michael was another St. Francis Yacht Club commodore who for years was the West Coast's representative in yachting's national establishment, where he headed the North American Yacht Racing Union and the Cruising Club of America, and served on the New York Yacht Club's America's Cup Committee. A lawyer, Michael also was a skilled machinist, and in this second role he made the *Bolero-Baruna* rivalry important for all of sailing. When their original winches proved underpowered and fragile – "egg-shelling" was an apt metaphor for the tendency of their drums to crack – Michael and Tim Moseley, the owner of the Sparkman & Stephens cutter *Orient* (ex-*Courante*), formed a company called Barient (a marriage of their boats' names) to develop the first strong, geared winches.

That was important, but what most excited San Franciscans was the high level of racing of their ever-increasing fleet of wooden classics from Olin Stephens's drawing board (and often from Henry Nevins's yard). "From 1955 to 1970 the best big-boat racing in the world was right here on San Francisco Bay," Bob Keefe claimed with only a little exaggeration. "Of course it was *Baruna* vs. *Bolero*, but it was also Jim Michael vs. his boyhood friend Dennis Jordan, two St. Francis Yacht Club commodores having after each other on Saturday afternoon right after lunch around the round table in the club's grill room. God, it was great. . . . I never remember a time when Michael and Jordan were not at the wheels of their respective yachts. And they were pretty damned good at what they did." They sailed with a flare that John Nicholas Brown would have admired, going out no matter what the weather and tipping their caps to each other when the boats passed at marks. *Bolero* generally had the edge, especially in a hard blow.

"Big, Bountiful, and Beauteous"

In 1962 Jordan sold *Bolero* to Southern California. *Baruna* remained in San Francisco; the two great yawls never raced each other again. Under Sally Blair Ames, a transplanted New Englander who was the boat's fourth owner, *Bolero* undertook

Bolero's most intensive period of ocean racing came in 1962-63 when she was owned by Sally Ames Langmuir, seen here with the crew before the boat's only transatlantic race (and a memorable encounter with whales). Arnie Schmelling is over the owner's left shoulder. At the far left is Peter Bowker and, behind him, at a safe distance from the ship's mascot, is Tom Hovey. (© MYSTIC SEAPORT, ROSENFELD COLLECTION)

the longest and most intense period of racing in her history. Over almost a year and a half, she covered some 15,000 miles in the Pacific, the Caribbean, and the Atlantic. Like John Nicholas Brown, Sally Ames was a wealthy New Englander with a saltwater heritage who had lost a father early. Frederick Lothrup Ames was the heir of a fortune derived from manufacturing shovels. While still a Harvard student, he raced a boat to Bermuda, and in 1927 he sailed a schooner from England to Newport via Iceland and Labrador and was awarded the Cruising Club of America's Blue Water Medal "for meritorious seamanship and adventure upon the sea." Taking up aviation, in 1928 Ames was in Mexico during a flying tour of North America when he met and promptly married a French-born singer, Maurice Mosette. She sailed with him and in 1930 became only the third woman to race to Bermuda. In 1932 Ames was killed when his plane crashed. Maurice Ames resumed her singing career, and with her daughter Sally ended up in Beverly Hills.

Although Sally did some summer sailing, she did not become serious about the sport until her 20s when she acquired a 75-foot Alden schooner, *Constellation*. In 1959, with a crew of 15 and a pet macaw named Felipe Segundo, *Constellation* won the big-boat class in the 2,225-mile Transpac Race from San Pedro to Hawaii. Sally Ames took the boat to Europe for a year of cruising and racing before returning to California and eventually purchasing *Bolero* for a reported $165,000.

Southern Californians were then used to big schooners, but not to a boat like *Bolero*. "A very impressive, massively large machine" was how she was remembered

THE QUEEN, FOUR OWNERS, AND TED TURNER | 121

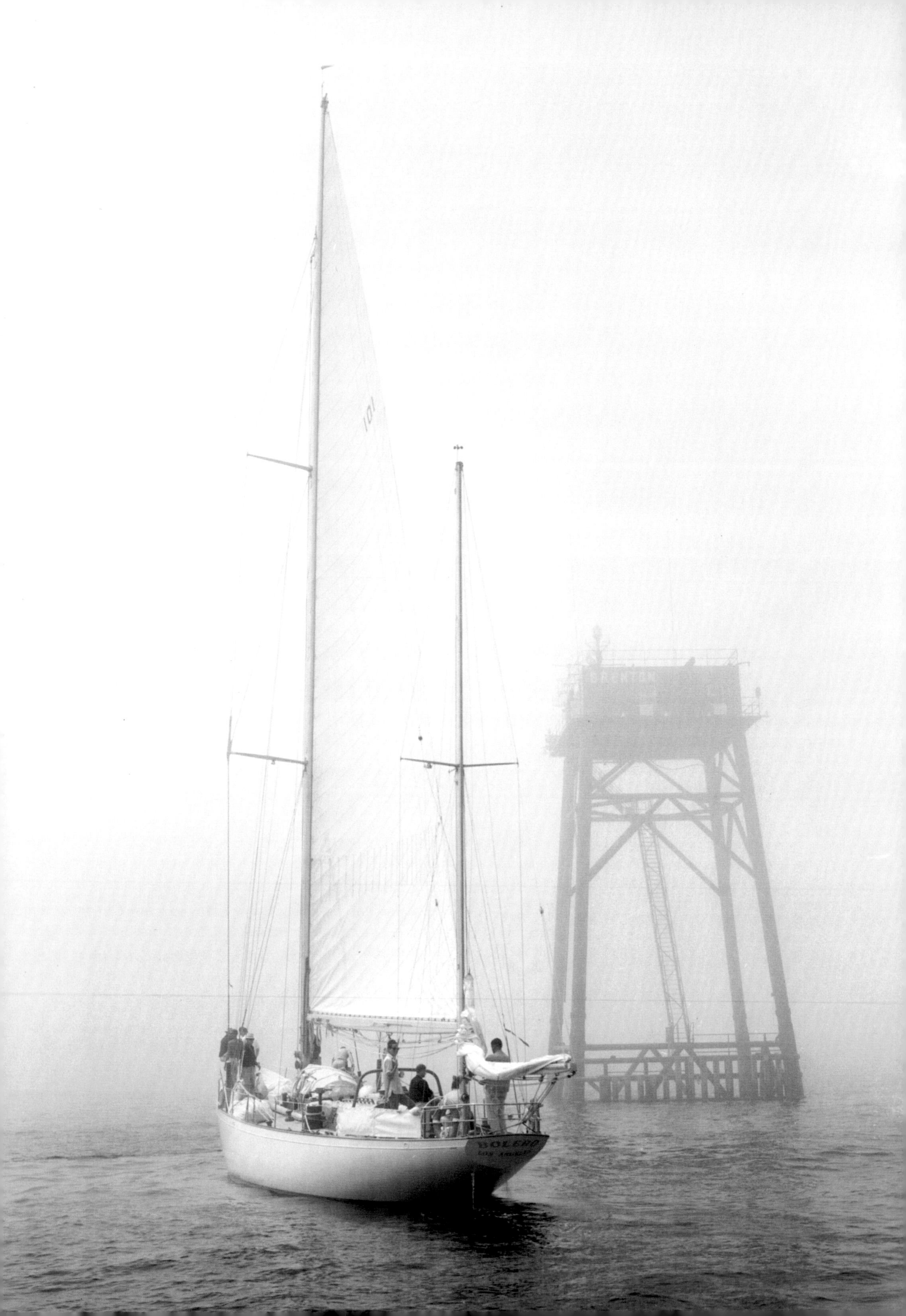
101
BOLERO

> "We were surfing down waves and several broke over the stern and filled the cockpit."

The old Brenton Reef tower peeks out of the fog as *Bolero* awaits the start of the eventful race to England in which she had "coming apart problems." Her sail number, 101, has been inherited from Denny Jordan. Despite almost 15 years of hard racing, her sheerline has not lost its original sweet curve.
(© MYSTIC SEAPORT, ROSENFELD COLLECTION)

by a former young catamaran sailor named Steve Dashew, whose family had once owned *Constellation*. *Bolero*'s navigator, Ray Wallace, went one better on the 1962 race down the coast of Baja California to Mazatlan, Mexico. Every time he signed onto the radio for morning roll call, Wallace exuberantly announced that he was calling in from *"big, bountiful, and beauteous Bolero."*

Bolero frequently matched up against a Philip Rhodes-designed 72-foot yawl, *Escapade*, owned by Baldwin M. Baldwin. In short races, in the 1,400-mile race to Mexico, and later in the 1963 Southern Ocean Racing Conference races off Florida, the two big boats usually were bow to bow. Racing more than 400 miles from St. Petersburg to Ft. Lauderdale, "as close as two prams in a swimming pool" (as a boating writer put it), *Escapade* nipped *Bolero* at the finish by just 90 seconds. *Bolero* turned the tables to win the race from Miami to Nassau by a mile (and take the overall prize as well), and then beat *Escapade* to Montego Bay, Jamaica, by eight hours. At that, Baldwin went back to California, sold *Escapade*, and bought *Bolero*'s near-sister, the former *Venturer*, which he renamed *Audacious*.

As *Bolero* was flexing her muscles on the racing circuit, a sailor wrote of her owner that "Her charm and joy of living have stimulated the racing scene even in Florida, where the unusual is often accepted as commonplace." Unusual Sally Ames Langmuir (who had married) certainly was. Tall, vivacious, and part-Yankee, part-Californian, she was one of very few women who raced in big boats, much less owned one that was so successful. Acknowledging that she did not know enough to take charge, she recruited a capable crew headed by a footloose Englishman and former airplane ticket agent named Peter Bowker, who went on to a long, distinguished career as an ocean racing navigator. One of the regular crew was Arnie Schmeling, a California policeman and a nephew of the German boxer Max Schmeling, who had beaten Joe Louis for the world heavyweight championship and later was the trainer for Dennis Conner's America's Cup crews. A nagging problem was the owner's affection for animals. When the ship's cat got underfoot and shed hair, some sailors threatened to throw it overboard, though Sally seemed most upset by Bowker's tactic of ignoring the animal. Yet the crew could not have been that unhappy; when a cousin of Sally's, Oliver Ames, visited *Bolero*, he found the crew humming the tune by Maurice Ravel that carried the same name as the boat.

After the Montego Bay Race, *Bolero* went up to Annapolis and raced from there to Newport on the familiar but now reversed course. In the end of June 1963, she drifted across a fogbound starting line ahead of 13 other boats headed toward England's Eddystone Light, 2,800 miles to the east. The transatlantic race – her fifth ocean race in seven months – offered some unusual activities. A curious big ship altered course to take a look and came so close that her steep wake left *Bolero*

In the sixties *Bolero* regularly and successfully raced under a young crew from Connecticut. Here, in 1967, she races off Block Island under her striped nylon light sails. (© MYSTIC SEAPORT, ROSENFELD COLLECTION)

rolling wildly and her spinnaker wrapped around the headstay. On another unlucky day, *Bolero* was approaching the geographical location marking the southern limit of ice when some of the crew thought they heard bergs coming at them. "We were all positioned around the boat staring into the fog when I saw a whale surface off the starboard quarter," one of them, Tom Hovey, recalled. "It made a growling sound as it surfaced, and then a mate appeared. They were swimming parallel to us and submerged." The next thing they knew, scratching sounds emanated from the keel. "The whole boat shuddered and then they were gone."

After the flirtation with the whales came a series of gear failures. "We tore every jib and spinnaker on the boat as well as the main," said Hovey. "We had a sewing machine and someone who knew how to use it, thank goodness." One night as *Bolero* ran fast under a tiny storm spinnaker in towering following seas, Hovey was left all alone in the cockpit taking his trick at the helm, with the rest of his watch dry and warm in the deckhouse. "It blew harder and harder as the hour progressed and I yelled for someone to come up but they couldn't hear me. We were surfing down waves and several broke over the stern and filled the cockpit." He added wryly, "Luckily my watchmates had the doors bolted shut so they wouldn't get wet."

By the end of her 17-day, 17-hour race, *Bolero* had broken both spinnaker poles, blown out all her spinnakers, and had the main halyard jam and almost had the headstay pull off the mast. Despite what the American yachting writer Alfred F. Loomis called her "coming apart troubles," *Bolero* was first to finish and third on corrected time.

Her bad luck resumed during racing in England. One day while racing off the Isle of Wight, she ran aground on an uncharted obstruction that turned out to be a section of a Mulberry, a D-Day artificial harbor that had probably toppled off a barge carrying it across the English Channel to the invasion of Normandy in 1944. "We had managed to park our bow on a wall!" Bowker recalled with amazement. This wall chewed up the oak forefoot. *Bolero* was hauled, and the damaged area was cut away and replaced. Then, after the start of the Fastnet Race, the mainsail pulled the track off the upper part of the mainmast. In a wonderful bit of seamanship, Bowker turned a spare halyard into an improvised jackstay, or temporary stay, behind the mast, and hoisted the top of the mainsail on it.

Amid all this excitement there was one flaw: Sally Ames Langmuir was not very happy; Bowker would refer to her sympathetically as a classic "poor little rich girl." In late September 1963 she died suddenly, evidently due to an accidental overdose of sleeping pills. She is memorialized at Stonehill College's Sally Ames Fitness Center, on the site of the Ames family's estate in Massachusetts.

"The Boat Made Me a Hero"

Accounts by *Bolero*'s sailors on Long Island Sound tingle with the usual awe and excitement. Betty White raved after the 1965 Block Island Race about the "wonderful express train ride." Bob Smith (the artist-writer who memorably observed that anything that flapped on *Bolero* could be lethal) experienced the greatest of all sensations when he signed aboard for what he thought would be a long, overnight 100-mile race down Long Island Sound to Block Island. It turned out to be far faster, and far more thrilling as *Bolero* blasted along, "Throwing red spray to port and green spray to starboard (what a sight!)." Averaging more than 11 knots, she reached Block Island well before dawn – so early, in fact, that the finish line was not yet established for the good reason that no race official had even fantasized that any boat would arrive so early. *Bolero*'s crew recorded their time at the finish buoy and proceeded to take the rest of the day off while the remainder of the fleet dribbled in.

Of another race, a sailor taking his first ride in *Bolero* as her navigator, Dev Barker, remembered, "I had never sailed on a boat with her sort of speed. I predicted we were going to hit all the tides wrong, but we were going so fast and so far ahead of all of our estimated times of arrival that we hit everything perfectly. The boat made me a hero because she was just so darn fast."

THE QUEEN, FOUR OWNERS, AND TED TURNER | 125

"So There We Were"

The boat that many sailors were calling "the Queen" was sold again in the spring of 1964. Her fifth owner was Elizabeth Leahey White, from Darien, Connecticut, the widow of the man who developed the microfiche as a method for storing information. Like Sally Ames, she was an enthusiastic owner but more a passenger than a sailor. An amateur skipper named Ted De Boer gathered a crew of enthusiastic young men who called themselves "the River Rats" because most of them lived near the Three Mile River, in Darien and nearby Rowayton, and together they did well on various race courses.

From time to time Betty White chartered *Bolero* to crews to race to Bermuda or off Florida in the Southern Ocean Racing Conference. One charterer was Ted Turner. Still in his 20s and one of the sport's most successful skippers, the brash Georgian had been winning often in smaller boats before he chartered *Bolero* for the 1968 SORC. First, he had to get the boat to Florida through a brutal January cold snap. Recruiting a crew was a problem because, as he would say with characteristic glibness, "Anybody who knows enough to be of any use has too much sense to go." Once he had put his arm on six people, his second problem was getting *Bolero* clear of the ice pack surrounding Jakobson's shipyard in Oyster Bay, Long Island. For that he hired an icebreaker. Then he navigated Hell Gate and the East River into New York Harbor, and *Bolero* was back among ice again when a freighter came by and she followed it out to sea.

In five-degree temperatures and a hard northwest wind, *Bolero* flew down the coast and was just past Cape Hatteras when the wind came ahead into the southeast and blew up to 60 knots. Under bare poles, with the decks awash and leaking badly, with her engine stalled by dirty fuel, and with the crew pumping and bailing around the clock, *Bolero* drifted down toward Hatteras. "We were constantly under water now, even though we had all sail down," Turner told Bruce Kirby, the yacht designer and editor of a sailing magazine. "So there we were without sails, pumps, and power. We could have hoisted sail but we knew as soon as we did we would start taking on more water than we could handle with the buckets. During that time we got the water under control with an organized bucket brigade."

With everybody exhausted, some seasick, and Turner feverish with flu, he reluctantly called the Coast Guard, which sent out a 180-foot oceangoing tug. It seemed unlikely that the tug would arrive before *Bolero* fetched up on Cape Hatteras. One of those seers who has the habit of filtering any situation through romance, Turner looked at his exhausted crew, slumped over the pumps and buckets, and saw the dead Foreign Legionnaires in the movie *Beau Geste* who had been propped up with guns in their hands in an attempt to fool the enemy into thinking their fort was defended. Perhaps it was the extreme desperation of that image that persuaded him to make one last effort to set sail. Just as Turner was stirring, the wind clocked from southeast to south and began blowing *Bolero* away from the shoals.

Eventually she was towed into a slip, her crew patched her back together, and she made it to Florida in time for the St. Petersburg-Ft. Lauderdale Race, which

At the time he chartered *Bolero* for the 1968 SORC, Ted Turner was introducing small-boat intensity to ocean racing, and his results with the almost 20-year-old yawl showed just how good he was. To get there, however, he first had to double Cape Hatteras in a storm. (© MYSTIC SEAPORT, ROSENFELD COLLECTION)

she won on elapsed time. First to finish in almost all the others, *Bolero* twice was second on corrected time.

That was the end of *Bolero*'s successful serious racing career. As lighter, quicker boats arrived, she lost some of her old edge. She finished way down in the standings in the 1968 Bermuda Race – the last of the six she sailed – and by the 1970s she was in the charter trade, shuttling between the Mediterranean and the Caribbean. The interior was altered, a teak deck was laid over the leaky old cedar one, and, after she was dismasted near Madeira, a new rig was installed. *Bolero* had a new life in new waters.

John Nicholas Brown died in 1979 in the cabin of his last boat, *Malagueña*, at Annapolis, Maryland, soon after attending his son Carter's birthday party. The second *Bolero* Brown passed away six years later at Harbour Court. Anne's tombstone reads, "Historian, collector, musician, vivifier." In 1987 the Brown family sold Harbour Court to the New York Yacht Club as its Newport clubhouse. Among the many artifacts there are a bust of John Nicholas Brown by Joseph Coletti, Joseph Appleton's intricate model of *Bolero*, several rooms with names associated with the previous owners (including the Pirates Room, where one of the boys once slept), and a series of marks on the back of a closet door in the Commodore's Room that traces the growth of the three Brown children, year by year and inch by inch.

Bolero, meanwhile, was regressing into sad, relentless decline. In 1983 a new owner had the by-now 34-year-old yawl in Newport where, trolling for financial support for a restoration, he wrote to Anne Brown to invite her come aboard for a tour. He was neither the first nor the last dreamer who approached the Browns before the mid 1980s, when *Bolero* disappeared.

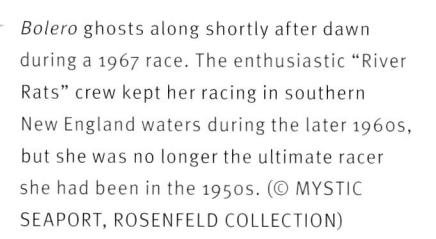

Bolero ghosts along shortly after dawn during a 1967 race. The enthusiastic "River Rats" crew kept her racing in southern New England waters during the later 1960s, but she was no longer the ultimate racer she had been in the 1950s. (© MYSTIC SEAPORT, ROSENFELD COLLECTION)

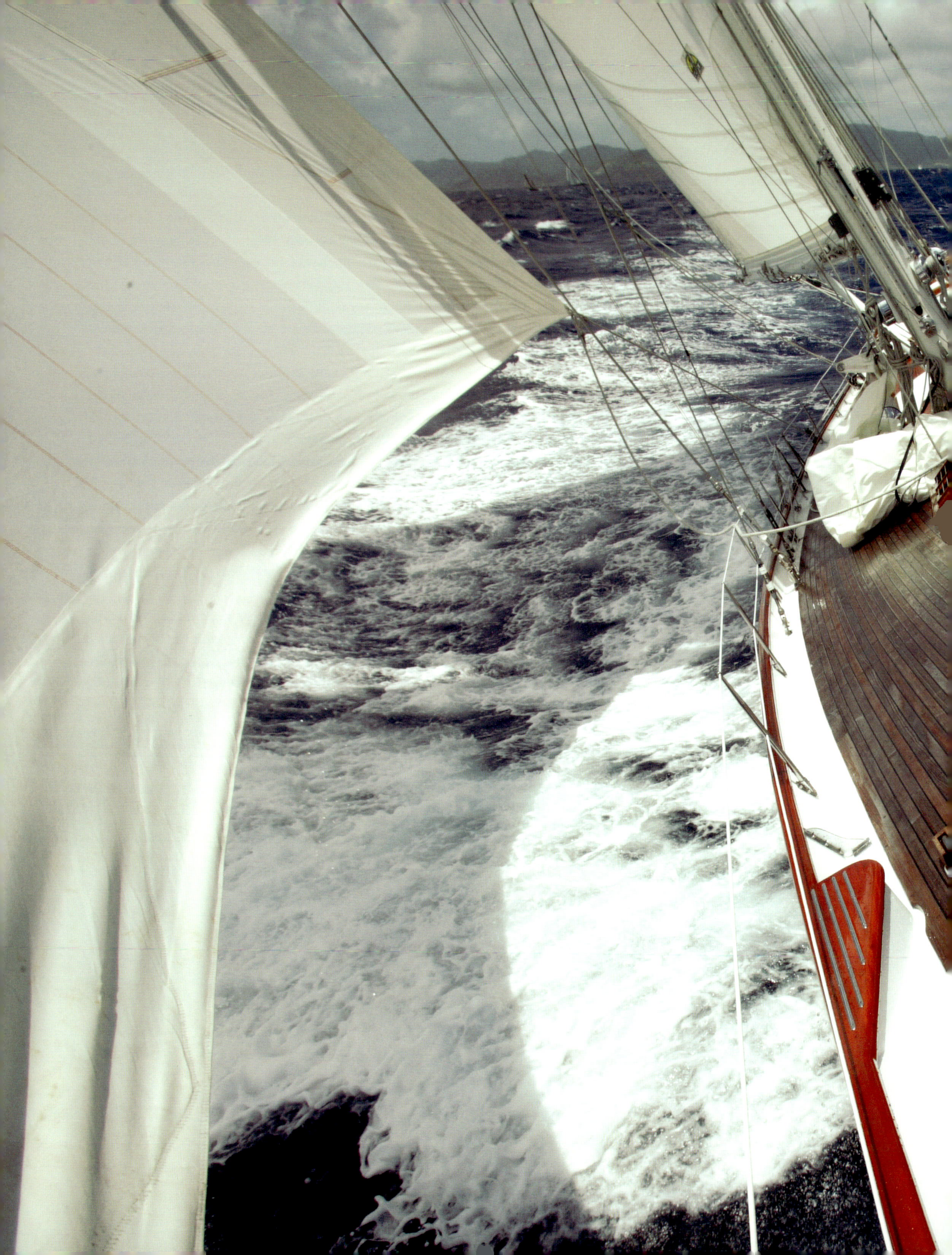

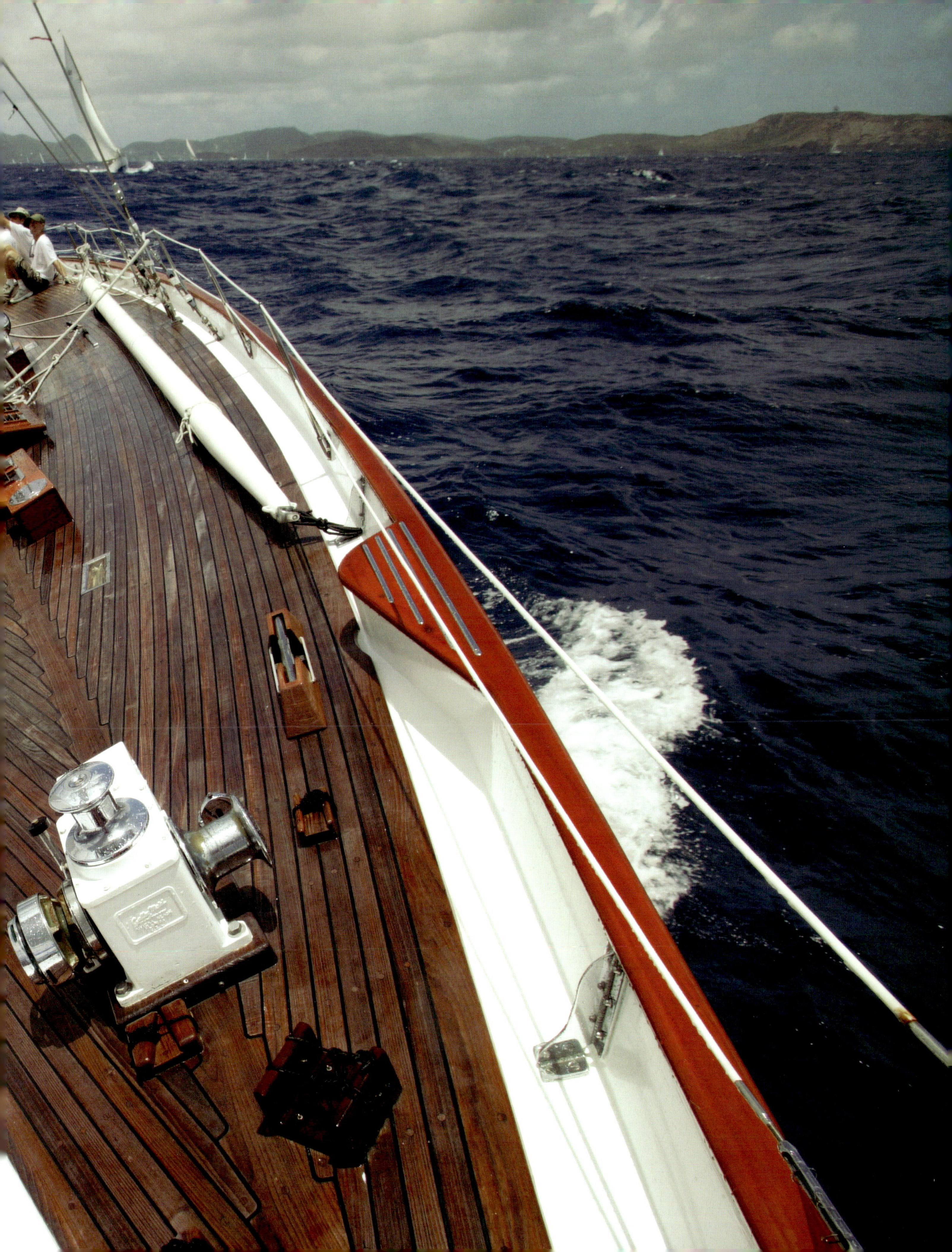

Her frames showing through the gaping hole left by the removal of her forefoot as a carpenter shapes its replacement, *Bolero* is part-way through her restoration at Pilots Point in 2002. At the left are Chip Barber, the boat's manager, and Hans Zimmer, head of the restoration team. (CHIP BARBER PHOTOS)

(Previous spread) In April 2004, fully restored, *Bolero* leads the fleet in Antigua Race Week. (© DANIEL FORSTER)

"Owning Bolero requires a commitment to her that has no corruptions of monetary considerations."
—George C. Welch, in *Bolero*'s Survey, 2000

Doing the Right Thing for the Boat

In the late 1980s, Peter Bowker was distressed to see *Bolero* lying up a creek in Fort Lauderdale with her keel deep in the mud, her paint peeling, and her masts, steering wheel, and many winches nowhere in view.

Bolero was at the end of a decade-long trail of tears on which a succession of owners with more dreams than dollars had been struggling to bring the boat back to her old form. Because they sometimes wrote to her original owners asking for encouragement, the Browns knew more about her decline than they would have wished. "The pattern was, somebody would buy it with stars in their eyes, and would run out of money," Nick Brown said. In moments when he was tempted to retrieve the family's old flagship from ignominy, he remembered the burden that went with being a "*Bolero* Brown."

There finally appeared a man with the necessary resources and ambition to make the big leap successfully. Gunther Sunkler, an Austrian-born businessman and sailor, had once glimpsed *Bolero* at a distance and was smitten. When he was in Fort Lauderdale one day in 1989, his lawyer drove him down to the river and told him, "There's the boat you have always wanted. There's your *Bolero*." Did Sunkler want to buy her? "I hesitated for a second because it was hard to find any beauty under that mess," Sunkler later told Charles Mason of *Sail* magazine. "But I had seen *Bolero* many years before, and I had done a lot of research on the boat. Even then I could see the magical qualities that she always had."

The magic ended quickly enough when Sunkler discovered that the masts, winches, and just about everything else of value had either been stolen or was in hock in lieu of payment to suppliers and former workmen. After chasing down and paying off liens, Sunkler had his boat. In the spring of 1993, a tug pulled her out of her silted-up berth, and, with her spars laid on deck, *Bolero* went up the Intracoastal Waterway to Chesapeake Bay for a refit.

Her fundamental condition seemed good. While many older wooden boats lose the grace of their sheer, *Bolero*'s ends were not drooping and her middle was

> "You cannot justify intelligently what I'm doing."

not humped. Other than that, to quote a sailor who saw her then, *Bolero* was "positively decrepit." The first try, at a boatyard in Oxford, Maryland, displeased Sunkler because the labor seemed to be going into disassembling her hull to find more problems, rather than fixing the obvious trouble at hand. He moved the boat to Georgetown and hired a team of workmen who worked under his supervision. She came away with (among other things) some new planks and refastening, repairs to the stem and mast step, fiberglass reinforcement for some frames, a layer of epoxy on many areas, new plumbing and electrical and hydraulic systems, and a number of cosmetic improvements. Repainted a gleaming black, *Bolero* was recommissioned on June 10, 1995.

When not tied up at Sunkler's Schaefer's restaurant on the Chesapeake & Delaware Canal, she was sailing on the Chesapeake Bay or in the Caribbean. Hinting that the major refit had cost over a million dollars, Sunkler described it as "a labor of love," adding, "You cannot justify intelligently what I'm doing."

"I Love the Stories"

When Sunkler eventually put *Bolero* up for sale, among the many people who was interested was a Bostonian named Edward Kane, who took a look with Mitchell Gibbons-Neff (called Mitch Neff), a yacht broker who was president of Sparkman & Stephens. "I don't know how or why Mitch and I hooked up on *Bolero*, but sometime in 1996 or '97 I slipped out of a University of Pennsylvania trustees' meeting, Mitch picked me up at a street corner in Philadelphia, and we drove down to the Chesapeake & Delaware Canal to look at her." Along the way, Neff told him of the boat's history. Kane was deeply impressed by the people who, seemingly through a mystical confluence of events, had united their efforts and dreams into constructing this yacht.

Sunkler's asking price was high and Kane did not buy the boat. But his interest remained keen. "I guess a restoration of a big boat was always in the back of Ed's mind," his wife, Marty Wallace, said in 2004. "I first heard about *Bolero* from him years ago, and when she became available at a good price, he asked me what I thought. I said, 'Fine, if that's what you want to do.'"

Despite different backgrounds, Ed Kane and Marty Wallace and the Browns shared several characteristics. They all loved boats and sailing, and were intensely private, committed to the priority of family, and passionate about doing things well on their own – often contrarian – terms. In one way or another, all were involved in the arts. Despite his demurrals that he had no aesthetic sensibility, Ed collected marine oil paintings and creamware. Marty was president of the board of governors of the Concord Museum outside Boston, where many artifacts of Ralph Waldo Emerson, Henry David Thoreau, and the New England Renaissance are collected and on display.

Born in a suburb of Philadelphia in 1949, the same year *Bolero* was launched, Ed Kane attended public schools, and his summer job was in a quarry. "We were

> "Sailing
> I can always come
> back to."

struggling to be middle class, but we were an overachieving family." His brother became a doctor, and Kane became a successful businessman. At the University of Pennsylvania in the late 1960s and early '70s, Kane started out a science major and ended up in political science and history as the cultural revolution of that time swept in. After graduating with honors, Kane served as an officer in army intelligence for two years before joining the flood of veterans to Harvard Business School. "I'd read a Horatio Alger novel at Penn and decided I wanted to make money somehow, but it wasn't something I dwelled on a lot. I wanted *respectability*." Surviving on the minimal funds available from the G.I. Bill, he wore his old army uniforms to class because he could not afford new clothes. He majored in finance and did well under the case method and grilling by professors because, he said, "I'd spent 15 years being harassed in high school football and the army, and it helped that I was in good physical shape." After graduation, he went to work for a Boston bank that was financing high-tech companies, and with that he got his start in venture capital that led him to a major insurance company and then his own business as a private equity investor.

One day at business school, Kane decided to learn to sail. He could not explain his motivation except that he was fascinated by the thought of doing something wholly different. "I'm a contrarian. I didn't go for a hike for 15 years after Infantry OCS, so if I'd been in the navy I never would have been interested in sailing. There was just something about it. I'd tried lots of sports before, then I'd lose interest. Sailing I always came back to."

His first boat was a skimpy Cal 25 fiberglass sloop that he bought in 1979. In it he had his first date with Marty Wallace, a Harvard Business School graduate and Pennsylvanian with a similar background. They cruised along the New England coast with a dog and bravado. "We sailed overnight to the Cape Cod Canal and went down to Block Island and the Vineyard. These were exotic places to me," Kane recalled with relish. "One year we headed off from Marblehead for a month in Maine with just a compass and a chart. No electronics, no VHF radio. We navigated by dead reckoning. We caught mackerel and cooked them on the Coleman stove. After four years we traded in the Cal for a Cape Dory 28, and that's when we also started chartering in the Caribbean."

They sold that boat when Marty became pregnant with their second child, but when their son and daughter were older, in 1990 they found a second-hand Bristol 47.7 centerboard sloop designed by Ted Hood. After a couple of coastal races, *Airborne* settled down into a serious, wide-ranging cruising routine. "Over the course of the next 10 years we turned that into a real cruising boat. In the fall and winter we cruised the Chesapeake, went down the Intracoastal Waterway, did the Bahamas, the Abacos, Key West, Cuba. We went around to New Orleans."

"Ed talked me into all that stuff," Marty said. "I'd ask, '*Take the boat to the Bahamas? Are you crazy?*' But that was really good. My son has sailed almost the whole east coast of North America, from Nova Scotia to Florida. We dragged our kids to every single fort. *Airborne* was absolutely the perfect family boat, very safe and dependable." One year *Airborne* circumnavigated the Adirondacks by way of the Hudson River, New York State Barge Canal, Lake Ontario, the St. Lawrence River, the Richelieu Canal, and Lake Champlain. The next summer she circumnavigated Newfoundland. While not a boastful man, Kane had an understandable pride in his achievements that occasionally burst out: "I was the first person to bring a boat into St. Pierre et Miquelon in the new millennium."

Their specialty was exploring old cruising grounds in modern ways. Sometimes it was just Ed and Marty, and from time to time Ed cruised accompanied only by a satellite phone that was his link to his office. "It almost doesn't matter where you are these days," he said. "We often left the boat in a harbor near an airport and called in a small plane to pick us up and fly us home. Sometimes the runway was nothing but a grass strip. We'd anchor and secure the boat, call the plane, which would arrive in a few hours, and then fly to Boston. Three weeks later we'd fly back, turn the key, and get cruising once again. I found some magnificent harbors this way that weren't in the cruising guides."

In 1990 Kane joined the New York Yacht Club, in part because its anchorage off Harbour Court—its Newport clubhouse and John Nicholas Brown's former private home—was handy to Boston and its nearby waters offered a warmer, longer sailing season than northern New England's. Like many people, Kane found the club a little intimidating. "The first time I took the helm of *Airborne* on a race in the New York Yacht Club Cruise, it was like the first time ever that you go hiking – and you're climbing Mt. Everest." Reading up on the club's history and rituals eased his anxiety. "I was always interested in the regalia and the formalities of sailing. I love the stories of the Brown family's house flags, with the design of the stripes and colors changing with each generation."

Here, Ed Kane's individualism is in full display. This admirer of tradition is also the sort of fellow who is demonstrably uncomfortable when wearing a tie or the usual yacht club gear. When sailing his world-famous yacht *Bolero*, he can usually be found in a practical, understated outfit of faded T-shirt, and well-worn boating shoes and wrinkled khakis.

Among the similarities between the two families was that the couples who headed them had an intriguingly parallel blend of skills and aptitudes. Like the Browns, Kane and Wallace were adventurers, had different senses of humor (exuberant with John and Marty, very dry with Anne and Ed), and approached projects in different but compatible ways. With a characteristic chuckle, Marty described herself as "a fussy control-oriented person" devoted to what she called "*Bolero*-type projects, fixing things that nobody can see." Kane usually worked differently: "I like the challenge of putting together the syndicate for a restoration project, and the intrigue of the personalities involved, the mix of people. And I love the historical research. It's Marty who's the builder and artist. She really loves ripping things apart and rebuilding them. I am not a project person. I have no artistic or creative instinct whatsoever. It's everything I can do to get my shirt and pants to match." Asked if he would he like to build a new boat, he responded quickly, "Not at all. I don't have the ability to look at plans and understand them. With a restoration, you know what's there – at least if there's enough boat left to restore."

"If Someone Didn't Rescue It, She Was Gone"

"Normally Eddie doesn't like project sorts of things," Marty said. "But he *really* likes that these boats are preserved and sailing." By "these boats," Marty Wallace referred to *Bolero* and also to another classic.

Early in 2000, while he was negotiating to buy *Bolero*, Kane was approached about joining a group of New York Yacht Club members who were planning to restore another, even older boat to take to the America's Cup Jubilee, the cup's 150th anniversary regatta in England. This was *Marilee*, a nearly 75-year-old Nathanael Herreshoff sloop that was one of the four survivors of the New York Yacht Club 40 class built between 1914 and 1926, using the same method that the gifted and genial Rufus Murray brought to the Nevins yard.

Nicknamed "the fighting 40s" because, despite a cloud of sail, they rarely if ever were reefed, New York 40s won Bermuda races in the 1920s. In 2001 Captain Nat Herreshoff's grandson, Halsey Herreshoff, sailed one of them, *Rugosa II* (winner of the 1928 Bermuda Race), across the Atlantic to race at the America's Cup Jubilee. He later cruised in Scandinavia and Greece before recrossing the Atlantic in 2005. But *Marilee* was in no such condition. "If someone didn't rescue it, she was gone," said one member of the New York Yacht Club group, Larry Snodden.

Kane recalled, "I asked my wife if she were interested in joining a syndicate to restore a 40-foot boat, and she said yes." It turned out that things weren't so clear-cut. The boat was 59 feet long (40 feet was the waterline length), and the New York Yacht Club group – including Kane, Snodden, Peter Kellogg, Mitchell Shivers, William Waggoner, and Ann Hutchins – were not a formal syndicate. They were, however, committed to getting a handsome classic yacht sailing again under the burgee of the New York Yacht Club, and that was good enough for Kane.

His first look at the boat was discouraging. "It was leaking all over the place. There was nothing about this boat that I found aesthetically pleasing." The hull was encased in a layer of fiberglass, there was a yawl rig, and most of everything was a mess. Starting from there, the nine-month restoration of *Marilee* at the William Cannell yard in Camden, Maine, was dedicated to the ideal of authenticity. The fiberglass covering came off, a gaff sloop rig went in with wooden spars fashioned at the workshop of the Independence Seaport Museum in Philadelphia, and 70 percent of the hull was replaced using the same materials that Herreshoff used in 1926 with the exception of synthetic sails and bronze straps and fastenings in place of the old steel or copper ones. Otherwise, the boat was *Marilee Redux*.

The effort schooled Kane in the protocol of classic yacht restoration. "I learned quickly that budgets and costs are meaningless. You spend the first third of your money essentially making the boat valueless. You're taking a seaworthy boat and making it unseaworthy. One-third to one-half of the way into the project, all the money you've spent has been flushed down the toilet, and you need the rest of your money to make the boat decent again. It's not like restoring a house, where at least the land has value. The fact is that you have to gut so much of the boat. When I took my wife to look at *Marilee*, she asked, 'What have you got us into?'"

With Ted Hood at the helm, the restored 75-year-old New York 40 *Marilee* reaches fast at the 2001 America's Cup Jubilee. *Marilee* taught Ed Kane the fundamental ground rule of yacht restoration, which is that normal analytical logic is not always relevant. "Budgets and costs are meaningless," he would say. (© DAN NERNEY)

Kane discovered that good yards know how to anticipate such shock. "There's a turning point when the boat starts to look *a lot* better," he recalled with a smile. "With *Marilee*, the first things they put back on were the deck beams – all of them beautifully varnished. That was very smart of them. My wife looked at them and said, 'This is going to be very beautiful, isn't it?' The message to the yards during a restoration is this: 'Find a little bit of boat to make look better quickly. Give the owner who's writing the checks an idea of what it's going to look like.' That's really central to the process." Kane pointed out his office window to the huge construction site that was downtown Boston. "It's like in the Big Dig. They put a lot of grass on all the mess."

"Something Broader was Happening."

The notion that there should actually be such a thing as an authentic restored classic wooden yacht was novel to most Americans before the 1990s. Most people interested in old wooden boats were content to buy one for a song, patch it up, and sail it very cautiously. If upkeep became too expensive, the sailing became less frequent and less adventurous, and the boat finally was put into storage or left on her mooring to collect seagull droppings until another dreamer came along to buy her for a smaller song.

Another view was that these boats should be restored to their former glory. In America, outside of Mystic Seaport and a few other museums, the torch for this radical notion was carried in America by *WoodenBoat* magazine. It was founded in 1974 by Jonathan Wilson, who cleverly combined an aura of neo-hippy romanticism (his first office was so deep in the woods that the telephone had to be installed on a tree) with page after page of detailed, technical advice about wood and boatbuilding. A few boatyards specialized in wooden boat construction and restoration, a few consultants and writers (most notably Wilson, Maynard Bray, and Matt Murphy) flew the restoration flag, and there were gatherings sponsored by Mystic Seaport, *WoodenBoat,* the Museum of Yachting in Newport, the Herreshoff Marine Museum, the Wooden Boat Center in Seattle, the Thousand Island Museum, and other organizations.

All this was a modest activity compared with what was going on in Britain and Europe, where boats dating back to the turn of the century were carefully restored and then raced in regattas and rallies specifically for classic yachts. Most of these events include judged competitions in which prizes were awarded for the quality and authenticity of restoration and for the boat's polish, the top prize being the coveted *Grand Prix d'Élegance.*

Beginning in the mid 1990s Europeans began to look to America for boats, especially prewar boats designed by Sparkman & Stephens and built by Henry Nevins. Cantiere Navale dell'Argentario, a yacht yard at Porto Stefano, Italy, that was managed by Frederico Nardi, restored a Nevins-built Sparkman & Stephens Twelve-Meter, *Nyala*, and then in 1997 – around the time Ed Kane was first looking at *Bolero* – they did the Stephens family's old *Dorade*, which had been on the American West Coast for 60 years. Later came *Stormy Weather*.

Besides the charm and history of the boats themselves, another link to wooden boat construction was Olin Stephens. After he retired from Sparkman & Stephens at the age of 72 in 1980, he and his wife, Susie, moved to Northern New England, where they spent the summer in a house that he designed and his son Sam built on the top of a small mountain in Vermont. Come the first snow, they decamped across the Connecticut River to a home in a village in New Hampshire.

Stephens remained active in the sport, although he was deeply disappointed in the evolution of yacht design toward a breed of boat that was lighter, wider, and faster than *Bolero* and her cousins. The boats sailed more *on* the water than *through it*. Stephens himself liked to sail fast; in his racing days, he had pressed exceptionally hard. Yet he was pointedly critical of the new type as uncomfortable, unattractive, unsuitable for going to sea, and even unsafe. His opinion seemed to be confirmed by sinkings and loss of life in the 1979 Fastnet race, after which he made a damning statement: "Some modern ocean racers, and the cruising boats derived from them, are dangerous to their crews." He then helped manage an important and eye-opening scientific study of the problem of capsize by keel boats.

His standpoint was that of the philosophical skeptic. "I'm a little bit dubious about progress, but I'm certain about change," he said at one of the events celebrating Sparkman & Stephens's 75th anniversary in 2004. "Progress is to me a concept that is dubious in a philosophical sense. In other words, mechanical advances may or may not contribute to pleasure and happiness in life or sailing."

Yacht restoration attracted new notice with the return of several J-Class sloops from the 1930s, including *Cambria* (right) and the 1930 America's Cup challenger, *Shamrock V* (left). Still competitive among themselves, restored yachts large and small race in classic yacht regattas or in special classic yacht divisions of major races. (© DAN NERNEY)

Stephens found hope in the classic yacht movement in Europe, where he had many friends. He was unaware of serious interest in the United States outside of maritime museums until the late 1980s, when a determined young woman named Elizabeth Meyer bought the hulk of the Charles E. Nicholson-designed, 1934 British J-Class America's Cup challenger *Endeavour* and proceeded against all odds to recreate her. Stephens's initial interest was mainly on the technical level, but in time he saw, as he put it, that in *Endeavour* and other restorations, "something broader was happening."

Elizabeth Meyer had something to do with that. She went on to found the International Yacht Restoration School, in Newport, which became a center for a whole community based around wooden boats. After spending time in this world, Marty Wallace compared a classic yacht regatta with a small town in the 1950s, except that instead of grandparents sitting out on the front porch, owners of all backgrounds and types were on their boats, ready for a chat with another crew. "There's instant bonding. No matter what they are in their other life, we have something to talk about. You can spend the summer going from event to event – the classic regattas and the International Yacht Restoration School annual cruise (that's the best) – and everybody encourages you to climb aboard and enjoy these wonderful boats."

Olin Stephens found that out as well. Once Argentario had restored *Dorade*, her owners flew Stephens over for the launching. There he was deeply moved to discover that she was exactly as when he raced her in the 1930s, right down to a storage bin that he and Rod had arranged for the cutlery. "Because she was like the original, my experience when I went aboard in 1997 was personal and deeply emotional," he said in an interview I conducted with him in 2004, when Stephens was an exceptionally alert 96 years of age. "They had replaced the steering wheel with a tiller, just as she had when I first sailed her, and when I took hold of this tiller a feeling went over me like a wave. I came up breathing the same air as everyone else and was soon thinking analytically again, comparing one boat against another. But I was deeply moved." While sailing in *Dorade* in races on the Mediterranean, he discovered an entire fleet of classics. In due course, more of his favorite designs were brought back to their original condition.

Prepare to Say Goodbye"

As appealing as restorations seemed from a distance, they could be hazardous to one's bank balance if not one's mental stability. For some people, restoring an old boat made of natural fibers is not a practical matter but a soulful activity; even the most straight-laced women and men believe that, as standards of integrity go, fixing up a wooden boat is at the top of the list for the simple reason that good wood is akin to good character. ("Only a sweet and virtuous soul, / Like season'd timber, never gives," wrote George Herbert in his poem "Virtue.")

The cost can be high, however. That much was learned by a friend of mine who took a shine to the idea that he could replace the transom on his catboat. He went down to the local boatyard and asked how hard this would be.

"Do you have a wife and family?" the manager asked. "Yes I do," replied my friend, somewhat surprised. "How about a job?" "Yes. I'm a banker." "Own a house?" *Of course* he had a house. My friend was beginning to get a little irritated. The boatyard manager paused. "Well, then, prepare to say goodbye to *every single one of them*." Rather than sacrifice all to an obsession that he was unprepared to pursue, my friend paid the boatyard to replace the transom.

The disappointments inherent in this hobby can be brutal. In 2000 I raced to Bermuda in the 64-year-old, 53-foot Philip Rhodes-designed keel sloop *Kirawan*, built in 1936 by a good yard in Brooklyn in the manner of a composite Nevins boat. "Practically trussed from side" was one favorable judgment on her strong wood-and-bronze structure. She won the 1936 Newport-Bermuda Race after beating for 500 miles into a gale. Ending up on the West Coast, *Kirawan* was raced (even all the way to Tahiti) and cruised extensively. She was fading into disuse when a Hollywood movie producer, Sandy Horowitz, became enamored of her, bought her, and had her fitted with a teak deck and a handsome new interior. The carpenter, Tom Adams, made some structural repairs, but they were limited by the fact that the boat usually was afloat. "I bought her to sail, not to refit," Horowitz later explained.

Emotionally committed to his wooden sloop and her history ("This boat leads, I follow"), Horowtiz brought her east for the 2000 Newport-Bermuda Race. I was in the crew. In the windy early part of the race, *Kirawan* was averaging over eight knots and enjoying a big lead in the Classic Yacht Division when the lovely tiles on the sole of the head began to creep up on each other. This persuaded us to slow the boat down, but not long afterwards the navigator, sitting at his station, felt a squirt of dampness on his knees. Inspection revealed daylight shining through several feet of gaping seam on the windward side. Adams went over the rail in a harness attached to a halyard and filled the open seam with polysulfide sealant. (For this feat, Adams was the first recipient of the Cruising Club of America's new seamanship prize, which was named for Rod Stephens.) When the wind died, costing us our lead, the boat came upright and we were happy to see the leak slow.

Returning to North America, *Kirawan* (which, ironically, means something close to "peace of mind" in Persian) was hauled out and discovered to have 165 fractures in her frames. Tom Potter, who did the restoration at his yard in North Kingstown, Rhode Island, believed that most of these cracks occurred long before our race and may have been caused by the tight-fitting single layer of mahogany planks that literally pulled the frames apart. Almost 5,000 hours of work later, the boat was reframed, replanked, and back in sailing condition. In the meantime, the relationship between Horowitz and Adams had soured.

"One of the Wacky Things in My Experience"

Marilee's story was happier. After her launching at Camden in May 2001 (where she survived the parting of the cable on the ways) she was shipped to Cowes, England, for the America's Cup Jubilee regatta. In an elegant act of sportsmanship, the Royal Yacht Squadron was celebrating the 150th anniversary of its *losing* the cup to the visiting New York schooner yacht *America* by holding a large international regatta. On the first day, in a strong breeze, *Marilee*'s boom broke. She still finished well, and after she returned to her slip several sailors slung the broken boom on their shoulders and carried it down to a local yard, where a long length of pine was located and used to craft a new spar. In the race around the Isle of Wight that commemorated *America*'s famous victory in 1851, *Marilee* – steered by the sailmaker and yacht designer Ted Hood – had the best corrected time in the fleet. She went on to race some more in the Mediterranean and Caribbean before she was sold to a European owner.

Ed Kane would call the *Marilee* project "one of the wacky things in my experience." He ended up paying more than he had expected, and the organization was surprisingly loose. "We never had a formal written agreement – it was all on a handshake. And the economy was sliding out from under us." Yet he was pleased to say that everybody came out of it as friends. What made it work, he thought,

> "We never had a formal written agreement—
> it was all on a handshake. And the economy was sliding out from under us."

Marty Wallace and Ed Kane (right), with their children, Nat and Ellie, and syndicate member Bill Wagner (center) accept one of the prizes that *Marilee* won at the America's Cup Jubilee. With them is Halsey Herreshoff (a grandson of the boat's designer, Nathanael Greene Herreshoff), whose own New York 40 edged out *Marilee* for the Jubilee's overall win. At that time, *Bolero* was about to begin what everybody expected would be a modest rehab, but everybody was surprised. (© DAN NERNEY)

was the fact that the restoration had a deadline that kept it from getting bogged down in details. He would have liked more recognition from the New York Yacht Club, which would have encouraged other restorations, but in the end he found the exercise extremely satisfying. "We won about everything you can win, the owners could always sail when they wanted to, and the boat was used a lot. Boats tend to be *under*sailed, not *over*sailed."

As *Marilee*'s restoration project developed, Kane was getting serious about taking on a second wooden boat. Gunther Sunkler had been dropping his asking price for *Bolero*, and in October 2000 Kane was prepared to make an offer pending the results of a survey. For the job Kane retained George C. Welch, a former manager of a full-service boatyard who was certified as a surveyor by the National Association of Marine Surveyors. Welch liked Sunkler and he also found things to like in the refit, though he acknowledged that much of the work that had been done was cosmetic.

Because a thick, tough layer of epoxy covered many parts of the boat, Welch was unable to employ what he called "invasive" and "destructive" methods of inspection. By close visual examination and poking at wood from the inside and outside, he turned up softness in the stem, more rot elsewhere, broken or loose fastenings, damaged fittings, and a mizzenmast step so rotted out that Welch recommended that the mizzen not be set in any breeze stronger than light air. In his 27-page report to Kane, Welch told Kane that once these and a few other problems were addressed, *Bolero* would be in good enough shape for coastal sailing or an offshore passage. He also recommended further inspections.

One of a marine surveyor's jobs is to report on the boat's condition. Another is to advise on her value. Here, Welch repeatedly emphasized that *Bolero* must be regarded as something other than a commodity: "*Bolero* is a famous yacht," are the first words of his report, which goes on to say: "*Bolero* is a striking yacht with magnificent proportions of grace and shape…. She is a famous yacht, fine period piece, and the acme of her type, with a history of remarkable feats of performance…. She is a classic museum piece of twentieth-century American yachting and is of inestimable historic value…. One's decision to purchase and own this type of vessel should not be approached by financial analysis."

He issued a warning that might have been made by Henry Nevins, Olin or Rod Stephens, or John Nicholas Brown: "To own such a boat," Welch insisted, is to assume a "custodial obligation and responsibility" not only to the boat, but to history. Whatever Kane paid for *Bolero*, it would be a fraction of the eventual price in various currencies – dollars, time, sweat, and a heavy sense of obligation. To translate that simply, to own this boat responsibly was to be not just a "*Bolero* Kane," but "*Bolero*'s Kane."

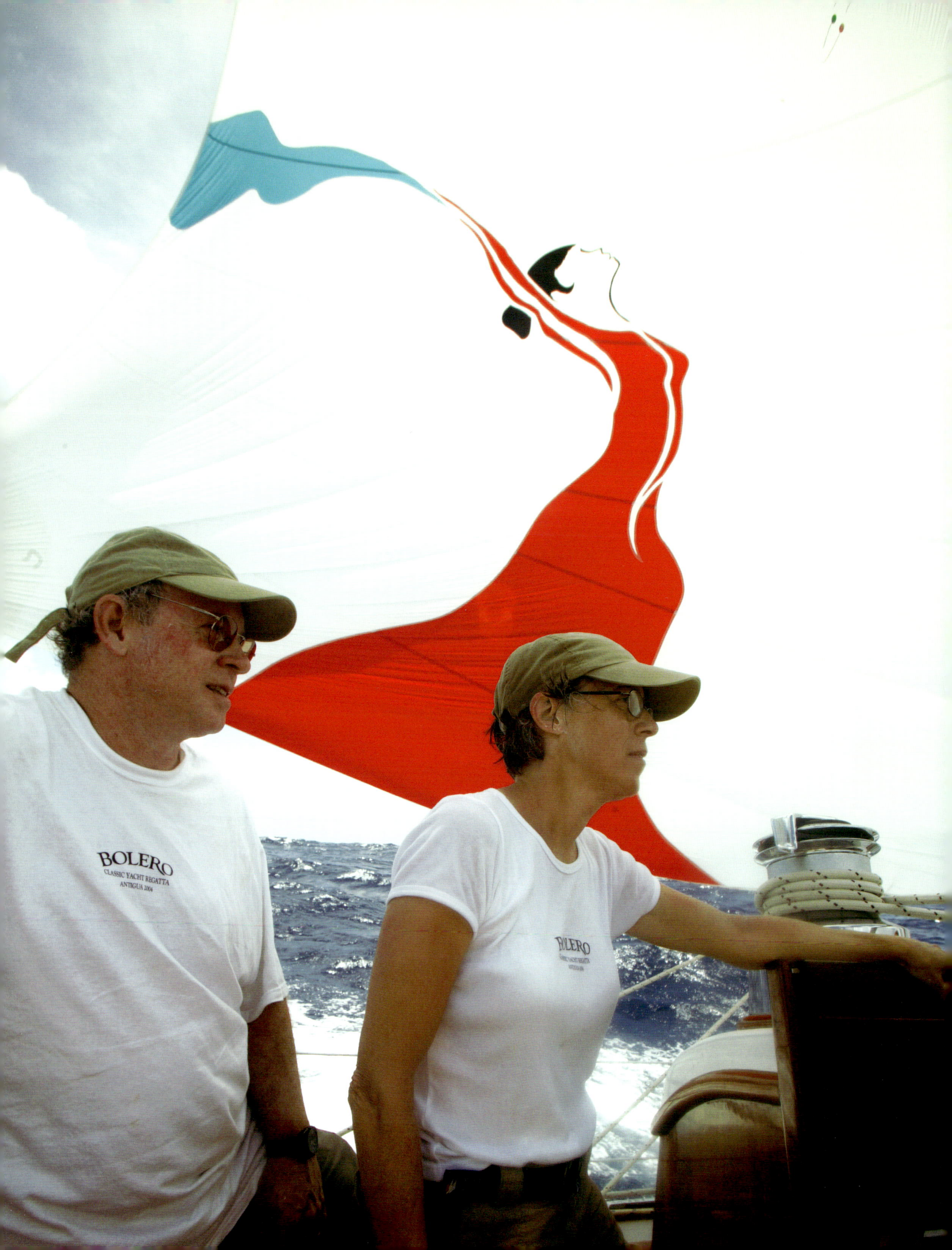
BOLERO
CLASSIC YACHT REGATTA
ANTIGUA 2004

"It's not just a question of installing a new wooden frame." ⁓Edward Kane

10 *Bolero*'s Kanes

Though they had owned boats for many years, Ed Kane and Marty Wallace (here under Bolero*'s dancer) were taken aback by aspects of a big yacht's restoration, with all its surprises. "There goes my garden!" she exclaimed after a new structural problem appeared. (© DANIEL FORSTER)*

There were tears in Gunther Sunkler's eyes at the closing when Ed Kane bought *Bolero* for $475,000 in February 2001. Kane, Mitch Neff, Chip Barber (a professional boat manager), and Hans Zimmer (a yacht restorer) then took the boat to a yard in Oxford, Maryland. When Kane brought Marty Wallace down to look at their new acquisition, the response, as he liked to tell it, was familiar. "She asked, '*What have you got us into?*' – exactly the same thing she said when I showed her *Marilee*." Marty was especially unimpressed by the boat's amenities. "My first impression was that it had thick, hideous cushions that were too heavy to pick up." She cheered up when she went cruising. "She just seemed so livable and comfortable. I love the way she's laid out, with all that privacy in the deckhouse, and that big main saloon. I'd never sailed a wooden boat of her generation, so *Bolero* was a revelation. She was so wonderful to sail. *This* is why people like wooden boats."

Kane's first hint of what was involved with owning an icon came that spring during a cruise on the Chesapeake Bay by members of the New York Yacht Club. Before then, when he invited friends on a cruise he habitually overbooked. "If we wanted five guests, we'd ask 10, maybe 20 people. But with *Bolero*, it was the other way around. If we asked 10 people, 20 people showed up. The boat was *packed* for that cruise. We had people sleeping everywhere." After some summer cruising, in early September *Bolero* was delivered to Brewer's Pilots Point Marina, in Westbrook, Connecticut, for what everybody believed would be a relatively modest patching up costing, at most, $200,000. "I didn't *have* to do a restoration," Ed said later. "This was a functioning, clean, gorgeous boat. The problems were below the waterline. I couldn't go offshore, but the boat *could* do coastal Maine and back and forth to Ft. Lauderdale." Marty Wallace put her initial caution behind her. "My whole goal was to do the right thing for the boat. I didn't want people asking, 'Why didn't they fix the mizzenmast step?'"

To prepare himself, Kane took a course in planking at the International Yacht Restoration School, where he was a trustee. That knowledge of the complexities of woodworking would become extremely valuable to him over the next two years as his initial budget ballooned four-fold.

The extent of *Bolero*'s elaborate metal-and-wood composite construction became obvious as the planking, forefoot, and deadwood were peeled away in search of rot and corrosion. Some repairs were simple, while others demanded extensive rebuilding. (CHIP BARBER PHOTO)

"I Get These Blank Stares"

Bolero went to Pilots Point because of a meeting of minds between the head of the yard's boatbuilding and restoration operation, Hans Zimmer, and Ed Kane while they were making the winter delivery on the Chesapeake Bay. Zimmer was there because the yard's manager, Rives Potts, was considering taking on the refit but first needed to know if Kane would stick with what might turn out to be a big, expensive project. "I wanted Hans to see if he was the type of person we wanted to do business with. Did he love boats? Did he love *Bolero*? Was he prepared to make the commitment to do the job right?"

As a longtime boatyard manager and lifelong sailor, Potts well understood the importance of making a strong commitment to doing things right. His perspective had been enhanced in a brief encounter with Rod Stephens back in 1980, when Potts was in charge of maintaining (and also sailed on) Dennis Conner's Twelve-Meter *Freedom* in the America's Cup trials and races. Stephens, who a generation earlier had been known as "Rod-God" and had been a ubiquitous presence in boat yards, was not at Newport. Stubborn and vocally critical of new trends, he had been shunted to the sidelines by younger sailors and designers. Olin Stephens saw that his brother's feelings were hurt and asked Potts if Rod could be helpful around the boat.

Potts had a rigging problem. When the running backstay supporting the mast was cast off during a tack or jibe, it tended to jam in the deck block and stop the boom from going out. This drastically slowed Conner's aggressive pre-start maneuvers. When Potts apprised Stephens of the problem, the older man not only understood it immediately but, with his typical intensity, reached back into his long memory to come up with a solution. The problem, he told Potts, was that he was using the wrong kind of block. Instead of one fixed in an upright position, he needed a block that could flop over to the same angle as the line's. "See, like that," he said, pointing to a nearby boat, a pre-war Sparkman & Stephens Twelve-Meter, *Nyala*, that still carried exactly such a block that Stephens had put on her more than 40 years earlier. Potts replaced the block, and the problem went away. A quarter century later he was able to say that his good deed had taught him a heartfelt lesson: "That's when I discovered there's nothing new in boats. Different materials, maybe, but no new ideas."

Raised sailing on Fishing Bay, Virginia, near the mouth of the Rappahannock River, Potts graduated from Virginia Military Institute. Boat-crazy, he did a lot of ocean racing, honed an aptitude for rigging and construction, and ended up at Pilots Point. Located in a well protected cove off Long Island Sound near the mouth of the Connecticut River, it was the sort of facility that Henry Nevins's accountant dreamed of when he tried to talk Nevins out of the boatbuilding business. Its well-maintained 50-acre facility has a large service area for painting and maintaining boats, a marina with almost 900 slips, and a playground, a swimming pool, and other amenities to attract families. While the yard has done some boatbuilding, it specializes in boat restorations. It performed some work on *Marilee*, did more on

In a time of depleted hardwood forests, finding good wood is an even greater challenge in the early 21st century than in the time of Henry Nevins and Rufus Murray. Oak logs were eventually located, and here Frank Rapoza shapes one in the traditional way to form the boat's timbers. (CHIP BARBER PHOTO)

Halsey Herreshoff's *Rugossa II* and *Bolero*'s near-sistership *Windigo* (ex-*Venturer*, ex-*Audacious*), and constructed wooden masts for a number of classic yachts, including the big L. Francis Herreshoff-designed ketch *Ticonderoga*.

"Restoration work gets the guys excited," said Potts, and there was plenty to be excited about when the yard's biggest restoration project arrived. "Doing *Bolero* was very important for us in many ways. In fact, I think *all* the boats of that generation are very important. I get these blank stares from younger people when I mention Nat Herreshoff and Olin Stephens and boats like *Bolero*. I've just seen that too often. That's why it's so important that Ed Kane came along."

A laconic Southerner, Potts became a fan of Ed's deadpan, self-deprecatory humor. He liked to repeat the instructions that Kane had given him when he brought in his cruising boat, *Airborne*, for maintenance. "Don't fix it up too much," he said. "We want to use it like an old station wagon."

Potts was sure the deal to restore *Bolero* was cinched when he sent Hans Zimmer down to the Chesapeake that cold February. "Hans helped Ed and Mitch Neff deliver *Bolero*, and he charmed them." Like so many actors in the *Bolero* story, Hans Zimmer knew what he wanted to do when he was still a teenager. Born in 1941 in Germany, he studied boatbuilding at trade school because, he said, "I wanted to sail, and the only way to afford it was to build a boat." He emigrated to Sweden in order to avoid the military draft (ironically, that was the reason why Nils Halvorsen, who lofted *Bolero*, had fled Sweden for the United States half a century earlier). While working for the boatbuilder Halberg Rassey, Zimmer learned boatbuilding from the bottom up – "lofting, setting up keels, everything." When Swedish taxes got too high, Zimmer, who is something of a libertarian, designed and built a 31-foot boat and sailed it to Italy, where he built boats. Later he crossed the Atlantic to the Caribbean, and at Bequia in 1976 he came across a ragged, dismasted old ketch that on close look turned out to be a 37-year-old English Twelve-Meter called *Flica II*, likely the last boat built by the 140-year-old William Fife yard in Scotland. Zimmer bought and rehabbed *Flica*, sailed her up to New England, and took a temporary job at the Pilots Point yard repairing the mast of an old New York Yacht Club 50 called *Spartan*. He abandoned the project in order to get *Flica II* back to the Caribbean, but a storm at sea forced him back, and there he stayed. When Halsey Herreshoff began bringing boats down to Pilots Point, he did their restorations.

Hans Zimmer loved boats deeply, but was a realist. Like Rod Stephens, he seemed to be one of those skeptics who is convinced that Murphy—the man or woman behind the famous law concerning the universal tendency toward chaos

—was an optimist. When we raced together in *Bolero* in the classic yacht regattas off Newport in the summer of 2004, and the sailors were choosing their assignments, Zimmer every time went for the running backstays, the adjustable tackles and wires supporting the mast. Make a mistake with a jib sheet and even the main sheet, and you will survive. But if the running backstay is not snugged down hard in a timely fashion in hard conditions, the mast may go over the side. In the light conditions we had, *Bolero*'s oak-tree-trunk size aluminum mast could reasonably be expected to survive on its own, but Zimmer was there to snug down the runners after every tack, even in a calm.

Pilots Point yard manager Rives Potts (right, with Ed Kane) had aggressively sought on the job and was as surprised as everyone else when it turned out to be so complex. "There was always new stuff being discovered," Kane ruefully looked back. (CHIP BARBER PHOTO)

"There Goes My Garden!"

After *Bolero* was hauled in early September 2001, the armor of epoxy that had thwarted George Welch's efforts to make a proper "invasive" survey was peeled away to reveal bare wood. Zimmer and his assistants opened up the boat by pulling four pairs of double planks from the side and cutting away six more planks forward. Alas, the exploratory surgery exposed more problems than anybody had feared, almost from stem to stern. Half the stem – the massive length of oak supporting the bow – had been cut away sometime in the past, very likely due to stress, worms, and rot. Now the whole stem had to be replaced. So did the forefoot, the transition from the stem into the wooden keel that, thanks to the grounding on the Mulberry in England in 1963, had two layers. Moving aft, Zimmer came to the very front part of the wooden keel, at the joint with the forefoot. This is the most stressed area in a wooden sailboat because, as he explained, "The bow is pulled up by the headstay, the ballast keel does not flex, and the mast pushes down at a rate several times the boat's displacement." He found the joint worm-damaged, split, and soft. Aft of that, at the back end of the keel, there was more trouble at the joint between the sternpost (slanting upward just ahead of the rudder) and the horn timber (the stern's backbone). This joint "has opened up more than can be tolerated," he told Kane.

As if it were not enough that that part of *Bolero*'s spine was eaten away, Zimmer had to report that the stainless steel water tanks were badly rusted – an indication of a serious problem with electrolysis. Everybody was surprised. "What *Bolero*

A victim of stress, worms, rot, and damage in England in 1963, the old stem comes off. Behind it lies the gap left by the forefoot. (CHIP BARBER PHOTO)

told me once again is that I don't know much," said Mitch Neff, who added – with the rueful tone of voice of someone who has been surprised far too often – "Welcome to my business." Neff believed the culprit was electrolysis, which damages both metal and wood. "I would not be one to second-guess Mitch," said Stephens, who speculated that at some stage the electrical system had been inadequately grounded.

So much for a simple refit. "There was always new stuff being discovered," said Kane, shaking his head. Rotten frames, broken fastenings, split frame ends – the list ran on. "There were millions of things like that," Zimmer said later. "Add it up, and the price is climbing and climbing." The $200,000 project became an $800,000 project. After one conference, Rives Potts heard Marty Wallace exclaim, "There goes my garden!" Kane could be quite funny about it in a darkish sort of way. "When I bought *Bolero*, it meant I had three boats – *Airborne*, *Marilee*, *Bolero*," he looked back. "Since we could use only one at a time, this was pretty expensive, but at least I knew where they all were." At an illustrated talk at a meeting of the Cruising Club of America, when a photograph of *Bolero* came up he ran his finger down the leech of the mainsail and said, 'This is the angle my finances are taking.'"

Some repairs were relatively simple, like substituting polypropylene water tanks for the old rusted metal ones. But finding and cutting massive quantities of seasoned white oak for the stem, forefoot, and keel was not as easy in 2001 as in Rufus Murray's day. The new forefoot alone required an 18-foot log, 30 to 36 inches in diameter, with just the right bend so the grain would follow the curve of the hull. By early October three suitable logs were found at a cost of $10,000. One was well-seasoned Iroco, an African variety of oak, that was left over from the construction of the schooner *Amistad* at Mystic Seaport. In the end, Zimmer chose a white oak log, off which came the stem, forefoot, smaller bits for floor timbers and frame ends, plus a new piece for the wooden keel.

The sort of person who could make moving a mountain seem easy, Zimmer described the replacement of the forefoot this way: "You just pull the fastenings, then relieve the frame ends where they fasten to the keel, and she comes right out." With the new wooden keel in place, the new forefoot was then jiggled into place with the help of a forklift. Once the forefoot was installed, it was time to put in the new stem. Then they lifted the boat off the lead keel by driving in wedges, but first setting up a transit on deck with a laser to check that she was lifting off evenly.

As the hull slowly rose, to everybody's surprise the big centerboard, which presumably had been removed years earlier, was seen sticking out of the top of its slot. Facing yet another unanticipated expense of $40,000, Kane and Wallace decided that if *Bolero* was going to be the same old boat, she should have her centerboard. It took two days for a chain saw and chisel to open up the bottom of the slot so the board could be dropped out, polished up, and reinstalled (with a

The hull hangs suspended over the wooden keel under which the old centerboard was discovered. (CHIP BARBER PHOTO)

hydraulic hoisting mechanism because the original worm-gear system could not be found). An inspection of the lead keel revealed a large area filled with putty where the boat very likely had grounded hard at least once in her history. They cleaned up the cavity and filled it with 600 pounds of molten lead as new ballast. Up in the hull, *Bolero* looked like an albino porcupine; the holes left when the old fastenings were removed were filled with thousands of white pegs so moisture would not collect to cause rot.

Work stopped temporarily in mid-February 2002. The original idea had been to have the boat ready for the Bermuda Race, but when so many problems turned up, the goal shifted to June 2003. Zimmer would describe the restoration as "a 12-month project spread out over 18 months."

"These *Dorade* Vents Are No Darn Good"

The project was anything but solitary or, for that matter, noncontroversial. "One of the things I enjoyed about the process was not so much the technical part, but the *people* I worked with," Kane would say. Zimmer's team varied in size depending on the stage of the restoration, but it totaled eight men: Jeff Barnett, Chuck Celone, Phil Crouthamel, Greg McPhee, Charlie Newcomb, Frank Rapoza, Jim Rolston, and Eben Whitcomb. In the group were an electrician-mechanic (Barnett), a machinist-metal fabricator (Rolston), and several carpenters. Rapoza, who had done boat restorations at Mystic Seaport and other yards, played a crucial role in the woodwork. Displayed in Kane's and Wallace's living room is a treasured half-model of the boat that was built of wood from her restoration and was signed by the work crew.

Because *Bolero*'s community was old and broad, it was not surprising that many men and women turned up to watch and offer comments. Kane was flattered. "There's something about doing a restoration that puts you on the line and makes you a *player*. It puts you on the inside of the game. You're taken more seriously as a yachtsman than a guy who's just bought a boat. You become a magnet. Once I bought *Bolero*, people came to me from all over. There was this constant stream of yachting luminaries." One very tactful visitor was Olin Stephens, age 95. "He came to take a look and I was thinking how nice it would be to get him on deck," Kane recalled. "Then I looked up and saw him scampering up the ladder faster than I could do it." According to Zimmer, "He immediately sprung up the ladder, took a look around, and commented, 'These Dorade vents are no darn good. They aren't going to work unless you put drain holes in them.'" While admiring the restoration, Stephens was a little discontented with some post-1949 additions, notably the hydraulic sheet winches that emitted a distinctly unclassical whine.

Bolero Restored

Some detail photographs taken in 2005 show the restored boat to be as simple and seamanlike as the original. (Left, top to bottom). The skylight and kerosene lamp in the saloon; the owner's berth, no longer in its own stateroom; the saloon with a John Mecray print of *Bolero*. (Above, top to bottom) The navigation station in the deckhouse; the repaired metal mizzenmast step. (© DAN NERNEY)

BOLERO'S KANES | 149

Other visitors were less tactful. "At least 200 people came through here and said they'd sailed in the boat," Potts said, shaking his head. "They sometimes could be a bother. Ed was saying, 'Everybody in the New York Yacht Club is telling me what to do.'"

Advice and assistance came also from John Nicholas and Anne Brown's three children who, naturally enough, shared a deep emotional connection with the boat. Nick Brown indicated that he would be disappointed if *Bolero* were not restored as exactly as possible to her original condition, including *Bolero* Blue canvas. When Carter Brown wrote the foreword for a book collecting the plans of *Bolero* and other Olin Stephens designs, he asserted an art historian's authority to the proposition that *Bolero* was a work of art. The book, titled *Lines* and published early in 2003, was lovingly organized by Knight Coolidge, a friend of Olin Stephens's and a contributor in many small ways to *Bolero*'s rebirth. (Carter Brown died in June 2002 so never saw the restored boat afloat.)

The Pilots Point crew reassembled in September 2002 and got to work on the planking, much of which had to be replaced. The inside surfaces of many planks neighboring the water tanks or the metal strapping were so soft that Zimmer could scrape away wood with his fingernails. The new planks had to be shaped with care because the boat had shrunk a little around the Monel ring frames.

First, though, Zimmer had to find some good mahogany, which had become elusive due to global conservation efforts. Zimmer (muttering about how Greenpeace was getting in the way of good boatbuilding) eventually found suitable Peruvian mahogany at a lumberyard in Massachusetts. He was proud that all the joints between the planks were scarfed and glued together without a single reinforcing butt block inside the hull.

In mid October 2002, Zimmer finally was able to get to work replacing the broken mizzen mast step, which the survey had indicated might be the boat's worst problem. The last plank went in with due ceremony two days before Christmas, and a month later, under a coat of white primer, *Bolero* was dropped into the icy water to swell up so she could get her outer coat of paint in whatever color the owners preferred.

Black or white topsides? Here was a lightning rod. Under the Browns, she had been black, which required regular repainting or touching up. Later owners painted the topsides a more easily maintained white until Gunther Sunkler returned to the original black. "Some total strangers would call us up and ask us, 'What color are you going to paint her?'" Marty Wallace recalled with mild annoyance. White would be more practical on a boat that would spend the winter in the Caribbean because the hull would be cooler. But black would be more traditional.

As often happened, the last word was hers. "Finally the day came in the spring of 2003 when we had to decide. Ed called up and asked me, and I said 'black.'" That choice pleased many people, but when it came time to choose a color for the transom, Kane made the less popular decision of having it varnished. "The contrarian in me made me do it," he said with a grin.

With her original cockpit and steering wheel (with a rim around its spokes), the restored *Bolero* leaves the rest of the fleet behind at Antigua Race Week. It was one of the regattas she won in 2004, her first serious racing season in years. Ed Kane's and Marty Wallace's biggest sacrifice was to commit *Bolero* to racing when they would rather be cruising. "This boat wants to race," he said. Hydraulic winches make sailing handling relatively easy. (© DANIEL FORSTER)

"Racing Isn't What Gets Us Up in the Morning"

There is a school of thought that a restored classic or an heirloom should be precisely like the original, even going so far as to have cotton sails (or at least synthetic sails that look like cotton). But Ed Kane and Marty Wallace wanted *Bolero* to be a boat they could use without too much trouble. They had already gone through the exercise of an ultra-loyal restoration when they helped bring up *Marilee* very close to her original state.

Once was enough. "I'm not interested in restoring *Bolero* to her original state," said Marty. "It's not like *Marilee*, whose concept was to restore her to 1926. What a pain in the neck it was to sail that boat!" Roller-furling headsails and power winches were an easy call because they allowed young (and not so young) people in a small crew to handle her big sails with relative ease. When *Bolero* appeared for her recommissioning ceremony at Harbour Court in June 2003, these modern sail-handling aides were there for all to see, along with canvas that was colored khaki, not *Bolero* Blue. Marty, with the assistance of Candy Langan, an interior designer (and the wife of Sparkman & Stephens's former chief designer), had redesigned the cushions and much of the interior to make them look much like the simple originals. At the same time, she added amenities to appeal to her family when cruising, including a flat-screen television with DVD player that could be hidden inside a traditional locker when not in use.

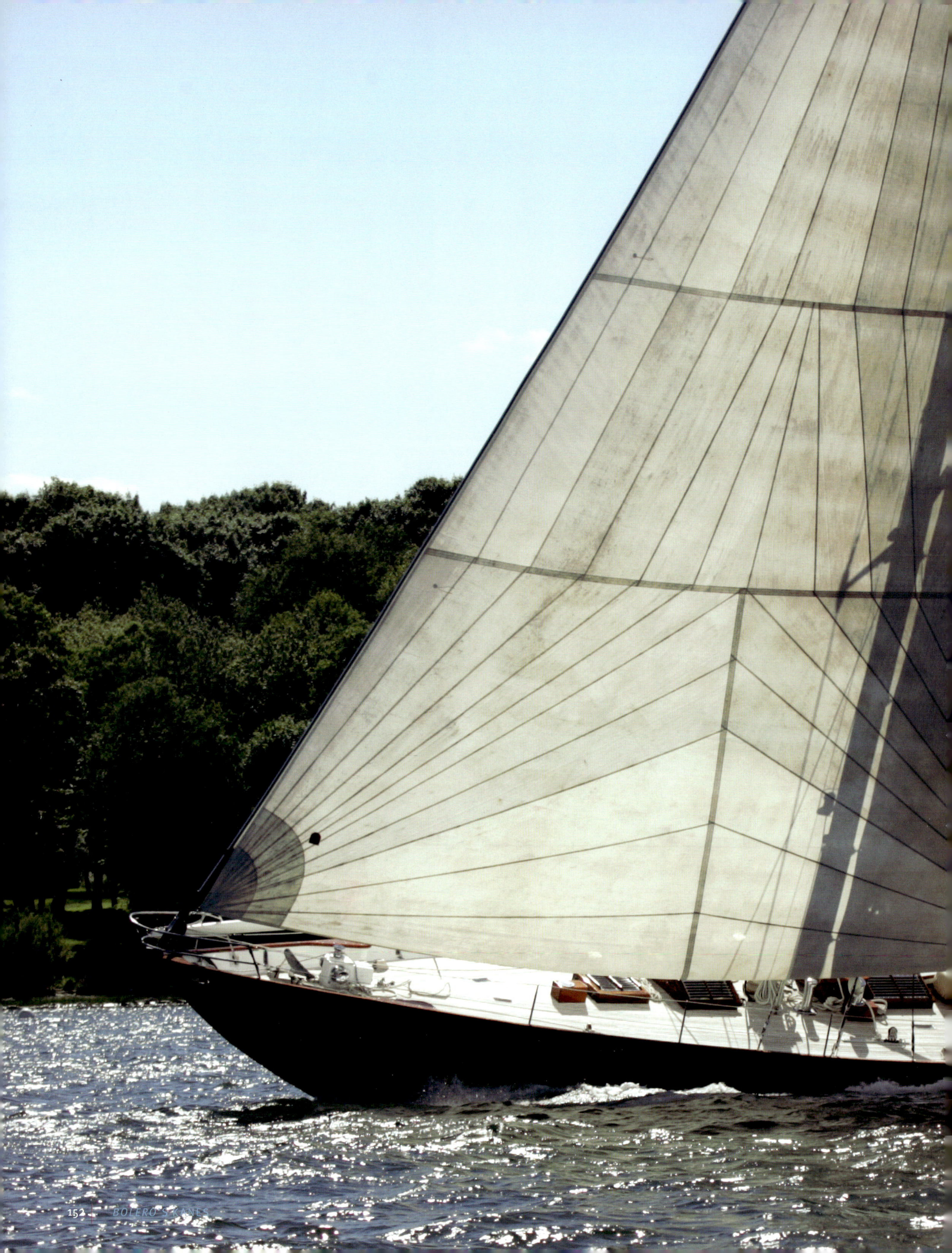

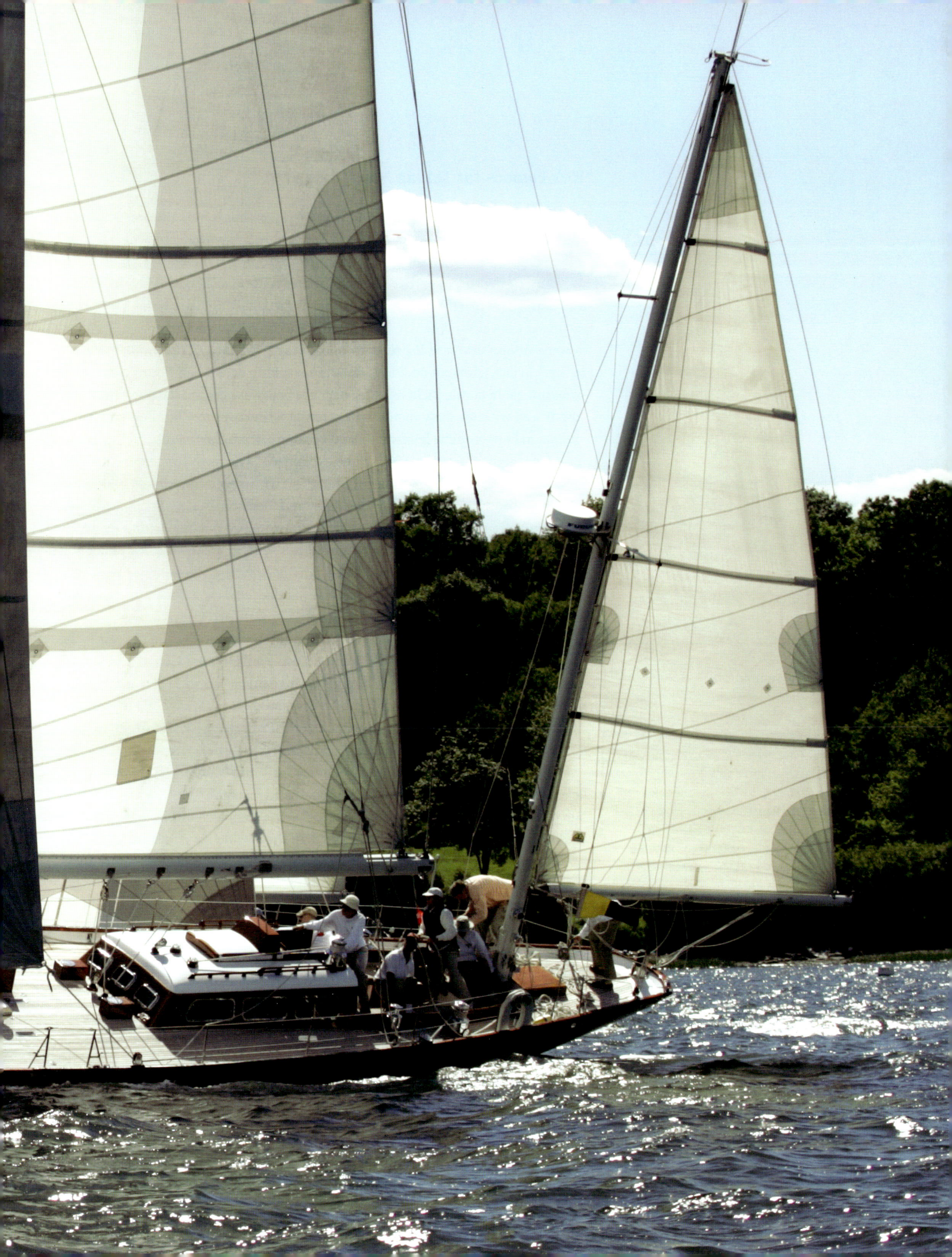

"He's Famous for Taking Naps"

Appearance is but one measure of authenticity. Another is how the object is used, and here Ed Kane was loyal to *Bolero*'s heritage in a way that can accurately be called self-sacrificial.

Among the surprises that Kane confronted with *Marilee* concerned the boat's use. "I asked my partners, 'We're not going to race this thing, are we?'" The rather surprised answer was that, yes, the boat would be raced, and hard, too. This led to some disappointment because, to quote Marty Wallace, "Eddie didn't take to racing." In fact, she went on, "He's famous for taking naps when *Bolero*'s in a race." True enough. In classic yacht regattas, once the boat was near the starting line, Kane quietly and without show handed the steering wheel over to Chip Barber, a navy veteran and very capable helmsman, and became just another member of the crew.

"I never got the racing bug," Kane explained. "The most fun about racing is the cocktail party afterward. Once I'm out there with a big crew, being on the helm doesn't mean anything to me." While Marty and their son, Nat, and daughter, Ellie, ably trimmed sails, Ed Kane, a very able seaman, helped out here and there while happily watching his boat and her competitors sailing, meanwhile keeping up a running commentary on the race. Occasionally he would slip below to read one of the history books he's devoted to and (yes, indeed) take a snooze while his boat raced and, often, won.

When the race was over and *Bolero* was on her mooring (which in Newport was off the Museum of Yachting, across Brenton Cove from Harbour Court), Marty and the children gathered below for a chummy board game or a session of reading while Ed helped put the boat away with the professional captain, Marty White, and the amateur crew. Later, the Kanes went ashore for the regatta party, and they returned for more family time together before an early bedtime with books.

"Racing isn't what gets us up in the morning," said Marty. "When we bought *Bolero*, my fantasy was to go to the Vineyard and just stay on the boat." It was a sign of Ed's and Marty's loyal dedication to *Bolero*'s complete restoration – physical and otherwise – that they raced her more than they would have preferred. In 2004, her first full sailing season since the restoration, they sacrificed a large part of their cruising schedule, put up with a crowded boat, bought an expensive jib solely for racing, and entered four different classic yacht regattas, three at Newport and one at Antigua – all so that the boat they considered a family cruiser would satisfy the demands of its pedigree. "*This boat wants to race*," Kane said emphatically. "You know how it is when a boat gets going, like using a passing gear on a car? If classic yacht racing ever gets going in the U.S. as it is in Europe, this boat would dominate."

As it was, *Bolero* did fine. In the 13 races she sailed in 2004, she had six first-place finishes and four seconds – a record in short races that was almost as good as the one that John Nicholas Brown put together over long distances. In fresh winds at the Antigua Classic Yacht Regatta in April, she won the Mt. Gay Rum Trophy as the top boat in the most competitive class. Two months later, in lighter conditions, she won her class with a 1-1-1 record at the New York Yacht Club's 150th

(Previous Spread) The restored *Bolero* sprints along the Jamestown shore during the New York Yacht Club's 150th Annual Regatta on Narragansett Bay in 2004. In her first racing season in 40 years, she won six out of 13 races on the classic yacht circuit. Chip Barber is at the helm, tactician John Rousmaniere stands at the companionway near Marty Wallace, and skipper Marty White trims the jib. With her modern full-battened sails and hydraulic winches in place of the old coffee grinders, she looks just as sleek as in her early years. (© DAN NERNEY)

Olin Stephens, *Bolero*'s designer and former watch captain, came out one day in 2004 and called some wind shifts that helped win a race. To his right is author John Rousmaniere. (© DAN NERNEY)

Annual Regatta, where she also was top boat in all classics classes. In judged events, meanwhile, she won several prizes, most notably the top prize in the *Concours d'Elegance* at the Sparkman & Stephens 75th Anniversary, at Mystic Seaport.

Kane analyzed the situation and his feelings about it and came away with an original perspective on boat restoration: "My advice to anybody considering the process – and I've met a lot of people with the means and time available to do it – is this: When you look back at this valuable experience, you see it's not just a question of installing a new wooden frame. *It's the people.* You're taking some risks, and risk pulls people together. You don't just end up with a boat and prizes. You end up with a collection of people."

It was the people, but the reason they were together was the boat. When *Bolero* raced, Kane was often content not to be aboard. "I'm happy to stand on the dock and watch her sail off," he said. Sometimes he stayed on shore, but more often he sailed on one of his boat's competitors. He was not being diffident or contrary. It was just that he wanted to look at the one object – the single work of art – that united all the intriguing, complex, and creative men and women who have made up this story. What pleased him had long been pleasing thousands, and that was watching *Bolero* under sail, making a brave sight.

Notes

KEY: JNBP, John Nicholas Brown Papers, John Nicholas Brown Center for the Study of American Civilization, Brown University, Providence, Rhode Island.

Chapter 1

Epigraph: via Edward Kane from Condor Smith and Ezmarelda Hammerton, the first captains of the restored *Bolero*.

"The man who": Nevins, "On the Building of a Yacht," *Yachting*, May 1935. "Commodore John Nicholas Brown": "general ship's maintenance," *Bolero* log.

"The presence": *Boston Globe*, July 3, 1949.

Anne Brown: Sailing Journal.

"Flotillas," "Olin's lines": J. Carter Brown, Foreword.

"Romping along": Bill Robinson, "Smallest Winner… Biggest Fleet," *Yachting*, August 1964.

"Bolero Browns": Anne Brown, "Goodbye, *Bolero*."

Chapter 2

"Sailors frequently": Stephens, "Trends in Yacht Design, 1920-1986."

"A comfortable": J. Carter Brown, Foreword.

Cutter: René de Kerchove, *International Maritime Dictionary*, 2nd ed. (New York: Van Nostrand, 1961).

Taylor on costs: Livingston, *Sailing the Bay*.

"A ship is": Loveridge, "*Bolero*."

"These two studies": Sparkman to Brown, August 20, 1946, Yachts/*Bolero* MSS I, Box A, folder F 2, JNBP.

"Personally": Stephens to Brown, September 13, 1946, Yachts/*Bolero* MSS I, Box A, folder F 3, JNBP.

Chapter 3

Epigraph: Theodore Roethke, "Words for Young Writers," *On Poetry and Craft* (Port Townsend, WA: Copper Canyon, 2001).

"Visions transcending": Samuel Eliot Morison, *The Maritime History of Massachusetts* (Boston: Houghton, Mifflin, 1921).

"I felt": Doll, *Heart of the Hilltop*.

"My first," "I grew up," "He was less": Brown obituary, *Providence Journal*, October 11, 1979.

"Their candles": Hedges, *Browns of Providence Plantations: The Nineteenth Century*.

"World's Richest Baby": *Saturday Evening Post*, August 23, 1947.

"The serious," "Were you": Loveridge, "*Bolero*."

St. George's chapel: Doll, *Heart of the Hilltop*; Cram, *My Life in Architecture*; Cram, "Ordeal by Beauty."

Windshield: Neumann, *Richard Neutra's Windshield House*; Neutra, *Survival through Design*; Neutra, *Nature Near*; Fred A. Bernstein, "When Modern Married Money," *New York Times*, February 3, 2002.

Dances: Anatole Chujoy and P. W. Manchester, comp., *The Dance Encyclopedia*. rev. ed. (New York: Simon and Schuster, 1967).

"I want": Brown to George B. Buck, Jr., July 27, 1959, B. 43 Yachts, Miscellaneous, *Tango*, JNBP.

Government service, "Affable but shy": Sidney Shallett, "Capital Portrait," *New York Times Sunday Magazine*, January 12, 1947.

"The ability": *New York Times*, February 1, 1949.

Krock: *New York Times*, March 6, 1949.

"A Naval": Chauncey Stillman to Browns, August 12, 1952, *Bolero* II, 1952 Bermuda Race folder, JNBP.

Chapter 4

Epigraph: Stephens, *All This and Sailing, Too.*

Alden: Robert W. Carrick and Richard Henderson, *John G. Alden and His Yacht Designs* (Camden, ME: International Marine, 1984).

Lines Comparison: Sparkman & Stephens Collection, Ships Plans Library, Mystic Seaport.

"Though *per se*": Stephens in plans section, *Yachting*, January 1928.

"I was lucky": Stephens, *All This and Sailing, Too.*

"You just try": Robert W. Carrick and Stanley Z. Rosenfeld, *Defending the America's Cup* (New York: Knopf, 1969).

"The imperturbable": Fox, "Across the Atlantic in *Dorade*."

"*Dorade* had no trouble": Loomis, *Ocean Racing.*

"He did not": Ogilvy, *Larchmont Yacht Club.*

"Shy and," "Yacht Designer": *Scribner's*, June 1938.

Chapter 5

Epigraph: Roderick Stephens Jr., interview, 1991.

"I had to": Nevins to W.P. Stephens, January 3, 1946, W. P. Stephens Papers, Collection 91, G.W. Blunt White Library, Mystic Seaport.

"The relationship": Tracy Kidder, *House* (1985; reprint, Boston: Mariner-Houghton Mifflin, 1999), 233.

Fishers Island One Design Class: contract and specifications, Charles D. Mower Collection, Ships Plans Library, Mystic Seaport.

Wood as construction material: Scheffer, *et al.*, "A Technical Comparison of White and Red Oaks"; Wilson, "Making a Choice"; Jagels, "Wood Technology."

"All's Well": *Business Week*, September 4, 1954.

Fiberglass: Daniels Spurr, *Heart of Glass: Fiberglass Boats and the Men Who Made Them* (Camden, ME: International Marine, 2000).

"The saddest day": *Yachting*, December 1962.

"A very congenial": Leonard Halvorsen, interview, 1994.

"These 'Clammers'": Payne, *City Island.*

"It's what": James B. Simpson, *Simpson's Contemporary Quotations*, 1988.

"From high forehead": *New Yorker*, September 10, 1938.

Herbert Lee: interview, 1992.

Nils Halvorsen: oral history.

Marjorie Young: Brian Kologe, "Sweet Lines," and Constance Andrews to author, October 4, 2004.

Odyssey: bill in Nevins Collection, vol. 7, City Island Nautical Museum.

"Champagne appetite": Nevins to W.P. Stephens, January 3, 1946, W. P. Stephens Papers, Collection 91, G. W. Blunt White Library, Mystic Seaport.

Donald C. Starr: *The Schooner Pilgrim's Progress: A Voyage around the World, 1932-1934* (Salem, MA: Peabody Essex Museum, 1996).

Audits: Audit Company of America report for 1925, March 17, 1926, Nevins Collection, vol. 7, City Island Nautical Museum.

Chapter 6

Epigraph: Rod Stephens comment to author, 1976.

Halvorsen: Nils Halvorsen oral history.

"A missing": Dana A. Story, *Growing up in a Shipyard* (Mystic: Mystic Seaport, 1991).

"Laying her": Nevins, "On the Building of a Yacht," *Yachting*, March 1935.

"Stern deck": Plan 711-5, Sparkman & Stephens Collection, Ships Plans Library, Mystic Seaport.

"Main Deck Framing": Sparkman & Stephens Collection, Ships Plans Library, Mystic Seaport.

Planking: *Yachting*, January 1936.

Sails: Records of Ratsey & Lapthorn, Collection 236, G. W. Blunt White Library, Mystic Seaport (my thanks to Debbie Pointer for passing on materials from this collection).

Rod Stephens memorandums: Sparkman & Stephens *Bolero* file, Yachts/*Bolero* MSS I, Box A, folder F10, and in addenda to Final Specifications, February 10, 1949, JNBP.

"It has been": log entry, July 10, 1935, *Stormy Weather* log, Roderick Stephens Jr. Collection, Collection 163, G. W. Blunt White Library, Mystic Seaport.

"I feel the beauty": Neumann, *Richard Neutra's Windshield House*.

Brown comments on Final Specifications: January 18, 1949, Yachts/*Bolero* MSS I, Box A, folder F 9, JNBP.

Names of screws: Wallace E. Tobin III, "Inside *Columbia*," *Yachting*, November 1958.

"I have had": Stephens to Lawton, February 8 and 9, 1949, Yachts/*Bolero* MSS I, Box A, folder F10, JNBP.

"We are getting": Stephens to Brown, January 11, 1949, Yachts/*Bolero* MSS I, Box A, folder F 9, JNBP.

"When you went aboard": Loveridge, "*Bolero*."

"She is not": Smith, "A Boat is a Boat."

Chapter 7

Epigraph: Brown to Stephens, August 16, 1971, Box 37, Sparkman & Stephens 1962-1971 file, JNBP.

"Out of commission": *Baruna* log.

"His Majesty": Keeper of the Privy Purse to Secretary of the New York Yacht Club, September 22, 1950, *Bolero* II box, 1950 folder, JNBP.

"A minute and": Engelina Dickerson in Kinney and Bourne, *Best of the Best*.

"It didn't take," "like me": Shields, *Cornelius Shields on Sailing*.

"No matter": John Rendel, "Sports of the Times: Sailing Man," *New York Times*, July 29, 1954.

Shields family history: see Neil F. Libbey, *Portside: An Early History of the Royal Cape Breton Yacht Club* (Baddeck, NS: Royal Cape Breton Yacht Club, 2003).

"The difference": Hoyt, *Addicted to Sail*.

"It dawned": Smith, "A Boat is a Boat."

Race results: New York Yacht Club Race Committee reports, Parkinson, *Nowhere is Too Far*, and Parkinson, *History of the New York Yacht Club*.

"It's a boat": *Providence Journal*, June 22, 1950.

"Ain't it": Taylor to Brown, June 30, 1950, Bolero II Box, 1950 Bermuda Race File, JNBP.

"The Stephens brothers": Joseph W. Appleton to Anne Brown, October 15, 1949, *Bolero* II Box, JNBP.

Log entries: Baruna and *Bolero* logs.

"At this point": Kinney, *You are First*.

"It left me": *Providence Journal*, June 22, 1951.

"A loud," Wall, "Down and Up Aboard *Bolero*."

"Were made": *New York Herald-Tribune*, August 13, 1954.

"What I am": Brown to Stephens, August 16, 1971, Box 37, Sparkman & Stephens 1962-1971 file, JNBP.

Chapter 8

Epigraph: Robert C. Keefe to author.

"Seasons warmest": Brown to Salen, December 22, 1955, *Bolero* II, sale folder, JNBP.

"I am sorry": Walter Dring Jr. to Brown, November 23, 1955, *Bolero* II, sale folder, JNBP.

Swedish ownership: English translation of "*Bolero*'s Bermuda Sail" (1956); Sven H. Salen, "Memories of *Bolero*," March 15, 1995.

"I stood": Keefe, "*Baruna* vs. *Bolero*."

"The best": Keefe letter, *Latitude 38*, October 2000.

Sally Ames Langmuir: "Only Woman Skipper: She May Win Race," *Los Angeles Times*, June 23 1959.

"Big, beautiful": "Alfred F. Loomis, "*Princess* Wins Mazatlan Race, *Yachting*, December 1963.

"As close as": Lew McMasters, "*Doubloon* Wins Tough Race to Lauderdale," *Yachting*, March 1963.

"Her charm and": A. Rulon Mansfield, "American Letter," *Yachting World*, March 1963.

"Coming apart": Alfred F. Loomis, "The Fastnet Race," *Yachting*, October 1963.

"Wonderful express": John Rendel, "*Bolero* Captures Conover Trophy," *New York Times*, May 31, 1965.

"Just charged": Smith, "A Boat is a Boat."

Ted Turner: Bruce Kirby, "Viewed from the Helm," *One-Design and Offshore Yachtsman*, February 1968.

Chapter 9

Epigraph: Welch, "*Bolero* Purchase and Sale Survey Report."

"The pattern": Wendy Mitman Clarke, "His Obsession: Restoration of *Bolero*," *Soundings*, September 1994.

"There's the boat": Mason, "*Bolero* Dances."

Classic yachts, *Marilee*: Robin Lloyd, "*Marilee*: A New York 40 Reborn," *Classic Boat*, August 2001; and Lewis Kleinhans, "New York 40s and 50s," *Sailing Craft*, ed. Edwin J. Schoettle (New York: Macmillan, 1928).

"Some modern ocean": Stephens, "Some Thoughts on Stability."

"I'm a little": *Ellsworth American*, August 8, 2004.

"At the time": Stephens and Rousmaniere, "Restoring the Classics."

Kirawan restoration: Nicholas Brown, "Reframing from the Outside," *WoodenBoat*, May/June 2004.

Chapter 10

Epigraph: Kane comment to author.

"Has opened up": Zimmer to Kane, September 22, 2001, Zimmer Collection.

Sources

Interviews and Correspondence

Oliver Ames, Henry H. Anderson, Constance Andrews, Charles H. Barber III, B. Devereux Barker III, Blake A. Bell, John B. Bonds, Peter C. Bowker, J. Nicholas Brown, Wendy Mitman Clarke, E. Kirkland and Helen Cooper, Steve Dashew, Anne Davidson, Mark P. Ellis, Robert S. Erskine Jr., Angela Brown Fischer, Edwin G. Fischer, Mitchell C. Gibbons-Neff, Richard F. Goennel, Albert H. Gordon, Joseph Gould, Halsey C. Herreshoff, Thomas B. Hovey, Kitty Hoyt, Bruce Johnson, William H. Dyer Jones, Jean Taylor Johnson, Edward W. Kane, Robert C. Keefe, Bruce R. W. Kirby, Susan A. Kline, W. Stephen Lirakis, Douglas Logan, Anita Mason, Carleton Mitchell, Keith Morgan, Thomas Nye, A. Rives Potts Jr., Deborah Rogers, James A. Rousmaniere Sr., Diana Russell, Christer Salen, Sven Salen, John E. Sanford, Larry Shepard, Olin J. Stephens II, Henry I. Strauss, Wallace E. Tobin III, Charles R. Ulmer, Martha Wallace, George C. Welch, Walter N. Wheeler III, Marty and Denise White, Harold Pratt Wilmerding, Marjorie Gladding Young Wolff, Hans Zimmer.

Selected Bibliography

Adair, L.A., and John Nicholas Brown. "Radar Signaling: A Simple Way to Make Your Presence Known." *Yachting*, April 1953.

Albion, Robert Greenhalgh, and Robert Howe Connery. *Forrestal and the Navy*. New York: Columbia University Press, 1962.

Barlow, Jeffrey G. *Revolt of the Admirals: The Fight for Naval Aviation, 1945-1950*. Washington: Naval Historical Center, 1994.

Baruna logs, G.W. Blunt White Library, Mystic Seaport,

Bolero logs, John Nicholas Brown Papers. John Nicholas Brown Center for the Study of American Civilization, Providence, Rhode Island.

Brown, Anne S. K. "Goodbye, *Bolero*." *The Rudder*, March 1957.

———. Sailing journal, 1949. John Nicholas Brown Papers. John Nicholas Brown Center for the Study of American Civilization, Providence, Rhode Island.

Brown, J. Carter. Foreword. In *Lines: A Half-Century of Yacht Designs by Sparkman & Stephens, 1930-1980*, by Olin J Stephens II. Jaffrey, NH: Godine, 2003.

Brown, John Nicholas. Autobiographical notes in 25th and 50th anniversary reports, Harvard College.

City Island: A Maritime History. New York City Maritime Heritage Preservation Study. New York: Department of City Planning, [2001?].

Cram, Ralph Adams. *My Life in Architecture*. Boston: Little, Brown, 1936.

———. "Ordeal by Beauty." In *Convictions and Controversies*. Boston: Marshall Jones, 1935.

Cunningham, Briggs S. Interview by Fred Calabretta, March 31, 1990, OH 90-1. Sound Archive, G. W. Blunt White Library, Mystic Seaport.

Doll, John G. *Heart of the Hilltop: The St. George's School Chapel*. Newport, RI: St. George's School, 2003.

Flood, Allen, and Robert Mullen. *City Island: History, Legend and Tradition, Yachting*. City Island, NY: 1949.

Fox, John D. "Across the Atlantic in *Dorade*." Unpublished manuscript, 1931.

Halvorsen, Leonard. Interview by Fred Calabretta, June 17, 1994, OH 94-12. Sound Archive, G. W. Blunt White Library, Mystic Seaport.

Halvorsen, Nils. Oral history, undated. Nevins Collection, City Island Nautical Museum, vol. 7.

Hedges, James B. *The Browns of Providence Plantations: The Colonial Years*. Cambridge: Harvard University Press, 1952.

———. *The Browns of Providence Plantations: The Nineteenth Century*. Providence: Brown University Press, 1968.

Hoyt, Norris D. *Addicted to Sail: A Half Century of Yachting Experiences*. New York: W.W. Norton, 1987.

Hunt, Morton M. "Up from Corker." *The New Yorker*, September 7, 14, 1957.

Jagels, Richard. "Wood Technology." *WoodenBoat*.

Keefe, Robert C. "*Baruna* vs. *Bolero*." St. Francis Yacht Club *Mainsheet*, 1982.

Kinney, Francis S. *Skene's Elements of Yacht Design*. 8th edition. New York: Dodd, Mead, 1972.

———. *"You Are First," The Story of Olin and Rod Stephens of Sparkman & Stephens, Inc.* New York: Dodd, Mead, 1978.

Kinney, Francis S., and Russell Bourne. *Best of the Best: The Yacht Designs of Sparkman & Stephens*. New York: W.W. Norton, 1996.

Kologe, Brian. "Sweet Lines." *WoodenBoat*, July/August 2004.

Lee, Herbert B. Interview by Fred Calabretta, March 11, 1992, OH 92-2. Sound Archive, G.W. Blunt White Library, Mystic Seaport.

Levy, Alan H. *Edward McDowell: An American Master*. Lanham, MD: Scarecrow Press, 1998.

Livingston, Kimball. *Sailing the Bay*. San Francisco: White Bridge, 1998.

Loomis, Alfred F. *Ocean Racing: The Great Blue-Water Yacht Races, 1866-1935*. New York: Morrow, 1936.

Loveridge, G. Y. "Bolero." *Providence Sunday Journal Sunday Magazine*, July 31, 1949.

MacGregor, Morris J., Jr. *Integration of the Armed Forces, 1940-1965*. Washington: U.S. Army Center of Military History, 1985.

McMenemy, Michael, and Debbie Pointer. "The Three Davis-Nevins Motorsailers." *WoodenBoat*, November/December 1990.

McNitt, Robert W. *Sailing at the Naval Academy: An Illustrated History*. Annapolis, MD: Naval Institute Press, 1996.

Mason, Charles. "*Bolero* Dances." *Sail*, December 1996.

Merrill, Owen P., Journal of Owen P. Merrill, RF 520. Manuscripts Collection, G. W. Blunt White Library, Mystic Seaport.

Neumann, Dietrich, ed. *Richard Neutra's Windshield House*. Cambridge: Harvard University Graduate School of Design, 2001.

Neutra, Richard. *Nature Near: Late Essays of Richard Neutra*. Ed. William Marlin. Santa Barbara: Capra, 1989.

———. *Survival through Design*. New York: Oxford University Press, 1954.

Nevins, Henry B. "Economy Versus Cheapness." *Yachting*, September 1933.

———. "On the Building of a Yacht." *Yachting*, March, April, May 1935.

Nicholas, Lynn H. *The Rape of Europa: the Fate of Europe's Treasures in the Third Reich and the Second World War*. New York: Knopf, 1994.

Nye, Tom. "Henry B. Nevins, Yacht Builder." Nevins Collection, City Island Nautical Museum.

Ogilvy, C. Stanley. *The Larchmont Yacht Club: A History, 1880-1990*. Larchmont, NY: Larchmont Yacht Club, 1993.

Parkinson, John, Jr. *The History of the New York Yacht Club*. 2 vols. New York: New York Yacht Club, 1972.

———. *Nowhere is Too Far: The Annals of the Cruising Club of America*. New York: Cruising Club of America, 1960.

Payne, Alice. *City Island: Tales of the Clam Diggers*. Floral Park, NY: Graphicopy, 1969.

Ratsey & Lapthorn Collection. Collection 53. Daniel S. Gregory Ships Plans Library, Mystic Seaport.

Report of the Committee on the Visual Arts at Harvard University. Cambridge, MA: Harvard University, 1956.

Rousmaniere, John. "Kenneth S. M. Davidson," "Olin J. Stephens II." *Encyclopedia of Yacht Designers*. Edited by Lucia del Sol Knight and Daniel B. MacNaughton. New York: W.W. Norton, 2005.

———. "*Kirawan Redux*: The 1936 Bermuda Race Winner Returns." *WoodenBoat*, January/February 2001.

———. *Sailing at Fishers: A History of the Fishers Island Yacht Club*. Mystic, CT: Mystic Seaport, 2004.

———. *Sleek*. Mystic, CT: Mystic Seaport, 2003.

Sauerbrey, Florence. "The Fighting Forties." *Maritime Life and Traditions*, Spring 2003.

Scheffer, Theodore C., George H. Engleith, and Catherine G. Duncan. "A Technical Comparison of White and Red Oaks." *WoodenBoat*, September/October 1974.

Shields, Cornelius. *Cornelius Shields on Sailing*. Englewood Cliffs, NJ: Prentice-Hall, 1964.

Smith, Bob. "A Boat is a Boat [*Bolero*]." *One-Design & Offshore Yachtsman*, October 1965.

Sparkman & Stephens. "*Bolero* Final Specifications," 1948 and 1949. *Bolero* Collection, Sparkman & Stephens, Inc.

Stephens, Olin J., II. *All This and Sailing, Too.* Mystic, CT: Mystic Seaport, 1999.

———. "Boatwrights Turn to New Materials." *New York Times*, January 12, 1947.

———. *Lines: A Half-Century of Yacht Designs by Sparkman & Stephens, 1930-1980.* Jaffrey, NH: Godine, 2003.

———. "Some Thoughts on Stability" and "Trends in Yacht Design, 1920-1986." *Desirable and Undesirable Characteristics of Offshore Yachts.* Edited by John Rousmaniere. New York: W.W. Norton, 1987.

———. "Where Performance Meets Aesthetics." *Sailing World*, November 2004.

Stephens, Olin J., II, and John Rousmaniere. "Restoring the Classics: A Conversation with Olin Stephens." *WoodenBoat*, July/August 2004

———. "A Legend Looks to the Future." *Practical Sailor*, November 1, 2004.

Stephens, Roderick S., Jr. Interview by Fred Calabretta, August 16, 1991, OH 91-4. Sound Archive, G. W. Blunt White Library, Mystic Seaport.

Stephens, William P. "City Island." *The Rudder*, July 1917.

———. *Traditions and Memories of American Yachting.* Brooklin, ME: WoodenBoat Publications, 1989.

Taylor, William H. "Henry B. Nevins, Master Yacht Builder." *Yachting*, April 1950.

Tobin, Wallace E., III. "Inside Columbia." *Yachting*, September, October, November 1958.

Wall, Dick. "Down and Up Aboard *Bolero*." *One-Design Offshore Yachtsman*, June 1968.

Welch, George C. "*Bolero* Purchase and Sale Survey Report," November 8, 2000.

Wilson, Jonathan. "Making a Choice." *WoodenBoat*, March/April, May/June 1976.

"Yacht-Builder [Henry B. Nevins]." *The New Yorker*, September 10, 1938.

"Yacht Designer [Olin Stephens]." *Scribner's Magazine*, June 1938.

Index

A

Adams, Tom 140
Airborne 133, 134, 145, 147
Alden, John 45
All This and Sailing, Too 51, 54
Aluminum 85
Ames Langmuir, Sally Blair 120-21, 123, 124
Ames, Frederick Lothrup 121
Antigua Classic Yacht Regatta 154
Appleton, Joseph 107, 127
Argyll 105
Astor Cup, 98, 99, 112
Audacious 123, 145

B

Barber, Chip 143, 154
Barker, Devereux 125
Barnett, Jeff 148
Baruna 11, 16, 22, 23, 24, 25, 26, 27, 39, 52, 53, 87, 97, 98, 99, 101, 105, 106, 109, 110, 111, 112, 119, 120
Black Watch 98
Block Island Race 125
Bolero blue 94-95
Bowker, Peter 123, 131
Brilliant 53, 74
Britannia 49
Brown, Angela 11, 12, 26, 27, 36, 37, 103
Brown, Anne Kinsolving 11, 14, 15, 18, 21, 22, 26, 27, 28, 30; background 35; 36, 38, 42, 43, 51, 61, 93, 95, 100, 105, 107, 109, 112, 127, 150
Brown, Carter 14, 18, 22, 36, 37, 38, 98, 100, 104, 115, 127, 150
Brown, John Nicholas 11, 14, 15, 18, 21, 26, 28; as Assistant Secretary of the Navy for Air, 27, 31, 40-41; as cultural advisor 40; concept for *Bolero* 21, 22, 25-27; family background 30; childhood 31; and St. George's School chapel 31-34; as philanthropist 34-35; as yachtsman 36; personality 37; and Windshield 38-39; elected to National Academy of Arts and Sciences 41; as New York Yacht Club commodore 41-42, 59; and radar 42; 45, 46, 47, 48, 61, 65, 68, 79, 83, 87, 89, 98, 101, 103, 104, 105, 111, 112; sells *Bolero* 115-16, 120, 121, 127, 154
Brown, Nicholas 14, 22, 36, 37, 40, 93, 100, 104, 110, 115, 131, 150
Burgess, W. Starling 71

C

Cantiere Navale dell'Argentario 137
Cape Hatteras 126
Caribbee 115
Cedar 83
Celone, Chuck 148
City Island, New York 61, 75-77
Coletti, Joseph 32, 127
Columbia 51, 53, 67, 85, 101
Conga 36
Constellation 121, 123
Corker 46

Cotton Blossom IV 98
Courante 21, 22, 23, 26, 39, 40, 97, 120
Cram, Ralph Adams 30, 32, 34, 38, 68
Crouch, George 66
Crouthamel, Phil 148
Cunningham, Briggs 53, 85
Cutter 23

D

Dashew, Steve 123
Davidson, Dr. Kenneth S. M. 51-52, 89, 104, 111, 116
Djinn 98, 100
Derecktor, Bob 81
Dickerson, Engelina 99
Dorade 47, 49, 53, 67, 85, 88, 89, 119, 137, 139, 148
DUKW 54

E

Eastern Yacht Club 15
Edlu 44
Endeavour 138
Escapade 98, 123

F

Fiberglass 67
Fife, William, III 49
Finisterre 48, 115
Fir 83
Fischer, Garry 103
Fishers Island 14, 15, 21, 26, 35, 36, 37, 38, 39, 61, 62
Fishers Island One Design 61, 62
Flica 145
Flica II 145
Fox, John 49
Fuller, A. Howard 52

G

Gauss, Arthur 13, 77, 79
Genoa jib 116
Gavotte 35
Gimcrack 52
Goennel, Richard 31, 46, 103, 105, 106, 109, 112, 116
Grand Prix d'Élegance 137

H

Haggerty, Patrick 53
Halvorsen, Nils 35, 55, 70, 71, 74, 75, 77, 79-80, 145
Harbour Court 31, 34, 35, 37, 43
Harvard University 31, 115
Henry B. Nevins Yacht Yard 11, 13, 16, 25, 27, 35, 45, 47, 49, 53, 59-74, 76, 77, 79, 85, 86, 103, 135
Herbert, George 139
Herreshoff, Halsey 90, 135, 145
Herreshoff, John Brown 36, 65
Herreshoff, Nathanael Greene 36, 48-49, 82
Hopak 36, 103
Horowitz, Sandy 140

Hovey, Tom 124
Hoyt, Norris D. 102, 104

I

International Yacht Restoration School 138, 143
Intrepid 53

J

Johnson, J. Seward 52
Jones, Dyer 37
Jordan, Dennis 119, 120

K

Kane, Edward 29; background 132-34; restores *Marilee* 135-36, 140-41; restores *Bolero* 141-50; 151, 154, 155
Keefe, Bob 104, 119, 120
Kidder, Tracy 59
King's Cup 98, 99
Kirawan 140
Kline, Susan 90

L

Langan, Candy 151
Lawton, Captain Fred 13, 14, 16, 93, 101-102, 103, 104, 116
Lee, Herbert 69, 70
Lemos, Albert 107
Locust 82
Lofting 78, 79

M

MacDowell, Marian Nevins 68
MacDowell Colony 68
Mahogany 62, 83-84, 150
Malabar 45
Malagueña 36, 127
Marilee 135-36, 140-41, 143, 144, 147, 151, 154
Mason, Al 46, 55
Masts 63
McPhee, Greg 148
Meyer, Elizabeth 138
Michael, James 25, 119, 120
Mistress 42
Mitchell, Carleton 48, 115
Monel 64, 84
Morgan, Henry S. 61
Mower, Charles D 61
Murray, Rufus 49, 59, 61, 65, 66, 80, 135, 147
Mustang 90
Mystic Seaport 46, 53, 65

N

Neff, Mitch 132, 143, 147
Neutra, Richard 37, 38, 68

Nevins, Henry B. 11-12, 13, 25, 27, 30, 35, 47, 49, 52, 58, 59; background 60-64, 65, 66, 67; character of 68; 69, 70, 71, 72; standards of 74; 75, 76, 77, 79, 80, 81, 82, 83, 84, 85, 86, 98, 101, 103, 107, 116, 120, 135, 137, 140, 141, 144
New York Yacht Club Annual Cruise, 15, 96-97, 98, 99; 16, 21, 37, 41, 42, 43, 59, 61, 82, 95, 107, 112, 115, 120, 127, 134, 135, 141, 143, 145, 150; 150th Annual Regatta 154-55
Newcomb, Charlie, 148
Newport-Annapolis Race, 1951 109-11; 1953 112
Newport-Bermuda Race, 1950 105-06; 1952 42; 1954 18; 1956 116-17; 2000 140
Niña 98
Nyala 137, 144
Nye, Tom 68, 77

O

Oak 65-66, 82
Orient 21, 39, 120
Orne, Percy 63

P

Paint 94
Pavanne 36
Pilgrim 72
Pilots Point 144-50
Potter, Tom 140
Piroutte 36
Plywood 64
Polka 36
Polly 59, 64, 74
Pomelion 71, 72
Potts, Rives 144, 145, 147, 150
Princess 36

R

Rapoza, Frank 148
Ratsey & Lapthorn 77, 86-87
Roethke, Theodore 29
Rolston, Jim 148
Roosevelt, George E. 42
Root, Elihu, Jr. 71
Rugossa II 145
Russell, Diana 90

S

Sails 86-87
Salen, Sven 103, 116-17
San Francisco, California 119-20
Saraband 36, 39
Schmeling, Arnie 123
Shag 36
Shields, Cornelius 61, 100-101, 103, 104, 105, 109, 116
Smith, Bob 95, 104, 125

Sparkman & Stephens 13, 21, 22, 24, 26, 27, 39, 40, 45, 47, 49, 51, 52, 53, 55, 56, 57, 59, 61, 67, 72, 79, 81, 82, 83, 84, 85, 88, 89, 90, 93, 94, 97, 98, 105, 107, 115, 116, 119, 120, 132, 137, 144, 151, 155
Sparkman, Drake 22, 26, 39, 47
Spruce 63, 83
Starr, Donald 72
St. Francis Yacht Club 119
St. George's School 31, 36; chapel 32-34
Stephens, Olin J., II, 11, 18, 22, 26, 27, 30, 39, 45, 46, 47, 48, 49, 50, 51, 53, 54, 55, 62, 65, 67, 70, 71, 72, 77, 79, 89, 93, 97, 100, 101, 103, 104, 105, 113, 116, 120, 137, 139, 144, 145, 148, 150
Stephens, Roderick S. Jr. 13, 14, 15, 16, 30, 46, 47, 49, 53, 54, 55, 65, 66, 67, 74, 79, 80, 81, 84, 85, 86, 87, 88-90, 93, 107, 139, 140, 144, 145
Stillman, Chauncey 43
Stone, Herbert L. 61
Stormy Weather 44, 45, 46, 50, 89, 137
Sunkler, Gunther 131-32, 141, 143, 150

T

Tango 36, 37
Tarantella 36
Taylor, Henry 11, 22, 25, 39, 87, 97, 98, 101, 106, 109, 111, 119
Taylor, Stillman 98, 109, 111
Teak 83
Ticonderoga 98, 145
Transatlantic race 123-24
Turner, Ted 115, 126

U

Uhle, Henry 55
Ulmer, Charles 77

V

Venturer 116, 117, 123, 145
Victory class 61
Vim 99, 107
Volta 36

W

Wallace, Marty 132, 133, 134, 135, 138, 143, 147, 150, 151, 154
Wallace, Ray 123
Watson, George L. 49
Welch, George C. 141
Wheeler, Walter, III 112
Whitcomb, Eben 148
White, Elizabeth Leahey 126
White, Marty 154
Wilson, Jonathan 137
Windigo 145
Windshield 30, 38-39, 85, 93
WoodenBoat 137, 139

Y

Yachting 84, 137, 154
Yard Class Minesweepers 66-67
Young, Marjorie Gladding 71-72

Z

Zimmer, Hans 65, 90, 143, 144, 145-46, 147, 148, 150

Index of Photographs from the Collections of Mystic Seaport

Page	Accession Number
10	1984.187.123328F
12	*top* 1984.187.123142F
12	*bottom* 1984.187.123147F
13	1984.187.123170F
14	1984.187.123330F
17	1984.187.142447F
18-19	1984.187.142432F
22	1984.187.73905F
23	1984.187.114560F
24	1984.187.129916F
39	1984.187.77010F
44	1984.187.74746F
47	1984.187.40292F
48	1984.187.73903F
50	1984.187.67194F
52	1984.187.78074F
54	1984.187.79865F
56	1984.187.73906F
62	1984.187.32697F
64	1984.187.74523F
65	1984.187.122686F
66	1984.187.103987F
67	1984.187.91460F
69	1984.187.122516F(a)
70	1984.187.122690F
71	1984.187.96027F
73	1984.187.96457F
76	1984.187.115881F
81	1984.187.122516F(b)
82	1984.187.63218F
84	*left* 1984.187.122692F
86	1986.106.31
88	1996.31.5288.19
91	1984.187.123304F
92	*bottom* 1984.187.123185F
96-97	1984.187.142435F
102	1984.187.136507F
108	1984.187.130415F
109	1984.187.129926F
113	1984.187.124433F
114	1984.187.185411
121	1984.187.174799
122	1984.187.174870
125	1984.187.179377
126	1984.187.191093_32
127	1984.187.184882-8A

Books of Related Interest from Mystic Seaport

Stanley Rosenfeld

A CENTURY UNDER SAIL

This exquisite collection of more than 200 black-and-white photographs celebrates the marriage of great yachts and the sea from the unique perspective of Morris and Stanley Rosenfeld, renowned throughout the world for their award-winning nautical photographs.

10" x 12", 287 pages, bound in cloth. ISBN 0-939510-71-5 $50.00

John Rousmaniere

SAILING AT FISHERS: A HISTORY OF THE FISHERS ISLAND YACHT CLUB

In this heavily illustrated volume, noted yachting historian John Rousmaniere recounts the history of recreational boating at Fishers Island, New York, with special emphasis on the Fishers Island Yacht Club, which was founded in 1928. Though small, this club has been home to many highly competitive sailors and is closely associated with several noted designs, including the Fishers Island One Design, Fishers Island Sound 31, Herreshoff 23-Foot Class, Luders 16, Rhodes 27, Bulls Eye, and International One Design. Classic powerboats are also featured in this social history of the evolution of a boating organization.

10 1/2" x 10 1/2", 160 pages, bound in cloth. ISBN 0-939510-93-6 $45.00

John Rousmaniere

SLEEK: CLASSIC SAILBOAT PHOTOGRAPHY FROM THE ROSENFELD COLLECTION AT MYSTIC SEAPORT

The Rosenfeld Collection at Mystic Seaport contains a million images emphasizing classic yachts. But even more than photos of boats, the collection represents the epitome of the art of marine photography, just as the subjects represent the ideals of the art of naval architecture. Here, John Rousmaniere interprets 79 images, taken between 1890 and 1954, that speak to the artistry of boats and the photography that captures them. Sleek and elegant describes both the vessels themselves and the striking photographic images, scanned from original prints and printed in duotone.

9 1/4"x 11 3/4", 144 pages, bound in cloth. ISBN 0-939510-90-1 $50.00

Olin J. Stephens II

ALL THIS AND SAILING, TOO

Olin Stephens is the most successful racing-yacht designer of the twentieth century, a legend in his own time almost from the day in 1931 when he and his brother Rod and father Rodrick Sr. finished a transatlantic race to England in the revolutionary 52-foot yawl *Dorade* a full two days ahead of the competition. His autobiography begins with youthful family sailing, moves on to Six-Metre designs and victories, to J-Boat experience in the 1930s, to war work in the 1940s, to America's Cup design and sailing from 1958 to 1983, and to a fleet of great cruising and racing yachts in between. This personal history of Olin and his brother Rod, of the renowned design firm of Sparkman & Stephens, and of international yachting in the 1900s, is informed, introspective, eloquent.

8" x 10", 280 pages. bound in cloth. ISBN 0-913372-89-7 $45.00